I0093716

THE REINVENTION
OF POLICING

THE REINVENTION OF POLICING

Crime Prevention, Community, and Public Safety

William R. Kelly

Daniel P. Mears

ROWMAN & LITTLEFIELD
Lanham • Boulder • New York • London

Acquisitions Editor: Becca Beurer
Assistant Editor: Elizabeth Von Buhr
Sales and Marketing Inquiries: textbooks@rowman.com

Credits and acknowledgments for material borrowed from other sources, and
reproduced with permission, appear on the appropriate page within the text.

Published by Rowman & Littlefield
An imprint of The Rowman & Littlefield Publishing Group, Inc.
4501 Forbes Boulevard, Suite 200, Lanham, Maryland 20706
www.rowman.com

86-90 Paul Street, London EC2A 4NE

Copyright © 2023 by The Rowman & Littlefield Publishing Group, Inc.

All rights reserved. No part of this book may be reproduced in any form or by
any electronic or mechanical means, including information storage and retrieval
systems, without written permission from the publisher, except by a reviewer who
may quote passages in a review.

British Library Cataloguing in Publication Information Available

Library of Congress Cataloging-in-Publication Data

978-1-5381-7919-2 (cloth)
978-1-5381-7920-8 (paperback)
978-1-5381-7921-5 (electronic)

Brief Contents

Contents

Acknowledgments

Fɪʀsᴛ, Kᴇʟʟʏ ᴡᴀɴᴛs ᴛᴏ ᴇxᴘʀᴇss his gratitude to his wonderful wife Emily for her continuous support and encouragement. Several undergraduate students at the University of Texas at Austin provided research assistance: Madalena Almanza conducted extensive background research on several key issues; she also coauthored Chapter 3 with Kelly. Gabrielle Jabour went above and beyond in providing excellent research summaries of a considerable number of materials. We also wish to acknowledge the very helpful assistance of Alexander Tsioutsias, Kitxia Juarez, Elizabeth Riordan, Ava Milligan, Jordan Harkins, and Nisha Bhatia.

Mears thanks Florida State University for providing a collegial environment that supports scholarship, and Emily Leventhal and Eli Mears, and many students, for their wonderful tolerance and willingness to act as sounding boards.

We both extend our profound gratitude to our editor Becca Beurer at Rowman & Littlefield and to Elaine McGarraugh for excellent editing of the manuscript. Thank you both for making this such a pleasant experience.

Preface

CONTEMPORARY POLICING IS IN CRISIS, a situation that has led to persistent calls to reform it. Unfortunately, many proposed solutions focus on piecemeal changes that, though potentially helpful, ignore a fundamental problem—policing relies on a largely reactive approach that does not in any systematic or comprehensive way focus on crime prevention. What does that mean? It means that most of what the police do, such as responding to 911 calls for service and employing directed patrols or hot spots policing, fails to address the causes of crime. Compounding this problem is the absence of any institution or agency charged with prioritizing the prevention of crime and ensuring that police efforts support this goal.

We argue that a better strategy exists, one that places responsibility on the police and other governmental and nongovernmental agencies and organizations for truly *preventing* crime. Remarkably, this idea can be found, at least in part, in the origins of policing. In the United Kingdom, Sir Robert Peel, widely considered to be a founder of modern policing, promoted passage of the Metropolitan Police Act of 1829. Peel commonly discussed crime prevention in speeches before Parliament and other venues. Indeed, crime prevention was codified in Peel's "New Police Instructions," which described the operations and mission of policing:

> It should be understood at the outset, the object to be obtained is the prevention of crime. To this great end, every effort of the police is to be directed. The security of person and property, the preservation of public tranquility, and all

the other objects of a police establishment will thus be better effected than by the detection and punishment of the offender after he has committed a crime.[1]

What happened? Why did crime prevention not take hold and infuse policing? One reason is a design flaw—the vision of policing centered too much on surveillance and an assumed deterrent effect, and too little on efforts that target the diverse causes of crime. Deterrence assuredly is one part of the equation, but if the field of criminology has demonstrated anything, it is that many other causes of crime exist. This is a simplified account, but the point remains—contemporary policing lacks any institutionalized commitment or systematic approach to crime prevention. It is designed to fail.

In this book, we diagnose this problem, along with many others, in American policing. We then turn to solutions, drawing on insights from scholars and other countries, especially those that have made strides in institutionalizing crime prevention. First, we call for a great many reforms to existing practices. The good news? Many changes can be made that can make a positive difference. Second, alongside of these changes, we call for a reinvention of the design and focus of policing and, concomitantly, the way that states, cities, and towns approach public safety. This change presents special challenges, but it is, we submit, the only way to create an appreciable impact in reducing crime and improving justice.

1

Our Broken Criminal Justice System and the Failure to Put Public Safety First

GOVERNMENT IS IN THE BUSINESS of developing and implementing public policies on a wide range of issues such as health care, economic and monetary policy, tax law, the environment, energy, infrastructure, safety of the food supply and medication, and personal safety, among many, many more. Sometimes government policy is a resounding success (absent proverbial naysayers and partisan politicians) and other times, for a variety of reasons, public policies fail.

The events of 9/11 are cited as a glaring illustration of the failure of government, as are other recent examples, including the financial collapse of 2008, the Bernie Madoff Ponzi scheme, Hurricane Katrina, numerous consumer product recalls, the Trump administration's handling of the COVID-19 pandemic, the absence of weapons of mass destruction in Iraq, and in turn, the war in Iraq, just to name a few.

Government policy failures are unfortunately common and often have profound consequences for public health, financial well-being, safety and security, and quality of life. However, we argue that one would be hard-pressed to find a greater public policy failure than the American criminal justice system. It is truly remarkable on a variety of dimensions, including: (1) longevity/sustainability (federal, state, and local governments have been at this for nearly fifty years); (2) scale (113 million, or 50 percent of, Americans have a family member who is or has been incarcerated in prison or jail); (3) the nearly unilateral focus on punishment (the United States has the highest incarceration rate and rate of correctional control in the world); (4) the racial and ethnic disparities in the justice-involved population (Black individuals are 50 percent more likely than whites to have a family member who is currently or has been incarcerated); and (5) the socioeconomic disparities among those who are in the justice system (adults with incomes under $25,000 are over 60 percent more likely than adults with incomes over $100,000 to have a family member incarcerated).[1]

Taking a step back and looking at the numbers, it is not difficult to see the U.S. criminal justice system as a tool for managing large numbers of people who enter the system because they have engaged in acts that lawmakers (Congress and state legislatures) define as criminal. Clearly, many of those criminal acts make perfect sense. Violent crimes like murder, sexual assault, aggravated assault, assault, and robbery and many property crimes like burglary, motor vehicle theft, theft, and major white-collar crimes are the kinds of things we want the government to address and protect us from.

However, these same legislators have gone into lawmaking territory that begs the question—what are the real intentions here for large numbers of justice-involved individuals who engage in petty crimes or low-level misdemeanors and felonies? What is branded as a system for keeping the public safe often looks a lot like a system for regulating the poor and minorities. A quick glance at the evidence reveals a set of institutions that deal with people for whom we lack appropriate alternatives, and defining their behavior as criminal is just a way to get them in the front door. We criminalize homelessness because we lack sufficient affordable housing. We incarcerate persons with a mental illness for lack of treatment options. We have fought a War on Drugs because lawmakers simply cannot concede that substance abuse is a medical disorder. We criminalize poverty, which is a profoundly important criminogenic factor, because we have failed to adequately mitigate disadvantage. Since there is a significant correlation between race and poverty, the criminal justice system also looks very much like a tool for regulating the poor and racial and ethnic minorities. Contributing substantially to this is the fact that racial and ethnic minorities are highly disproportionately arrested, convicted, and incarcerated for drug crimes, most of which are simple possession.

The Costly Failure of American Criminal Justice

Despite decades of quite concerted effort at all levels of government; massive capital investment; stunning collateral costs to families, communities, the economy, and victims; and a fundamental reengineering of law and procedure, the American criminal justice system simply has not been able to accomplish what most would consider the basic point of such a system—to reduce reoffending, prevent crime, and enhance public safety. First, we discuss the costs.

Recent estimates put the direct costs of American criminal justice at approximately $300 billion per year. That includes the costs of policing ($142.5 billion); corrections, which consists of prison, jail, probation, and parole ($88.5 billion); and the court system ($64.7 billion).[2]

On top of that, a variety of broader social costs are incurred by those who have been incarcerated, as well as their families, children, and communities. Monetizing twenty-two attributes including health consequences, lost income, homelessness, marital and family disruption, and increased criminality of children, among others, researchers estimate the total collateral cost of incarceration is $1.2 trillion annually.[3]

What has been ignored in much of the financial data about crime and criminal justice are the economic impacts of crime on victims. This requires a variety of assumptions regarding both tangible costs (for example, the value of property taken in a robbery or burglary) and intangible costs (such as the trauma, pain and suffering, medical costs, and diminished quality of life associated with violent crimes). Recent estimates of the cost of crime to victims, including both tangible and intangible costs and based on index crimes only, put the aggregate cost at between $250 billion and $325 billion annually.[4]

The economic price tag for the administration of criminal justice provides a rather sobering picture. An obvious question is what have we bought? Absent a sophisticated cost-benefit analysis, a short answer is extraordinarily high recidivism.

In 2019 in the United States, there were 5.8 million violent crime victimizations (rape, sexual assault, robbery, and aggravated and simple assault, excluding homicide) and 12.8 million property crime victimizations (burglary, theft, and motor vehicle theft).[5] The unfortunate reality is that the majority of these crimes were committed by individuals who have been through the criminal justice system at least once before. Specifically, we have a reoffending rate of approximately 85 percent and a reincarceration rate of 55 to 60 percent.[6] It is important to note that these are official statistics that represent people who were caught. Considering that the majority of crimes are not reported to the police and for those that are, a majority do not lead to an arrest, it is safe to assume that the real reoffending rate is closer to 100 percent.

In addition to the fact of reoffending is the cost associated with each recidivism event. An Illinois study estimates that a criminal reconviction costs $151,000, part of which is the direct cost to the criminal justice system (police, courts, jail), part the economic impact on victims, and part the indirect costs due to reduced economic activity (for example, loss of employment).[7]

Based just on the simple metric of recidivism in combination with the economic impacts of crime and criminal justice, it is impossible to come to any other conclusion—the American criminal justice system is an extraordinarily expensive, abject failure. The reasons for this failure are relatively simple. The criminal justice system was designed to do primarily one thing, which is to punish. If we look back over the past fifty years of tough-on-crime policies, including statistics like incarceration rates and rates of correctional supervision (both are the highest in the world),[8] we see that punishment has ruled the day. Unfortunately, punishment does not effectively change the behavior of the vast majority of individuals who commit crime. In fact, the evidence indicates that criminal justice involvement, especially incarceration in jail or prison, is criminogenic. It actually increases the likelihood of reoffending. This makes perfect sense when we consider the circumstances of the majority of the individuals in the criminal justice system.

Roughly 80 percent of justice-involved individuals have a substance use disorder, 50 percent have a mental health problem, and an unknown number suffer neurocognitive impairments. We can get a sense of the extent of the problem from the fact that 60 percent of individuals in prison and 55 percent of individuals on probation have had at least one traumatic brain injury, putting them at high risk of cognitive dysfunction. The comparable statistic for the general population is 8 percent.[9] Add to that the common consequences associated with living in poverty, such as educational deficits, poor medical and mental health care, exposure to trauma and environmental toxins, poor nutrition, and lack of opportunity such as employment. The result of all of this is large numbers of individuals with quite complex comorbidities. For example, results of the National Comorbidity Survey indicate that between 40 and 65 percent of individuals with any lifetime substance use disorder also have a lifetime mental health disorder. Among those seeking treatment for substance addiction, nearly 80 percent had a history of a psychiatric disorder. Two-thirds of those seeking treatment for addiction had a current mental health disorder. Alcohol abuse is also associated with a comorbid psychiatric disorder.[10]

The recent Centers for Disease Control–Kaiser Permanente Adverse Childhood Experiences (ACEs) Study sampled over 214,000 individuals regarding a variety of adverse experiences they may have had as children. These adverse experiences include emotional abuse, physical abuse, sexual abuse, violence, substance abuse, or mental illness in the household; parental separation/divorce; an incarcerated member of the household; and physical and emotional neglect. The results are grim. Nearly two-thirds report at least one ACE. Nearly one-quarter had three or more. Significantly higher adverse experiences were reported by minorities (Black and Hispanic), those with less than a high school education, incomes under $15,000 per year, and unemployed. The CDC-Kaiser study also reported a variety of behavioral, psychological/psychiatric, medical, financial, and educational outcomes associated with the number and intensity of the adverse experiences.[11]

The obvious question that arises from all of these prevalence studies of substance use disorders, psychiatric disorders, trauma, adverse experiences, neurocognitive impairments, poverty, and others is what is the link to criminality? Part of the answer can be found from a few decades of neuroscientific research and how various conditions, circumstances, disorders, and impairments affect the brain and brain functioning. Since we have written about this extensively elsewhere, we will keep it brief here, but it is certainly worth some discussion in light of the profound relevance for criminal justice policy.

Dopamine is a neurotransmitter that signals pleasure and reward in the brain. Under normal circumstances, dopamine assists the brain to learn. Unfortunately, ingestion of drugs results in an exaggerated release of dopamine, resulting in overlearning, which in turn leads to repeated use. That is largely the neurobiological pathway to addiction. But it is just the beginning of the effects of substance use on the brain.

Executive functions are a set of cognitive faculties that include attention, working memory, impulse control, cognitive flexibility, future orientation, planning, and regulation of emotions, among others. Executive functions are regulated largely in the prefrontal cortex of the brain. Neuroscientific research estimates that between 50 and 80 percent of substance abusers, especially addicts, have some degree of executive dysfunction. Although not necessarily causal, executive dysfunction certainly can facilitate criminality, considering impairments to self-control, attention, and delayed gratification.

Consider the criminality of juveniles. The age-crime curve depicts a well-established fact about offending, which is that the risk of criminal involvement is highest in the age range of 14 to the early 20s, then declines through adulthood. Although there has been considerable debate among criminologists regarding the relationship between age and crime, one cannot ignore the developmental trajectory of the frontal lobe of the brain. The prefrontal cortex (PFC) is the part of the brain where much of executive functioning is regulated. Neuroscientific research has demonstrated that the PFC is not fully developed until the mid-20s. That developmental pattern contributes significantly to understanding why, as the traditional explanation goes, Johnny made a bad decision when he broke into someone's car or assaulted someone. It was a bad decision, but may have been a result of Johnny's lack of impulse control or empathy.

Moreover, exposure to adverse experiences, environmental toxins, traumatic brain injury, and other assaults that tend to be associated with poverty and disadvantage significantly contribute to executive dysfunction through impacts on the prefrontal cortex. For example, children raised in poverty score significantly lower on assessments of memory, impulse control, achievement, IQ, attention, and language skills. Child abuse and neglect (what the CDC-Kaiser ACEs research addresses) are associated with executive dysfunction, lack of remorse and empathy, risk-taking, lack of impulse control, and a variety of psychological disorders like conduct disorders, PTSD, and personality disorders.[12]

Adrian Raine is a leading expert on the neuroscience of criminality. He concludes, "The best replicated brain imaging abnormality found to date across a wide variety of antisocial groups, across structure and function, and across different imaging methodologies is the PFC."[13] Raine continues implicating structural and functional impairments to the PFC and antisocial behavior:

> Neurological patients suffering damage to the ventral prefrontal cortex exhibit psychopathic-like, disinhibited behavior, autonomic and emotional blunting, and bad decision-making. Magnetic resonance imaging (MRI) research has shown that those with antisocial personality disorder have an 11% reduction in prefrontal gray matter. . . . Structural prefrontal impairments are paralleled by functional prefrontal impairments (i.e., reduced brain functioning) in a wide range of antisocial populations. Murderers have been found to show reduced glucose metabolism in the prefrontal cortex. This impairment also specifically characterizes impulsively violent offenders, suggesting that the prefrontal cortex acts as an "emergency brake" on runaway emotions generated by limbic structures. Brain imaging studies are supported by findings from neuropsychological, neurological, and psychophysiological studies, indicating robustness of findings.[14]

The prevalence statistics for justice-involved persons with a mental illness are staggering. In state prisons, three-quarters of women and 55 percent of men have at least one mental health problem. It is comparable in local jails, except that 63 percent of men have at least one disorder.[15] These rates are three to four times the rates in the general population, which begs the question, why is there such a concentration in the justice system of individuals who have a mental illness? Does mental illness make people more prone to engaging in crime? The answer is no.[16] The evidence is clear that a rather small percentage of crimes committed by persons with a mental illness are due to their symptoms. A greater proportion of crime committed by these individuals appears related to a comorbid substance use disorder.[17]

We also have to consider the state of public mental health treatment in the United States. The unfortunate fact is that we lack anything close to adequate treatment capacity. Access to treatment is also quite limited, especially for the uninsured and underinsured. The lack of treatment alternatives has resulted in what many experts have labeled the criminalization of mental illness, which in turn has transformed the criminal justice system into de facto mental health asylums. The Los Angeles County Jail is the largest mental health facility in California. As is the Cook County (Chicago) Jail in Illinois and most county jails in larger metropolitan areas across the country. In many respects, the criminal justice system houses so many individuals who have a mental illness because there are no other options.

But let's be clear. Just because the criminal justice system is the primary institution for housing persons with a mental illness does not mean it is also the primary treatment provider. Although some individuals with a serious mental health disorder may receive some treatment, the justice system was not designed and is not resourced to provide much in the way of effective treatment. Recent estimates indicate that only about one-third of persons in prison who have a mental illness receive any mental health treatment while incarcerated.[18] That is any treatment, which says nothing about the quality, length, or dosage of treatment.

The evidence demonstrably shows that criminality in most circumstances is not simply a matter of bad decision-making or hanging out with the wrong crowd. It is extraordinarily more complicated than that. Many individuals who end up in the criminal justice system often bring with them complex circumstances and comorbidities.

The assumption that underlies much of criminal justice policy over the past fifty years—that punishment will change the behaviors associated with crime—is clearly discredited by decades of scientific evidence. What is it about punishment that mitigates any of these criminogenic circumstances? Does being in jail "treat" schizophrenia or mitigate the effects of poverty or trauma? Does prison make the consequences of ACEs better? The obvious answer is no. In fact, punishment, especially incarceration, aggravates many of these disorders and impairments, especially mental illness. To make matters worse, the criminal justice system is not designed, implemented, or resourced with the appropriate budget or expertise to address these criminogenic circumstances and often complex comorbidities characteristic of those who enter the system.

Keeping individuals out of the criminal justice system is a critically important component of public safety. Criminal justice involvement is criminogenic, meaning that the risk of reoffending is heightened by what individuals experience while in the system as well as by collateral effects such as restrictions on employment, housing, credit, public assistance, health and mental health care, and education loans, among others. Public safety is severely compromised as we continue down this discredited path of punishment as the solution.

Another defining attribute of the American criminal justice system that severely limits opportunities for enhancing public safety is that, by design, the criminal justice system is reactive. The police respond to a criminal event and that often results in an arrest which, in turn, triggers a variety of responses by the prosecutor and the court, involving matters such as pretrial detention, conditions of release, what charges to bring, what to plea negotiate, and what sentence to impose. Corrections agencies are reactive as well when they impose punishment.

There is another very important consideration regarding public safety and the reactive nature of criminal justice. The police can respond or react only to what they know about. The vast majority of information about crimes comes from the public. Unfortunately, most crime is not reported to the police. The Bureau of Justice Statistics conducts annual surveys that among other things ask victims whether they reported their crime to the police. The results indicate that 41 percent of violent crimes and 32 percent of household property crimes are reported. So right off the bat, the ability of the criminal justice system to effectively improve public safety with this reactive posture is seriously disadvantaged. Moreover, most reported crimes are not solved. Under 50 percent of reported violent crimes are cleared by the police (45 percent) and only 17 percent of reported property crimes are cleared by the police, typically meaning arrest and referral to prosecution.[19]

All of this is after the fact of a crime. The unfortunate reality is that the criminal justice system is not positioned or resourced to proactively prevent crime. The policing expert David Bayley wrote twenty-five years ago that policing as currently configured does not prevent crime:

> The police do not prevent crime. This is one of the best kept secrets of modern life. Experts know it, the police know it, but the public does not know it. Yet the police pretend that they are society's best defense against crime and continually argue that if they are given more resources, especially personnel, they will be able to protect communities against crime. This is a myth.[20]

To be fair, the police do attempt to reduce criminal opportunity through strategies such as hot spots policing. But there is little in the way of reducing the risk of criminal justice involvement in the first place by, for example, mitigating individual-level criminogenic circumstances. Granted, there are some programs, such as pre-arrest diversion to emergency treatment for persons with a mental illness. Law Enforcement Assisted Diversion (LEAD) and Crisis Assistance Helping Out on the Streets (CAHOOTS), which we discuss in Chapter 6, are examples. They are, though, the exceptions.

In support of the punishment-focused, reactive posture of the criminal justice system is the argument that criminal justice policies were responsible for the crime decline of the 1990s and have taken us to the historically low crime rates we experience today. At first glance, that seems like a compelling theory—crime declined as arrests, convictions, and incarcerations increased. However, several studies have statistically estimated the relative role of the justice system in this sustained drop in crime, and although the estimates vary a bit, the consensus is that crime policy was responsible for somewhere between 10 and 20 percent of the decline.[21] Moreover, consider that essentially all of our

Western allies experienced similar crime declines during the same time period without implementing anything like our tough-on-crime policies.

The evidence we have briefly outlined here leads to the inevitable and unfortunate conclusion that despite what policymakers and elected officials have championed for decades, the American criminal justice system is effectively not in the business of public safety. Recidivism rates speak volumes about the efficacy of current policy, and there is little in our criminal justice repertoire, with the exception of some opportunity reduction strategies by police, that is aimed at proactive crime prevention.

Not only are we unable to effectively reduce recidivism and prevent crime, we suggest one would be hard-pressed to find anyone in the justice system who admits to being in charge of or has primary responsibility for reducing reoffending and preventing crime. The regrettable reality is that as currently designed and administered, criminal justice in the United States simply does not make public safety a priority.

The public agrees with this conclusion and has done so for at least twenty years. For example, a 2002 public opinion poll found that by a two-to-one margin, Americans want to address the root causes of crime, and two-thirds believe that the best way to reduce crime is to effectively rehabilitate those who are incarcerated. Importantly, the survey results reveal that "Americans see prevention as the most important function of the criminal justice system, and also the function that is most sorely lacking."[22]

A 2020 survey reports results that are consistent with the 2002 survey noted above. This more recent poll surveyed a variety of constituents including crime victims, people with mental health and substance abuse problems, individuals with prior criminal convictions, and voters. The bottom line is that these groups are in remarkable alignment in the belief that the American criminal justice system does not make public safety the priority it should be:

> Broad consensus exists at the neighborhood level and across different demographics: public safety policies and investments should prioritize violence prevention, recovery, mental health, reentry and the most effective strategies to stop the cycle of crime, more than incarceration. It's time for federal, state and local expenditures to match these urgently needed and popularly supported priorities.[23]

A 2017 survey conducted for the Urban Institute asked respondents what they believe are the primary barriers to increased public safety. The top responses included: "Not enough prevention programs to keep young people from turning to crime"; "Not enough reentry programs to help formerly incarcerated people"; "High unemployment"; and "Too many people being incarcerated for minor, non-violent offenses."[24]

Other recent polls affirm widespread dissatisfaction with the performance of the criminal justice system. A 2016 survey commissioned by the ACLU reported that over 90 percent of Americans believe the criminal justice system needs significant change, including a greatly enhanced focus on rehabilitation.[25] Another 2016 poll revealed that over 70 percent believe the main goal of the criminal justice system should be rehabilitation.[26] A 2020 NORC poll found that the majority of Americans (69 percent) believe the system needs either a complete overhaul (29 percent) or major changes (40 percent).[27]

Fundamentally Misunderstanding Public Safety

The evidence is overwhelming. The American criminal justice system is failing on multiple fronts. It is failing to effectively prevent crime. It is failing to effectively reduce recidivism. It is failing to effectively enhance public safety. It is failing crime victims since many victimizations are preventable. It is failing those who end up in the criminal justice system since most of the reasons for their criminality are ignored, perpetuating cycles of reoffending. It is failing taxpayers who must shoulder the unnecessarily excessive financial burden of paying for the administration of criminal justice. It is failing the economy as many justice-involved individuals are unable (often not allowed) to be economically productive and in fact many become permanently dependent on public assistance. It is failing in terms of fairness and equality as minorities overpopulate every aspect of the system. It fails routinely in terms of due process (absence or lack of adequate indigent defense, coerced confessions in the process of plea dealing, unreasonable bail and excessive use of pretrial detention, unlawful search and seizure and use of force, just to name a few).

Nothing about this is new or news. Experts, policymakers, many elected officials, the media, and the public have been well aware of the failings of American criminal justice for some time. The reasons are simple. Lawmakers decided fifty years ago that crime was largely a matter of making poor decisions or associating with the wrong people. How better to address these problems than rely on punishment? That logic seemed intuitive and perhaps even appealing due to its simplicity and seeming emphasis on accountability. As we will emphasize throughout this book, accountable government would prevent crime from happening rather than wait for it to occur, and then respond with expensive and ineffective strategies.

One would think that after thirty-plus years of contrary evidence, we would have charted a decidedly different course. Unfortunately, legislatures continue to expand the criminal law, increasing the number of behaviors that they decide should be handled by the justice system. It is breathtaking how easy it seems to simply add new "problems" to the criminal code and expect the police, the courts, and corrections agencies to somehow magically take care of it.

Take for example the efforts in Republican states to pass legislation in response to unfounded beliefs that there was significant voter fraud in the 2020 election. Legislatures used the fiction of voter fraud to ostensibly counter it, though the intent seemed to be focused on suppressing votes. Regardless, the relevance for us is that the legislation contained provisions for criminal liability. The evolving criminalization of abortion in many states in the aftermath of the Supreme Court's overturning *Roe v. Wade* is another example of a new "problem" for which the criminal justice system becomes the default enforcer.

This practice of continuously adding new things for the criminal justice system to deal with contributes to one of the major challenges facing the administration of criminal justice. Together with sky-high recidivism rates, this has resulted in extraordinarily overburdened police, courts, and corrections. We will discuss policing shortly, but a glance at prosecutor and public defender caseloads and court dockets provides all of the proof needed to justify or at least understand the fact that between 95 and 98 percent of all criminal convictions in the United States are arrived at through a negotiated plea. Although prison and jail populations have been declining modestly since 2010, and more so due to COVID, they still remain extraordinarily crowded and understaffed. It is not much better in the arena of community supervision, where probation and parole caseloads are typically way beyond what is recommended by professional organizations such as the American Probation and Parole Association and the American Bar Association.

Then there is the stunning practice of lawmakers of simply declaring the province of the criminal justice system matters that are obviously the domain of public health, such as substance abuse and mental illness. It does not take an expert to understand how profoundly counterproductive this is.

It is not surprising that the criminal justice system is broken. The multiple failures we noted above are the result of a variety of fundamental design flaws. Add to that a variety of ongoing legislative and policy lapses and we have the American criminal justice debacle.

Particularly troubling is the fact that many key decision makers in the criminal justice system fundamentally misunderstand the concept of public safety. When we dissect the criminal justice system, there is no department that is in charge of public safety. There are no officials who have the primary responsibility for public safety. It is as if somehow out of the mix of departments, agencies, offices, or whatever else we call the various divisions of the criminal justice system, public safety magically emerges. Public safety may be the wished-for outcome, but as the saying goes, hope is not a policy.

Not only does public safety not exist as a component of the criminal justice system, but our decades-long penchant for punishment deflects attention from key public safety drivers like crime prevention. We do very little on the crime prevention front, despite the obvious fact that crime prevention must be a mandatory priority of any institution purporting to preserve public safety. Much more on this later.

In light of all of the shortcomings, there is significant effort focused on reforming various aspects of the American criminal justice system. Academics, policymakers, elected officials, nonprofit organizations, the courts, and local, state, and federal governments are, to varying degrees, in the process of conceptualizing and implementing policy changes designed to improve procedures and outcomes. We have both written extensively about the failings of the justice system, evidence-based improvements, and methods for implementing reforms. Most of our work has focused on the courts and corrections. We believe it is now time to turn our efforts to policing, and in the course of proposing a reinvention of law enforcement, we intend to directly link policing and crime prevention in what we believe to be an effective path to public safety.

Why Focus on Policing?

Freddie Gray, April 19, 2015, Baltimore, MD
Sandra Bland, July 13, 2015, Waller County, TX
Jamar Clark, November 16, 2015, Minneapolis, MN
Philandro Castile, July 6, 2016, Falcon Heights, MN
Antwon Rose Jr., June 19, 2018, East Pittsburgh, PA
Javier Ambler, March 28, 2019, Austin, TX
Breonna Taylor, March 13, 2020, Louisville, KY
Michael Ramos, April 24, 2020, Austin, TX
George Floyd, May 25, 2020, Minneapolis, MN
David McAtee, June 1, 2020, Louisville, KY
Rayshard Brooks, June 12, 2020, Atlanta, GA
Marcellis Stinnette, October 20, 2020, Waukegan, IL
Daunte Wright, April 11, 2021, Brooklyn Center, MN
Mario Gonzales, April 19, 2021, Alameda County, CA
Andrew Brown Jr., April 21, 2021, Elizabeth City, NC
Patrick Lyoya, April 4, 2022, Grand Rapids, MI
Jayland Walker, June 27, 2022, Akron, OH

Many of these names are certainly familiar. And they are only a sample of citizen deaths at the hands of the police. Indeed, there were over 8,000 on-duty police fatal shootings of civilians from 2015 through 2022.[28] Although one-half of those killed by the police are white, the rate at which Blacks and Hispanics are killed is twice that of whites.[29]

The killing of Michael Brown in Ferguson, Missouri, in August of 2014 spawned Black Lives Matter and other local and national organizations protesting policing in America. Black Lives Matter has been in the national spotlight since Ferguson, and especially in the aftermath of the murder of George Floyd and the massive wave of protests during the summer of 2020.

It is probably not an overstatement to characterize policing in the United States as on the brink. Use of force, racism, lack of accountability, and a variety of other problems that we discuss in Chapter 2 have led to massive public protests on a level unseen since the 1960s. Civil and criminal litigation of police officers and police departments, calls to defund the police and reimagine public safety, and serious questions about the legitimacy of policing have rendered law enforcement a primary target in efforts to reform criminal justice.

Policing reform spans federal, state, and local efforts to address various issues with policing. For example, the federal George Floyd Justice in Policing Act was passed by the House, but never passed the Senate. The act was largely in response to the death of George Floyd and the events following his murder by Minneapolis police. The main provisions of the act focus on police bias and misconduct, excessive force, use of body cameras and dashboard cameras, prohibiting the use of chokeholds, and prohibiting no-knock warrants in drug cases.

The Council on Criminal Justice Task Force on Policing recently identified reforms to policing aimed to "keep communities safe."[30] The task force recommended prohibiting chokeholds, implementing duty to intervene laws requiring officers to intercede in situations where other officers are using excessive force or engaging in misconduct, and restricting or prohibiting no-knock warrants.

There has been a flurry of bills proposed in state legislatures. According to a 2021 analysis by National Public Radio, all fifty states participated in the prior year in the filing of 2,000 bills regarding policing. However, the result is described as a patchwork of reform coming in "bite-size portions," with most traction in blue states and metro areas.[31] Much like the George Floyd Act, what we are seeing in some states and some cities are restrictions on chokeholds and no-knock warrants, requiring that police officers wear body cameras, redefining use of force policies, and limiting qualified immunity for police. Specifically, between May 2020 and mid-April 2021, four states have limited immunity for police, ten have mandated body cameras, sixteen have prohibited the use of neck restraints, and five have restricted no-knock warrants.[32] A handful of cities are considering or have initiated some defunding of police departments (Austin and Seattle for example).

What we have seen so far in Congress, state legislatures, and city govern-ment has been nearly exclusively in response to events like the deaths of George Floyd and Breonna Taylor or issues that have been the subject of mass protests by organizations like Black Lives Matter (police accountability, racial bias, use of force). How policing will differ after these legislative efforts have run their course is obviously unknown at this point, but in all likelihood the changes will be piecemeal, crafted in response to particular circumstances that serve as a rallying cry for specific reforms.

The fact that legislative and policy changes have been reactive, after the harm has been done, is nothing new. Take for example the elimination of the death penalty in twenty-two states, due in part to over 3,300 exonerations since 1989.[33] The risk of making a mistake is a very persuasive motivation.

That is often the nature of the development and implementation of public policy and accompanying statutory changes. However, a reactive focus to spe-cific events can miss the bigger picture and lead to unnecessarily narrow change.

Improving Policing and Public Safety

Our goal in writing this book is in part to identify the litany of problems that plague policing, many of which have recently become top of mind for the public due to cell phone videos and body camera footage of things like use of force and death at the hands of the police. We believe that addressing these issues is important since they contribute substantially to the dysfunction of American policing. But again, there is a much bigger picture of policing and criminal justice reform.

Ronald Davis, who has served as chief of police and the head of the Com-munity Oriented Policing Strategies office under President Obama, is one of a relatively few experts who are advocating for a broader agenda of reform:

> After 30 years in local law enforcement trying to reform it, I would have to frankly say no, we cannot reform our current system. Reform over the few years has mostly been tinkering around the edges—a policy change here, a trend change there. But it didn't go far enough. . . . We're going to have to dismantle this thing all the way to the ground and rebuild it. The challenge, however, is that we have to do it while we are still flying the plane—because we do not have the ability to just stop police services and rebuild. . . . We need to understand what the community is saying: Quit tinkering around the edges, quit playing with policy changes, and do the uprooting changes that are necessary.[34]

It is sentiment like that expressed by Mr. Davis that motivates and informs our effort here. In some respects, it is quite simple. Yes, the problems with policing that we and many others have identified need to be mitigated. But those changes need to be substantive and substantial, not symbolic and piecemeal. Implementing those changes—eliminating unnecessary use of force, making police accountable, reducing racism in policing, enhancing the perceived legitimacy of the police in local communities—is absolutely necessary, but is not mission accomplished.

Those changes, as important as they are, do not get law enforcement where it needs to be in order to accomplish the goals of the criminal justice system. The transformational part of policing reform we are suggesting is expanding, not narrowing, the role of law enforcement, by placing substantial responsibility for crime prevention and public safety squarely in the hands of local police. Rather than defunding the police, we advocate for a broadening of the roles and responsibilities of law enforcement, while at the same time eliminating many of the functions police have no business performing.

We seek to develop a framework whereby local police can perform traditional, reactive roles such as responding to serious, violent crime on the one hand, and play a fundamental, leading role in proactive crime prevention and public safety on the other. We argue that the police are well positioned as the most visible agents of the government to zealously engage and collaborate in evidence-based strategies for preventing crime and enhancing public safety. This will involve a dramatic reinventing of policing as we know it. As such, we are taking police reform well beyond the boundaries of what most other proponents offer.

We absolutely understand that any effective effort to improve public safety cannot focus just on the police. Indeed, the effectiveness of the police depends on a host of factors that lie outside of policing. Ultimately, what is needed is a reinventing of policing and the structure and functioning of criminal justice more broadly. Without comprehensive police reform, the benefits will be quite limited. And without police reform, changing the courts and corrections will achieve little. Prioritizing public safety—crime prevention, in particular—is, we argue, the key.

What, though, led to our particular concern about policing and interest in examining its flaws and its potentials, and what needs to be done to improve it? One is the obvious problem that ineffective policing presents for society. Another is the national and ongoing debate about problems with policing and what should be done to address them. Still another is that, in many respects, our work has circled around policing without directly confronting its importance for systemic approaches to improving crime and justice. We both have undertaken research on crime theories and causation, crime prevention, sentencing, prisons, reentry, public opinion, and, more generally, problems with America's approach to criminal justice and solutions to these problems.[35] But despite intensively investigating almost all aspects of criminal justice and corrections, and some work on policing as well as how police decision-making may influence the courts, we had not systematically undertaken an assessment of policing or focused exclusively on it.

We recognized that we do not bring several decades of lived experience evaluating only policing and the variety of topics that attend to it. But we realized that our combined research experiences—and our focus on systemic factors that affect the operations and impacts of criminal justice and corrections—provided a unique vantage point from which to appraise the current state of policing and to identify ways to improve it. That includes recognition that the police operate within larger social, cultural, political, and systemic contexts. Much the same can be said about the work of the courts and those who work in corrections. Accordingly, any attempt to diagnose and solve problems involving the police requires attention to these contexts. In what follows, we build on this insight and are fortunate in being aided and abetted by tremendous advances scholars have made in recent decades in the study of policing.

Structure of This Book

Chapter 2 describes the litany of problems that plague contemporary American policing and what these problems mean for what is needed to improve society's approach to policing and, more broadly, public safety. Although public safety can encompass or touch on many dimensions—such as fear of crime, perceptions of fairness and justice, and disparities in criminal justice system responses—our primary focus will be on crime. As we emphasize throughout, however, any attempt to increase public safety through reduced crime necessarily entails and requires improvements in public perceptions of and experiences with the police. It also requires efforts that focus on improving equity in how government agencies and communities—not just the police—address crime. The coproduction of public safety, with communities and a variety of public institutions serving as partners in crime prevention and reduction, is essential for creating not only a safer society but also a more equitable and just one.

Chapter 3 discusses how we got to a place where we invest tremendous resources in policing—and in the courts and corrections—yet do so without making public safety our fundamental priority. We use this historical backdrop to highlight the pressing need for a new way to approach policing and, even more importantly, public safety writ large.

Chapter 4 steps back and presents a clean-slate look at what a smart approach to public safety would look like. Put differently, setting aside the exclusive focus on the police, what would be the contours of an effective and cost-efficient approach to public safety if public safety, in fact, was the fundamental priority? We present a comprehensive strategy, or framework, for what such an approach would entail. This framework provides a further basis for identifying the problems in contemporary policing and, more generally, our approach to public safety. It simultaneously provides guidance on how we can improve policing as we know it (discussed in Chapter 5) and make crime prevention and public safety the priority of policing and a variety of other public and private agencies and organizations. The ultimate goal of the new model we propose is to reduce crime and recidivism, and enhance crime prevention and public safety (discussed in Chapter 6).

Chapter 5 takes the framework from Chapter 4 and identifies a myriad of ways in which we can reform traditional policing to avoid harm and improve public safety.

Chapter 6 builds on the reforms identified in Chapter 5 and develops a more substantial set of approaches that collectively amount to a reinvention of policing. These go well beyond improving traditional policing and require, quite literally, a new model for the structure, goals, and activities of policing. This new approach conceptualizes policing as an institution that is part of a broader collaborative model of crime prevention and public safety.

Chapter 7 steps back and introduces "justice" into the discussion. Many criminal justice policy discussions focus primarily on recidivism and crime, but justice is central to American democracy. This chapter argues that public safety contributes to more justice, and that improved policing—including the coproduction of safety with communities—depends on processes that can decrease disparities and increase justice.

Chapter 8 concludes by highlighting key points and approaches to improving policing, to improving public safety, and, in turn, to improving justice. It then highlights "big" takeaway points for guiding a systemic and comprehensive approach to improving policing and public safety, as well as the challenges and barriers to accomplishing what we have proposed.

2

American Policing

A Litany of Problems

M ANY PROBLEMS WITH POLICING, some more serious and visible than others, have contributed to the recent nationwide call for police reform, including defunding the police. What reform looks like is highly variable, due in no small part to political differences in what reform should entail. As one example, for some people, defunding means literally cutting off funding to police. Others want to see some portion of police funding shifted to other services. Still others advocate wholesale reengineering of policing. One commonality exists amidst such differences: The fact that policing is a top-of-mind issue among the public, policymakers, and elected officials speaks volumes about policing problems, perceptions about the police, and the need for action.

Our goal in this chapter is to identify key problems with policing, many of which contribute, in various ways, to bringing us to this critical juncture in the history of policing. The premise in documenting these problems is simple—without clarity about what is wrong, how can we develop viable or effective solutions? To date, too many surface-level critiques have been leveled, and they consider only one or two problems. Failure to recognize the litany of problems that exist, however, will doom policy efforts to failure, and the end result will be more, not less, crime, victimization, injustice, and public frustration and anger with the police and criminal justice system. Accordingly, this chapter will help lay the foundation for, first and foremost, identifying the need for systemic change that attacks the myriad problems that confront contemporary policing and, indeed, all of criminal justice.

As we will see in Chapter 3, many of the same forces that have produced dysfunction in the criminal justice system more broadly have also contributed to the flawed state of modern policing. At the same time, there are some problems unique to policing. The implication is simple—if we want to improve policing, we must address a diverse range of problems, including those that are police-specific and those that emanate from broader problems in the institutions and systems that putatively exist to promote public safety. The focus on the police is, however, crucial. Problems in policing can directly affect communities through, for example, injustice and missed opportunities to undertake or contribute to crime prevention. And they can do so indirectly through ripple effects in what individuals face as they progress through the courts, into the correctional system, and back into communities.

We want to emphasize that the problems that we identify do not characterize all police departments. There is much that is good and effective to be found on the policing landscape. Furthermore, why problems may be greater in some departments or areas may depend on a variety of factors, including demographics of communities and police departments, crime rates, economic conditions, political issues, historical events and tensions, and much more. Yet, if we are to make genuine and substantial progress in improving policing nationally, a reckoning is needed. Once we take heed of the scope of the problem that confronts efforts to improve public safety, solutions can more readily be identified. Indeed, later in the book, drawing on lessons gleaned from this reckoning, we present a blueprint for fundamental changes to policing that can address many of these problems and, by extension, the crisis in policing—and throughout criminal justice—that has been brewing for many decades. As we will argue, police reform is one piece of a much larger set of criminal justice reforms needed to improve public safety. Put differently, police reform and criminal justice reform go hand in hand.

Critical Problems in Policing—Design Flaws

We begin with a set of critical problems that can be characterized as "design" flaws. When we build a house based on a flawed architectural plan, we can anticipate any of a variety of problems, including mold behind walls and in attics, plumbing disasters, risk of fires, and more. This basic idea holds for policies, programs, and agencies.[1] For that reason, we focus first on problems in the design and structure of policing, problems that arguably consign policing to be ineffective and inefficient, and even harmful.

Problem 1: Society Thinks That They Have a Crime Prevention Agency— They Do Not

At one level, it seems reasonable to assert that the criminal justice system, including police, courts, and corrections, is in the business of crime prevention. After all, what is the point of the police arresting individuals, the courts prosecuting and convicting them, and corrections punishing them if not to prevent crime? The unfortunate reality, underscored by extraordinarily high recidivism rates—82 percent of individuals released from prison are rearrested one or more times within ten years of release[2]—is that the criminal justice system does an extremely poor job of crime prevention.[3]

Looking at a metaphorical organizational chart of the criminal justice system, one would be hard-pressed to find someone in charge of crime prevention and reducing recidivism. That's because, remarkably, there isn't one.

To understand why, it is important to distinguish between crime prevention and crime control. Crime control is a phrase that captures the idea—more a philosophical or ideological orientation—that the criminal justice system should rely on deterrence and incapacitation. The "control" of crime does not have to rely solely on these mechanisms, both of which lead to a focus on punishment, supervision, and incarceration. But since at least the 1960s, "crime control" has been equated with this approach, even though one might rely on any of a broad array of policies and interventions to prevent crime in communities and recidivism among those who come in contact with the criminal justice system.

The crime control or tough-on-crime approach has defined the past fifty years of American criminal justice policy, and has been a failure. It did little to appreciably prevent crime, reduce recidivism, or increase justice. And, at the same time, it led to dramatic, large-scale increases in spending on expanding the scale of criminal justice and corrections.[4]

Policing has been part and parcel of this growth and failure. Nearly twenty years ago, the National Research Council (NRC) Committee to Review Research on Police Policy and Practices assessed the research on the crime control effectiveness of policing. They concluded:

> Contemporary policing has relied on an operating model emphasizing reactive strategies to suppress crime. The Committee's assessment of several decades of research is that there is weak or, at best, mixed evidence regarding the effectiveness of what we have defined as the "standard model" of policing.[5]

This conclusion is worse than it seems. Consider, for example, that investing in ineffective police strategies constitutes a missed opportunity to invest in ones that are effective. That amounts to an increase in crime relative to what would have happened if we invested in effective crime prevention strategies. Consider, too, that the assessment does not consider the harms—including emotional or physical harm or death, mistrust of the police, and delegitimization of criminal justice—that can arise from unprofessional, poorly implemented, or unlawful policing.[6]

The standard model of policing, which is closely tied to policing organization, systems, training, and culture, has as its foundation the response to calls
for service. As Lum and Koper noted nearly fifteen years after the NRC's report,

> Because this approach to policing is so dominant, and because it is so engrained
> in uniformed patrol and in the mindset of almost every officer who shares that
> experience, characteristics of the standard model permeate and shape other
> systems within policing. These systems include academy and post-academy
> "field" and "in-service" training; incentives, promotions, and rewards; systems
> of management, supervision, and accountability; and leadership. The model's
> reactive, individual-case, procedures-oriented approach is not only reflected in
> these systems but is also fostered and nurtured by them. For example, training
> focuses on learning correct procedures, how to apply appropriate force to make
> an arrest, and how to investigate a situation. Even the physical training in acad-
> emies is carried out from the perspective of arrest and use of force and is seen
> as central to those roles.[7]

To be sure, in recent years police departments across the nation have begun
implementing new, evidence-based strategies—including hot spots policing,
which focuses attention and resources on small areas where crime is concentrated; proactive, directed patrols; and problem-solving policing—that can be
effective at reducing crime. We will discuss these later in the book. For now,
though, the central point is that the dominant model has been and remains
reactive policing. That leads ineluctably to a focus on responding only after
a crime has occurred. Indeed, the preponderance of police effort is reactive,
such as responding to 911 calls. As Lawrence Sherman has written, "The rise
of telephone dispatch transformed both the method and purpose of patrol.
Instead of watching to prevent crime, motorized police patrol became a process of merely waiting to respond to crime."[8] Many accounts confirm this assessment. For example, the Vera Institute analyzed 911 data and allocation of
police time and found that most police time went to responding to 911 calls.[9]
Most of the calls were for noncriminal matters.

Crime prevention is entirely different. It relies on strategies to, well, prevent
crime from occurring in the first place. We will discuss prevention later in the
book. For now, though, consider three primary approaches to crime prevention
identified by Welsh and Farrington: developmental prevention, community prevention, and situational crime prevention.[10] Developmental crime prevention
focuses on mitigating the risk associated with trauma, mental health, the effects
of ACEs, and other developmental risk factors. Community crime prevention addresses community-level social factors and institutions that can increase the risk
of criminal involvement (e.g., families, schools, neighborhoods, organizations).
Situational crime prevention focuses on reducing criminal opportunity and de-

creasing the risk of offending. All of these strategies share the goal of preventing crime prior to criminal justice involvement.

In short, a central problem in modern policing is that society thinks it has an institution designed to prevent crime. Or it thinks that this institution, by responding to crime after it has occurred, appreciably reduces overall crime. The police, though, are not charged with—nor are police agencies designed for—preventing crime.

There is, in fact, no public safety agency whose mandate is to prioritize crime prevention or the coordination of diverse institutions, agencies, and efforts to prevent crime and ensure that sanctions and interventions contribute to crime reduction. Why does that matter for police reform? Because the police can hardly be effective at contributing appreciably to crime prevention efforts if (a) it is not actually their primary mandate; (b) they operate independently of a broader, comprehensive approach to public safety; and (c) their time is diverted to activities that either have little to do with crime prevention or are simply ineffective.

Problem 2: The Police Do Little to Address Known Causes of Offending or Crime

The primary focus of crime prevention, as we are using the term, is preventing crime from occurring in the first place. That requires addressing the underlying causes and correlates of offending, not simply deterring or incapacitating those who commit crime.

We and many scholars have written about the criminogenic circumstances, disorders, and impairments that are fundamentally related to criminality.[11] Most are obvious—mental illness, substance abuse, neurodevelopmental and neurocognitive impairments, poverty, and family disruption, among many others. A wide variety of local jurisdictions have developed diversion programs to address many of these factors. Drug courts are some of the earliest attempts and are widespread. Other diversion programs, whether in the form of specialized or problem-solving courts or some other format, are certainly positive shifts away from punishment and toward behavioral change. Having said that, these efforts at rehabilitation are still the exception and many lack sufficient funding, operate with little accountability or evaluation, or are ineffective.

Much the same can be said about the causes of crime at a community, city, or county level. A diverse array of factors can contribute to higher rates of crime. These include social and economic disadvantage (e.g., high rates of poverty, unemployment, and family disruption) as well as weak informal social control institutions (e.g., the limited presence of churches, businesses, volunteer organizations, and the like, as well as low levels of collective efficacy) and weak formal social control institutions (e.g., ineffective polic-ing).[12] The police do nothing to address these diverse factors, even though ef-forts to improve community conditions can help reduce crime.[13] It is the case that community policing initiatives exist and, indeed, are widely prevalent. However, their design often does not include a focus on addressing com-munity conditions that give rise to crime, and they frequently face substantial implementation challenges, especially in high-crime communities where citizens may mistrust the police.[14]

Later in the book, we will present the argument that the police are well positioned to engage in crime prevention strategies by being in direct con-tact and working with individuals, families, and communities. However, contemporary policing does not come even close to realizing that possibility. The design of policing, the competing demands on officer time, their reactive posture, and lack of training and resources—all of that makes it difficult for police to be in the business of addressing the causes of offending (e.g., among at-risk populations) or the causes of crime rates (e.g., among areas at risk of or experiencing high rates of crime).

Problem 3: Goals and Mission Creep

Any program or organization with an unclear mandate will be ineffective.[15] Indeed, without clarity about a program's goals, it is hard to know how to evaluate its effectiveness. That certainly characterizes policing, and can be seen in the conventional, but incorrect, view that the police exist to promote public safety through crime prevention. They don't. Or rather they do, but only in the quite narrow sense of responding to crime. Let's view the matter this way: We expect a family doctor to not only cure disease but also help us to take steps to prevent it. The conventional view of the police is that they protect us from crime. In fact, though, as we have argued, the police do almost nothing to prevent crime—they merely respond to it. And often they do so in ways that will not "cure" offending and may even contribute to it.

So, we begin with a situation of ambiguity about the goals of policing. Is it to prevent crime in communities? To reduce offending among individu-als who perhaps have actually committed a crime? To respond to the policy priorities of prosecutors, pursuing gang crime when prosecutors show an interest in pursuing such crime, drug crime when they seem inclined to ad-dress this particular type of offending, or some other crime? To patrol school hallways to reduce crime? Or to help youth? To empower communities to fight crime on their own?

Then, added to that problem is mission creep. Over many decades, law en-forcement has been called upon to shoulder an increasingly diverse range of issues and circumstances that have little or nothing to do with crime. Use-of-time surveys illustrate how the roles and responsibilities of police have greatly expanded over time. As Alex Vitale, in an op-ed in the *Washington Post*, has observed,

> Police spend most of their time on noncriminal matters, including patrol, paperwork, noise complaints, traffic infractions and people in distress. An observational study in *Criminal Justice Review* shows that patrol officers, who make up most of police forces, spend about one-third of their time on random patrol, one-fifth responding to non-crime calls and about 17 percent responding to crime-related calls—the vast majority of which are misdemeanors.[16]

Mission creep (which we discuss in the next chapter) stems from a failure to clarify the goals of policing and ensure that law enforcement agencies are designed and funded to achieve these goals. It also stems from a failure of government to find and fund better alternatives for addressing social problems like mental health crises, medical calls, truancy, students who are disruptive in school, traffic, and community disorder, among many others. The end result? Policing that cannot do much to prevent crime, that is not well-equipped to substitute for societal failures to create institutions to address a variety of social problems, and that becomes increasingly at risk of contributing to crime and injustice.

Problem 4: Lack of Clarity about How Large Police Departments Should Be

A common debate and challenge in police departments around the country centers on police force size. If crime goes up, the largely unchecked assumption is that we need more police. One will look long and hard, however, to identify calls for police force reductions, even when crime declines. The exception, of course, is the emergence in recent years of calls to defund the police.

How large should police forces be? Put differently, how many police officers do we really need? To answer that question well requires clarity about the precise goals of policing, the scope of the problem (e.g., crime) in society, the causes of the problem, and so on. For example, consider two identical communities. In one, the main causes of increased crime stem from insufficient housing and employment opportunities, while in another it stems from gang-related drug production and dealing. In the former community, investing in strategies to alleviate the housing and employment problems might be indicated more so than investing in the police. In the latter, perhaps investing in more police might make greater sense.

What justifications actually generate police force expansion? Not the above type of assessments but instead comparisons to other equally sized jurisdictions, pointing to increased crime, and policymakers looking for quick fixes. The politicization of crime control contributes to the latter. Political candidates paint their opponents as "weak" on crime and themselves as the obvious choice for public safety. One of the most unmistakable ways to make this point is to campaign on clear-cut polarized platforms, along the lines of "Vote for me. I'm for the police. And keeping you safe. But not my opponent, who wants to free criminals and cut funding to the police." This type of rhetoric arguably helped in the election of George H. W. Bush to the presidency. In a now-famous television advertisement, he showed a profile of Willie Horton, who was furloughed on Massachusetts governor Michael Dukakis's watch.[17] And one of President William J. Clinton's signature criminal justice policies was to call for and fund the hiring of 100,000 more police officers nationwide during his time in office.[18]

The problem ultimately is not police expansion but rather the lack of clarity about the goals of policing and the best design or structure of policing to achieve those goals. It includes as well a lack of research-based information about the causes of crime, which is critical if in fact the police are to play a prominent role in preventing and addressing crime.

Problem 5: Increasingly Militarized Police

Over the past fifty-plus years, local law enforcement has become increasingly militarized. This is most often seen in displays of SWAT (Special Weapons and Tactics) operations, which typically involve the use of military equipment and heavily armed and protected officers. How we got to this point is a topic we will take up in detail in Chapter 3.

The militarization of local police is a concern for a variety of reasons. When police have military equipment, they tend to use it in situations that may not require it. An extensive analysis of the use of militarized SWAT by the ACLU found that these special tactics and weapons were originally intended for hostage and active shooter situations, but that the police increasingly have been using them for much less dangerous activities, such as serving warrants and drug searches.[19] The ACLU analysis found that the vast majority of SWAT deployments that they studied were for executing a warrant, typically for a drug investigation. They found that under 10 percent of deployments were for hostage, barricade, or active shooter situations.

Fredrick Lemieux, a Georgetown University criminologist, has observed that the use of SWAT has trickled down "to much more ordinary operations, like drug busts and patrolling areas with high concentrations of crime."[20]

Research by Peter Kraska supports these conclusions. The traditional function of SWAT teams entailed reacting to high-risk, dangerous situations, but Kraska found in his research that 80 percent of SWAT deployments instead entailed drug raids. As he highlighted in describing the evolution in militarized policing, "PPUs [Police Paramilitary Units] changed from bring a periphery and strictly reactive component of police departments to a proactive force actively engaged in fighting the drug war."[21]

Militarized policing was sold as a way to enhance public safety, fight crime, and protect police officers who were engaged in dangerous situations. The reality is different. A study of over 9,000 police departments in the United States by Jonathan Mumolo found that police militarization has reduced neither violent crime nor police officers assaulted or killed.[22] Moreover, this militarization of law enforcement has occurred without public oversight.

Problem 6: Lack of Coordination with Courts and Resistance to Reform

It should come as no surprise that the criminal justice system is not a system. Rather, it is a set of silos that to a disturbing degree operate independently of each other and can work in opposition to one another. Such is the case with law enforcement and the courts.

The police, along with prosecutors and judges, have pursued a largely tough-on-crime approach over the past five decades. That accords with the notion of the police as "crime fighters," with the prosecute, convict, and "lock 'em up" priorities of many prosecutors and judges. Changes, however, have been under way that put the police in conflict with court actors and with calls to approach crime in a different way.

Criminal justice reform has become a primary focus of many policymakers and elected officials at the federal, state, and local levels of government. However, law enforcement agencies, and their unions, by and large appear to be out of sync with these efforts. Although police agencies in general have continued down a crime-fighting, paramilitary path, many prosecutors and judges are increasingly promoting reforms that place less emphasis on arresting and prosecuting every individual who commits a crime and more on diversion to treatment and rehabilitation.[23]

As one example, it is not uncommon for law enforcement to resist prosecutor-driven shifts toward not prosecuting minor misdemeanors. Bail reform has also been opposed by police agencies and unions. One of us (Kelly) interviewed a number of reform prosecutors for his book, *The Crisis in the American Criminal Courts.*[24] These prosecutors, elected on platforms of criminal justice reform and increased police accountability, highlighted that one of the key barriers to implementing change was opposition by law enforcement agencies as well as police associations and unions. For example, a common reform measure is to shift to not prosecuting low-level drug possession. The police and their union representatives typically criticize these efforts as "soft on crime" and, in turn, as contributing to higher crime rates.

Reform-minded prosecutors have argued for greater police accountability in matters like use of force and killing of civilians. But many unions have created substantial roadblocks to its implementation. After Derek Chauvin was charged with murder in the death of George Floyd, Lieutenant Bob Kroll, the union president for the Minneapolis Police Department, criticized the prosecutor and other local officials for firing the four officers involved without due process. Kroll said, "It is despicable behavior." As the *New York Times* noted, "Mr. Kroll, who is himself the subject of at least 29 complaints, has also chided the Obama administration for its 'oppression of police' and praised President Trump as someone who 'puts the handcuffs on the criminals instead of us.'"[25] Kroll also called the George Floyd protesters a terrorist movement.

In 2020, the U.S. Conference of Mayors took police unions head-on in claiming that the collective bargaining agreements that the unions negotiate are a primary obstacle to police reform.[26] The Chicago Task Force on Police Reform concluded: "The collective bargaining agreements between the police unions and the City have essentially turned the code of silence into official policy."[27]

Other impediments to accountability are civil service protections, the so-called Law Enforcement Officers' Bill of Rights, as well as specific legislative statutes. Professor Jill McCorkel, an expert on policing and police unions, states:

> Research suggests that these unions play a critical role in thwarting the transformation of police departments. . . . These agreements [the union contracts] do more than just establish basic parameters governing salaries, raises and overtime pay. They also dictate how investigations into officer misconduct will be carried out, the types of disciplinary measures available to departments and avenues of redress for officers seeking to overturn or evade sanction.[28]

Moreover, the various protections provided by union negotiations block civilian review boards from effectively overseeing police, keep much of police disciplinary proceedings out of the light of day, and prevent public access to personnel files and body camera footage.

Police unions' power exists largely because they typically enjoy the support of both political parties. Republicans tend to be pro-police and Democrats tend to be pro-union. That power further siloes the police from the courts and reforms. Of course, the goal is not for the police to somehow do the bidding of, say, prosecutors. It is for the police, along with the courts, to embrace changes that will promote public safety and justice. Change, though, cannot happen when key players staunchly resist it and insist on reinforcing the status quo.

Critical Problems in Policing—Harmful Impacts

We turn next to a different set of problems in policing, namely harms that may arise from the approaches to policing that have been taken. The first and most obvious is a failure to prevent or reduce crime. But other harms exist that constitute concerns in their own right and that can contribute to a failure to protect the public.

Problem 7: Failure to Prevent or Reduce Crime

Some people believe that the criminal justice system successfully reduces crime, and they might point to the crime decline of the 1990s, a period that ushered in historically low crime rates that we still have today. But it is a fallacy. For starters, property crime had been declining for decades and continued to do so before the move toward get-tough policies.[29] In addition, viewed from a historical perspective, the crime decline appeared to be simply a resumption of the prior trend—that is, a temporary rise and fall in crime occurred against a broader backdrop of continuity. There are still other ways to highlight the logical fallacy. We can look, for example, to crime trends in other Western countries. They followed essentially the same patterns as the United States, but with nothing like our tough-on-crime policies.[30]

Considerable research has tried to sort out the relative effects of various explanations for the crime decline.[31] The evidence provided by the Brennan Center for Justice shows that mass incarceration, the hallmark of American criminal justice policy over the past five decades, had a marginal impact on the decline in property crime (roughly 5 to 10 percent of the decline), and less than 1 percent of the decline in violent crime.[32] The Brennan Center's original state-level research and past studies they analyzed indicate a minor role due to increases in the size of police departments, with a relative estimated effect of somewhere between 0 and 10 percent of the crime decline. They concluded there was no effect since the year 2000. Research conducted by the *Washington Post* shows essentially no correlation between local, inflation-adjusted per capita spending on police and crime rates.[33]

The Brennan Center measured one city-level police characteristic, the use of CompStat by police departments. Although there are other tactics police departments use, such as hot spots policing and stop and frisk, that could conceivably have an impact, so much variation exists in their application that measurement ruled out an aggregate-level study. Separately, the results of the analysis of CompStat, which is a data-based method for police management and accountability to prevent and reduce crime, have identified only a modest impact of between 5 and 15 percent declines in crime in those cities that implemented it. These findings align with past research on the effects of CompStat.[34]

Such results do not necessarily mean that policing strategies are ineffective—or cannot be effective—at reducing crime at the local level. Consider hot spots policing, one of the most widely adopted policing tactics for crime reduction in recent decades. It entails a focused deployment of police patrol resources to relatively small areas that have high crime rates. The logic is simple: identify micro areas with particularly high crime and concentrate patrol resources with the goal of deterring crime by reducing criminal opportunity.

Policing experts like Anthony Braga and David Weisburd, as well as a National Academies panel on proactive policing, have recently investigated the effectiveness of hot spots policing in reducing crime. Relying on both original research and meta-analyses, the assessments show that hot spots policing can have statistically significant, small to modest effects in reducing crime in the area where it occurs.[35] However, research has not identified long-term crime reduction benefits, nor does it show effects much beyond the hot spots themselves; that is, there is no evidence of a diffusion benefit, such that the effects spread out across a broader area. Finally, although the research shows no displacement of crime to the areas immediately surrounding the hot spots, some studies have found displacement to more distant areas.

Another policing strategy that has played a central role in many jurisdictions is the focus on arresting individuals for low-level crimes, which tend to focus on public order offenses. However, arresting individuals for low-level misdemeanors has received considerable pushback in recent years in light of evidence that these arrest policies do not reduce serious crime and often do more harm than good.[36]

We are not saying that policing does not reduce crime. For example, when the police arrest someone, if that person is jailed, prosecuted, convicted, and incarcerated, they are incapacitated and temporarily prevented from committing crime. And we do not deny the modest effects due to efforts like hot spots policing, though displacement remains a concern. Furthermore, there is no question that society needs an institution that can respond when a crime occurs. However, on the whole, we have precious little evidence that policing—as currently practiced—produces appreciable crime prevention or reduction benefits.

We hasten to add that the failure of the police to prevent or reduce crime does not only stand as an indictment of policing, but also serves as an indictment of criminal justice and corrections, and of government in not devising a coherent approach to public safety. Indeed, one could make a similar point about prison systems. The fact that almost all individuals released from prison eventually recidivate can be seen as indicative of correctional system failure.[37] That can be viewed as a fair appraisal. Yet, it remains the case that correctional systems have no control over the communities to which individuals return or over the limited availability of rehabilitative treatment in prisons and jails or in communities.[38] The same applies to law enforcement agencies across the country—the police work within a structural context that does not create meaningful opportunities to prevent or reduce crime and, indeed, that inhibits their ability to do so.

Problem 8: Use of Force—Problems, Effectiveness, and the Ridiculous

Probably the most remarkable thing about police use of force is how little we know about the frequency, circumstances, and consequences of excessive use of force. Thanks to the work of the *Washington Post* and *Mapping Police Violence,* we do know how many civilians are killed by the police each year— about 1,100. The number of civilian deaths has been consistently in the 1,000 to 1,100 range at least since 2013. We also know that 112 children have been fatally shot by police since 2013, 135 unarmed Black males and females have also been shot to death by police since 2015,[39] and 1,000 fatal shootings since 2015 have occurred when police shot at people fleeing in cars.[40]

According to Mapping Police Violence, police use of lethal force is not related to violent crime. There is essentially no statistical relationship between city-level violent crime rates and rates of police killings. In fact, most police killings typically begin with traffic stops, domestic disturbances, mental health checks, and low-level misdemeanor situations.[41]

There is no way of knowing how many fatal police shootings are justified or not. We simply lack sufficient information on a case-by-case basis to even begin to make judgments about whether a shooting was necessary or appropriate. The courts are not much help. Only about 2 percent of police officers are prosecuted for murder in fatal shootings. Since 2005, 126 police officers have been arrested for murder or manslaughter. To date, 44 resulted in convictions, many for lesser charges. Only 7 have been convicted of murder since 2005.[42]

While information on the use of lethal force by police is quite limited, data on nonlethal use of force is nearly nonexistent:

> It's a source of on-going frustration among law enforcement executives, whose only nationwide data on police use of force comes from databases created by the *Washington Post*, and websites such as Fatal Encounters and Mapping Police Violence. In 2015, then-FBI Director James B. Comey told top policing officials he could get the latest box office data on popular movies, but "it's ridiculous—it's embarrassing and ridiculous—that we can't talk about crime in the same way, especially in the high-stakes incidents when your officers have to use force."[43]

In an attempt to rectify the absence of systematic, nationwide statistics on police use of lethal and nonlethal force, the FBI created the National Use-of-Force Data Collection program, launched in 2019. Unfortunately, many local police departments refuse to participate in or cooperate with this data collection effort. In 2019 and 2020, only 27 percent of police departments provided any information. The FBI will not release any data until the participation rate reaches 80 percent, and when and if the release occurs, it will be limited to the national level, and thus provide no insight on local-level lethal and nonlethal use of force.

A briefing before the U.S. Commission on Civil Rights titled *Police Use of Force: An Examination of Modern Police Practices* constitutes an indictment of the state of information on police use of force:

> Data on lower level uses of force, which happen more frequently than officer-involved shootings, are virtually non-existent. This is due in part to the fact that most police precincts don't explicitly collect data on use of force. . . . Without accurate data on police use of force, allegations by community members and actions by law enforcement not only sow distrust among communities and the police, making policing more dangerous, but also jeopardize public safety.[44]

Problem 9: Racism, Ethnic Bias, and Profiling

Probably the two most frequently cited criticisms of U.S. policing are (1) use of force and (2) racial disparities in vehicle stops and street stops, known as stop and frisk or stop, question, and frisk. Without question, there are tremendous racial and ethnic disparities in the criminal justice system, grounded historically in the criminalization of Blacks.[45] There is plenty of shared blame for this situation. That includes the police. But it also includes legislatures and Congress, which create criminal statutes and establish sentencing laws and criminal procedure; prosecutors, who decide who to prosecute and on what charges; judges, who make pretrial detention and sentencing decisions; and corrections (jails, prisons, probation, and parole).[46] However, the police control the front door of the criminal justice system,[47] so it is important that we investigate what is known about police decision-making and racial bias.

The Pew Research Center conducted a recent, nationally representative survey of police officers and the public. Several questions focused on race and attitudes about Blacks. Two-thirds of the officers believed that fatal encounters between the police and Blacks are isolated incidents. Nearly three-quarters of white police officers shared that view, but only 43 percent of Black officers did. Sixty percent of the public and the majority of Black officers think that these fatal encounters reflect broader problems. When viewing race relations in the United States more broadly, the vast majority of white police officers (92 percent) believed that the United States has made the changes necessary to assure equal rights for Blacks. Only 29 percent of Black officers shared that belief.[48] In short, separate from evidence about any objective level of discrimination, there exists evidence of substantial demographic and police-citizen divides in views about it. That, of course, has direct bearing on how the police view citizens but also on how citizens, as well as different social and demographic groups, respond to the police.[49]

In 2018, over 61.5 million individuals in the United States had contact with the police. Nearly one-half of these contacts were police-initiated. Of those 29 million police-initiated contacts, 84 percent involved vehicle stops and 12 percent involved street stops.[50] What is the role of race and ethnicity in these stops?

Racial profiling is understood as a police practice that uses race and ethnicity as a factor in deciding who is sufficiently suspicious to stop, question, frisk, and search. Racial profiling can occur in the context of vehicle stops or street stops. We discuss vehicle stops first.

Vehicle stops that involve racial profiling typically begin with the police observing a traffic violation, an extremely common event. Analyses show that nearly everyone commits a traffic violation of some sort within a limited time frame and driving distance. This vehicle stop then can serve as a pretext for a search for evidence of another crime, commonly drug possession. It is fair to say that the War on Drugs—along with the responsibility of the police to enforce drug laws—has played a very important role in perpetuating the use of racial profiling.

The U.S. Supreme Court has held that this type of policing does not violate the Fourth Amendment protection against unreasonable searches and seizures. Perhaps the most important case on this matter is the 1996 U.S. Supreme Court case *Whren v. United States*. In this case, the police had no evidence, and thus no probable cause, to believe that the petitioners were in possession of cocaine. Nevertheless, the officers used a minor traffic violation to stop the vehicle and conduct a plain-view search and discovered cocaine. The Court held that as long as a driver violated a traffic law, the police have a right to stop the vehicle regardless of their real intent, which was not traffic enforcement but drug enforcement. Whren opened the door for police stops for minor traffic violations, questioning without administering Miranda warnings, consent searches, and plain-view searches, all legal with regard to the Fourth Amendment.[51]

A common denominator in the *Whren* case and many pretext vehicle stops is the race of the driver or the occupants. However, the Supreme Court declared that racial profiling was not relevant to the Fourth Amendment. Rather, it held that racial disparity or racial discrimination was a matter for the Equal Protection Clause of the Fourteenth Amendment. Consequently, evidence obtained from searches and seizures based on a racially motivated, traffic law violation pretext stop could not be suppressed under the Exclusionary Rule. David Harris, of the American Bar Association, has described the barriers to obtaining relief in the courts for racial profiling stops:

> Legal challenges to racial profiling have been numerous, but the successes have been few, given the ways in which the Supreme Court has cleared the way for the police to operate. . . . Success in these suits [under the Equal Protection Clause] is always difficult; most fail—sometimes because plaintiffs have criminal records and would make bad witnesses, sometimes because they lack the resources or patience to carry a multiyear legal battle to a conclusion, sometimes because the evidence is equivocal.[52]

So, what does the research indicate about the extent to which Blacks and Hispanics are racially profiled for vehicle stops? The overwhelming conclusion is that although not every police department and not every police officer engages in racial profiling, racial profiling occurs and is quite prevalent. Blacks and Hispanics have a substantially higher likelihood of being stopped by the police compared to whites, and the threshold of evidence used to lead to a search is lower for Blacks and Hispanics compared to whites.[53]

Apart from the critical and problematic issue of discrimination and injustice, there is also the question of effectiveness. It turns out that racial profiling is counterproductive in at least two ways: It rarely leads to the discovery of illegal contraband, and so does not make us safer, and it creates deep fissures between police and communities of color, eroding trust in and perceived legitimacy of the policy, and, in turn, cooperation with the police. That can only harm public safety, with the harm more likely to be borne by Blacks, Hispanics, and other groups that historically have faced discrimination from U.S. society and the criminal justice system.

Nearly three decades after the first major research studies and lawsuits, and after much deliberation and discussion by federal, state, and local government agencies, racial profiling continues to exist and to be a focus of policy efforts. Many jurisdictions have implemented policies, procedures, and training programs to try to curb it. Today, police departments are required to collect data on traffic stops, including demographic information and details about questioning, searching, and discovery and seizure of contraband. It remains an open question how well the data are analyzed and the extent to which departments appropriately and effectively act on the analyses.

At the end of the day, police discretion governs the decisions officers make. It is also the case that suspicion lies in the eyes of the beholder, so it is difficult to determine when and if race or ethnicity played any role, a modest role, or was the driving factor in raising a concern that becomes the rationale for a vehicle stop.[54] This situation creates yet another layer of difficulty in identifying when and how racism or ethnic bias affects police-citizen interactions. It also highlights the challenges that confront efforts to train or retrain police to eliminate their use of race and ethnicity in decision-making.

Terry v. Ohio 392 U.S. 1 (1968) set the stage for warrantless stop and frisk or stop, question, and frisk in circumstances when a police officer observes someone acting in a suspicious manner that leads the officer to believe that the individual is or is about to engage in criminal activity. The *Terry* decision stipulated that the officer also had to have a suspicion that the individual may be armed and dangerous. Under these circumstances, the officer is required to interrogate the individual and, if the suspicion remains, can then conduct an exterior pat-down (frisk) search. The intent with *Terry* was the discovery of a weapon. And the logic was straightforward: The public safety interest in seizing a dangerous weapon in the hands of a suspicious individual was held to outweigh the Fourth Amendment warrant requirement for a lawful search. A subsequent 1993 U.S. Supreme Court decision, *Minnesota v. Dickerson 508 U.S. 366,* expanded the scope of a *Terry* search by allowing the lawful seizure of contraband in addition to or in lieu of a weapon. The Court in *Terry* and *Dickerson* created the opportunity for what would become in many jurisdictions the stop-and-frisk version of racial profiling.

A large number of studies have identified racial and ethnic disparities in street stops. New York City has been the subject of much of this research, but substantial racial and ethnic differences in who is stopped by police have been found in many other cities, including Boston, Washington DC, Philadelphia, Chicago, Los Angeles, Milwaukee, Minneapolis, and Baltimore, among many others. Although the differentials vary across cities and studies, the results clearly show that Blacks and Hispanics, compared to whites, face a greater likelihood of being stopped by the police.[55] For example, of the five million pedestrian stops made by the NYPD between 2002 and 2019, 85 percent were stops of Blacks and Hispanics.[56] In Milwaukee, stops of Blacks were six times that of whites.[57] In 2019 in Boston, nearly 70 percent of all pedestrian stops were Blacks, while Blacks constituted only 25 percent of the city's population.[58] Similarly, in Chicago, Blacks were the subjects of nearly three-fourths of all pedestrian stops, but constituted under one-third of the population.[59] The evidence also shows that police use a lower threshold of suspicion for Blacks and Hispanics compared to whites.[60]

Many studies have shown that Blacks and Latinos are substantially more likely to be searched (frisked) after being stopped than whites and are more likely to be subject to use of force by police.[61] Ironically, the vast majority of these stop-and-frisk searches are unproductive. New York City data indicate that in only 1 percent of searches of Blacks and Hispanics did the police find a weapon.[62] These searches also failed to generate evidence of a crime. ACLU analysis of New York City data for the last two decades shows that the "over-whelming majority" of individuals in stop-and-frisk stops are innocent.[63]

Intervention by the courts (e.g., *Floyd v. City of New York, 959 F. Supp 2nd 540* [S.D.N.Y.], 2013) appears to have had only marginal effects on racially driven stop-and-frisk incidents. In the *Floyd* case, the court found that the NYPD violated both the Fourth Amendment protection against unreason-able searches and seizures and the Fourteenth Amendment Equal Protection Clause in their use of racially motivated stop-and-frisk incidents. The *Floyd* case resulted in a dramatic drop in the number of stops and searches. At the height of its use in 2011, 685,724 stops were recorded, and 91 percent were of Blacks and Hispanics. In 2014, there were 45,787 stops. By 2019, there were 13,459. Unfortunately, from a constitutional perspective, the stops appear just as racially motivated as before *Floyd*. In 2014, 80 percent involved Blacks and Hispanics, and in 2019, the proportion rose to 88 percent.[64] And in 2021, 8,947 stops occurred, and 87 percent involved Blacks and Hispanics.[65]

Another important way in which race and ethnicity play out in policing is in the use of force and in the use of lethal force. The 2018 data referenced ear-lier on police-citizen encounters indicate that 1,254,300 individuals 16 years and older experienced threat of force or actual force by the police in that year. Blacks experienced threats or force at a rate 2.6 times that of whites. The com-parable differential for Hispanics was 2.4. Of those who experienced force, 51 percent believed the force to be excessive. There are significant differences by race and ethnicity here as well, with 44 percent of whites, 63 percent of Blacks, and 54 percent of Hispanics saying that the police used excessive force.[66]

Due to cell phone video, dash cam video, and police body cam video, we increasingly witness the use of lethal force against civilians. Do they inac-curately convey racial and ethnic differences in experiences with the police? It does not seem so, at least not in general. For example, analyses of data on police shootings clearly show that the risk of being killed by the police varies by race and ethnicity. Black Americans are 2.5 times more likely than whites to be killed by the police. The differential for Hispanics is between 1.5 and 1.9. Edwards and colleagues' statistical analysis of probabilities of being killed by the police concluded: "Police violence is a leading cause of death for young men, and young men of color face exceptionally high risk of being killed by the police. Inequalities in risk are pronounced throughout the life course."[67]

Such differences only begin to scratch the surface. Studies of intersectional-ity, for example, highlight how gender and race intertwine to create unique forms of marginalization among Black women, not only in American society but also in their experiences with the police and criminal justice system. Media accounts, for example, typically provide less coverage when Black women experience police violence, and, as Janice Joseph has highlighted, "the deaths of Black women have not sparked the same level of national and global outrage against police brutality as the killing of several Black men by police officers."[68] More broadly, research identifies the disparate experiences that minorities face in police interactions.[69]

Problem 10: Police Accountability, Citizen Oversight, and Qualified Immunity

Several of the problems we have already discussed, such as militarization of the police, use of force, and racism, all invoke a broader concern about controlling police misconduct and holding police accountable. Extensive media coverage of stop and frisk, racial profiling, police use of force, and civilian killings has brought the issue of accountability front and center. Yet, here is the sobering reality: There exist no uniform, nationwide standards for investigating and disciplining officers for misconduct.

Some jurisdictions have independent citizen review boards responsible for investigating cases of misconduct. These boards' independence gives them legitimacy compared to internal police reviews and can help enhance trust in law enforcement. However, citizen review boards appear to be the exception; indeed, most jurisdictions do not have independent review boards. And those that do exist lack much, if any, ability to impose consequences for misconduct. For example, as of 2016, only six of the top fifty largest police departments had civilian review boards with disciplinary authority.[70]

In addition to review boards, civil lawsuits can be brought under 42 U.S.C. 1983, a federal law that prohibits constitutional violations when police are acting in their official capacity. These lawsuits are either state or federal actions and represent the most common method for enforcing constitutional protections.[71]

One of the more contentious issues involving police misconduct, including unlawful arrest, profiling, use of force, and lethal police shootings, is qualified immunity, which protects government officials from being held personally liable for monetary damages in civil cases involving the violation of someone's constitutional rights. Police departments, associations, and unions claim qualified immunity is necessary to protect police in the course of making difficult, split-second decisions in dangerous or lethal situations. They also claim that without it, police departments would be decimated by resignations. No one would want to be an officer.

The substantial power of police unions and police associations can be seen in their role in opposing state efforts to eliminate qualified immunity. In the aftermath of the George Floyd killing, at least thirty-five states attempted to eliminate qualified immunity. All of the efforts died, due largely to the political power and influence of police unions and associations. Efforts at the federal level have suffered a similar fate. The only state that has successfully eliminated it as a legal defense is Colorado. To date, there is little evidence of the dire warnings by the unions.[72]

The Pew Research Center survey of police officers also addressed accountability and the disciplinary process. Under one-half (45 percent) believed that the disciplinary process in their department was fair. Strikingly, though, nearly three-quarters did not believe that officers who consistently do a poor job are held accountable.[73]

The apparent inability to adequately hold police accountable is not lost on the public. An April 2021 ABC News/*Washington Post* survey found that 55 percent of the public do not believe the police are adequately trained to avoid using excessive force. Here, again, stark racial divides exist. For example, 53 percent of whites, 83 percent of Blacks, and 67 percent of Hispanics believed that more should be done to hold police accountable for mistreatment of Black people.[74] A 2020 PEW Center poll found that two-thirds of respondents believed that civilians need to have the power to sue police officers to hold them accountable for excessive use of force or misconduct. Nearly 70 percent do not believe that police departments hold officers accountable when misconduct occurs.[75] And a 2020 CATO Institute survey revealed that nearly two-thirds of the public favor eliminating qualified immunity for the police.[76]

Critical Problems in Policing—Operational Issues

Next, we turn to what can be termed operational issues, or challenges, that undermine effective policing in contemporary America. These constitute the nuts-and-bolts of everyday policing. They are not by any stretch exhaustive, but convey the substantial barriers that exist to effectively preventing or reducing crime, generating appropriate and just decision-making, or creating greater public confidence in and satisfaction with the police.

Problem 11: Inadequate Officer Training

Many problems with modern American policing originate in the quantity and type of training officers receive. Training here refers to the initial academy instruction that cadets receive as well as ongoing field instruction after they graduate from the academy.

There are approximately 18,000 law enforcement agencies in the United States, yet there exist no universal or nationwide standards for police training.

Instead, state agencies set the minimum number of hours required to become a police officer. Meanwhile, local departments have considerable influence over the curriculum used to train officers.

The relatively small number of hours required to graduate from a police academy is, on the face of it, surprising given the enormous power that the police wield and the stakes involved, including the risk of violating individuals' rights and of death. Consider, for illustrative purposes, Texas, where the Texas Sunset Commission has the responsibility of assessing state agency performance. After examining the Texas Commission on Law Enforcement standards for police training, they provided the following sardonic assessment: "To qualify for a peace officer license, Texas cops need fewer hours of basic training than licensed cosmetologists and less than half the education required of air conditioning and refrigeration contractors."[77]

Texas is not an outlier. Insufficient training exists nationwide. For example, Georgia requires 408 hours of academy training, but 1,500 hours to become a licensed barber. Maryland requires 1,168 hours of academy training, while a licensed barber is required to have between 3,000 and 8,500 hours of training.[78]

A survey of 281 police departments conducted by the Police Executive Research Forum found that, on average, cadets received 107 hours of firearms and self-defense training, and only 8 hours of de-escalation training.[79] Separately, the Bureau of Justice Statistics (BJS) surveyed 681 police training academies. The average length of time in academy training was 833 hours. Assuming eight-hour days, that amounts to 104 days or just over three months of instruction.

Comparison to requirements in other countries paints an even starker picture.[80] The Institute for Criminal Justice Training Reform (ICJTR) analyzed the training requirements in over 100 countries. The United States had among the lowest required number of hours of any country. Many of our Western allies have training requirements that far surpass those in the United States. For example, the ICJTR research found that Portugal requires about 10,000 hours of training, Finland requires 5,500 hours, Germany requires 4,000 hours, Australia requires 3,500, England 2,250, and Canada 1,000.[81] For reference, a work year consists of about 2,000 hours. So, while a typical department in the United States might require only three months of training, Germany requires two years.

Not only are training requirements insufficient by a variety of standards, but it appears that officers do not always meet these minimum requirements. A troubling 2019–20 audit of the Los Angeles Sheriff's Department highlights that the vast majority of deputies had not completed required training. The Sheriff of Los Angeles County told the *Los Angeles Times* that "the Sheriff's

Department has made progress in training personnel since he took over the department in 2018. He said compliance with training requirements is at 37 percent, up from 22 percent when he started." [82]

The 2018 Bureau of Justice Statistics report compiled average number of hours of training in various areas. Those areas with the greatest average length of instruction included firearms skills (73 hours), defensive tactics (61 hours), patrol procedures (52 hours), criminal/constitutional law (51 hours), health and fitness (50 hours), and emergency vehicle operation (40 hours). Those areas with some of the lowest average number of instructional hours were mediation/conflict management (13 hours), problem-solving (16 hours), cultural diversity (14 hours), community building (11 hours), de-escalation (18 hours), nonlethal weapons (20 hours), ethics and integrity (12 hours), and stress prevention (9 hours). [83]

The distribution of instructional time in police academies highlights where departmental priorities lie. These priorities have real-world implications. For example, the disparities between weapons and defense training on the one hand and problem-solving, de-escalation, mediation, and conflict management on the other likely limit the options that police officers have when they encounter diverse situations. Furthermore, training will have lasting effects on an individual's approach to policing. As Chief Max Westbrook (ret.), a member of the Austin Police Department and a licensed academy instructor for three decades, once said to Kelly, "You never get a chance to redo the academy. First impressions are critical."

Historically, police academies operated as paramilitary institutions. Today, the evidence suggests that although the paramilitary approach persists nationwide, many academies have attempted to provide a more balanced approach, part paramilitary and part academic or adult learning. The 2018 BJS report shows that about one-quarter of the academies were mostly paramilitary, and 50 percent indicated they struck a balance between paramilitary and academic instruction. [84] Nevertheless, the type of training that typical cadets receive still leans heavily toward firearms and defense tactics and deemphasizes "soft skills" like conflict resolution, communication, use of emotional intelligence, and problem-solving.

The academy is not the end of officer training. Once they graduate, officers undergo field training, which is to say, instruction in a real-world setting. The 2018 BJS study reports that the average length of field training is just over 500 hours. In theory, field training makes good sense. The reality? In many departments, older officers lead field training, and they can and do perpetuate traditional, "old-school" approaches to policing. Derek Chauvin, found guilty of murdering George Floyd in Minneapolis in 2020, was a field trainer at the time of Floyd's death.

A recent analysis by the Marshall Project concluded that field training, like academy training, is highly problematic. One reason is the trainers:

> Field training officers are a big reason problems persist, according to current and former police leaders, academics and even the U.S. Justice Department. . . . The trainers get little formal instruction on how to mold young officers' behavior. Becoming a field trainer is seen as a mark of prestige and seniority, rather than a serious challenging job, law enforcement officers said. Critics say the low standards create poisonous field training programs that fuel a toxic street-cop culture, marked by too much aggression and too little accountability.[85]

To this point, we have focused on curriculum and length of instruction. But it is also important to assess who is being recruited to the academies and how candidates are screened. Donald Grady II (ret.), who spent more than thirty years in policing, including serving as a chief in several cities, has emphasized the critical importance of candidate selection:

> I cannot suggest to you a single training course that I could give someone that would change their thinking when it came to making a decision to shoot or not shoot when there is absolutely no threat to their person. This is not a training issue. This is an issue of who it is that we've decided we would allow to police our country. . . . There's a certain amount of aggression that they look for in a person. If you're too docile, I've known people to be rejected from police departments because they weren't aggressive enough. Why are we hiring people to do policing because of their level of aggression?[86]

You get what you recruit. If departments recruit aggressive individuals, that is the kind of officer they put out on the streets. If they recruit candidates with just a high school education, they risk getting individuals with less knowledge about problem-solving, different cultures, and critical thinking. To be sure, an education does not automatically confer such benefits, and plenty of people with a high school degree or no formal education can surpass college-educated individuals along a range of dimensions. The risk remains, however. If departments recruit in such a way that their workforce consists primarily of one group (e.g., white males), and not of other groups in a community, they end up with a workforce that is less likely to be able to understand or appreciate cultural, gender, or other differences relevant to effective communication and interaction with citizens.

Rank-and-file officers recognize problems with police training. The Pew Research Center conducted a survey of officers in 2017 and found substantial concern about training. Sixty percent stated their department has done only somewhat well or not well in training them adequately for their job.[87]

Training shortfalls, it should be emphasized, do not just affect police effectiveness in interacting with citizens and performing their job well. They can have life-or-death consequences for officers, and they can affect officers' physical and mental health as well as their families and their intimate and personal relationships.[88]

Problem 12: Police Discretion and Officer Supervision

Discretion is a hallmark of the American criminal justice system, and policing is certainly no exception.[89] Patrol officers have to routinely exercise judgment while responding to calls, assessing a wide variety of situations, conducting searches and seizures, interviewing witnesses and those who have been victimized or alleged to have committed a crime, evaluating evidence, determining whether use of force is necessary and, if so, how much to use, and determining what is an appropriate resolution, such as making an arrest, issuing a citation, or counseling individuals involved in a dispute.

It can be argued that discretion is necessary in effective decision-making, and that efforts to stamp out discretion can backfire.[90] Yet, when discretion entails bad decision-making—reflecting errors in judgment, stereotypes or biases, and so on—that can lead to ineffectiveness and discrimination. This is true in medicine and many other fields, and, no less, criminal justice.[91] As the examples above highlight, in policing, inappropriate exercise of discretion may lead officers to rely on inordinate and improper use of stop and frisk, have aggressive interactions with the public, engage in racial or ethnic profiling, or use excessive force. None of that promotes public safety or justice.

One approach to improving officer discretion is, of course, training. Another is field supervision. As our discussion above highlighted, problems exist in both areas. It is simply not known which of the 18,000 police departments and law enforcement agencies nationally provide adequate field supervision and feedback, much less whether these improve officer decision-making. We do know from research and litigation that effective supervision of patrol officers constitutes a significant problem. As one example, the U.S. Department of Justice investigated the New Orleans Police Department and noted:

> Front line supervision, especially of officers patrolling and responding to calls in the field, is a lynchpin of effective and constitutional policing. Field supervisors provide the close and consistent supervision necessary to guide officers' conduct and to help them learn from their mistakes. They are in the best position to recognize a problem with an officer's conduct and intervene immediately to ameliorate or prevent harm. . . . How a field supervisor conducts him or herself, and whether he/she requires adherence to policy and ethics, sets a tone of accountability and integrity—or not.[92]

Having emphasized the critical importance of supervision, the DOJ investigation concluded that the New Orleans Police Department failed to provide the supervision necessary to detect and prevent officer misconduct and to promote effective policing.

Consider another example: The federal government sued the Seattle Police Department (*United States of America v. City of Seattle*, in the U.S. District Court for the Western District of Washington at Seattle), which led to court monitoring to determine if the department was complying with a consent decree that mandated changes to field supervision of the use of force. Other cities that have been subject to consent decrees over field supervision and related policing issues include Los Angeles; Chicago; Baltimore; Cleveland; Yonkers, New York; Ferguson, Missouri; Detroit; Washington, DC; Pittsburgh; East Haven, Connecticut; Albuquerque; Steubenville, Ohio; and Warren, Ohio, among others.[93]

In short, supervision matters, and the courts have recognized that fact. At the same time, research has demonstrated that supervision approaches or styles influence such behaviors as making arrests, using force, and how officers implement community policing. For example, if a supervisor adheres to a more traditional, "old-school" approach to policing, he will promote more aggressive policing practices and denigrate or simply ignore alternative strategies, like community policing, when supervising officers in the field. Similarly, if the supervisor emphasizes arrests and citations as a metric of performance, that expectation will influence the officers he oversees. By contrast, supervisors who embrace community policing and problem-solving policing will tend to employ coaching and mentoring strategies.[94] Moreover, use of force is related to supervisor type, as is self-initiated proactive policing strategies, community policing, and problem-solving policing.[95]

Problem 13: The 911 System

According to the National Emergency Number Association (NNA), there are approximately 240 million 911 calls per year.[96] Police spend most of their time responding to these calls, most of which do not involve violent crimes or crimes in progress. It is, in many respects, that simple—the police spend too much time not on crime prevention or even responding to actual crimes, but on minor offending or incidents that entail no criminal activity at all.

These 911 systems rely on call-takers who listen to citizen input, ask questions, and make decisions. Sometimes those decisions are aided by computerized systems called CADs, or computer assisted dispatch. Whether using a CAD or not, call-takers exercise a considerable amount of discretion in interpreting what a caller is saying and making decisions about what to relay to the police or to the police dispatcher. The call-takers serve as the gatekeepers to the police, and the information they provide to the police determines how officers respond. In short, they occupy a unique and powerful influence over what the police do.

Sometimes, failures by call-takers to provide accurate information have tragic consequences. Consider the 911 call involving Tamir Rice, the 12-year-old Black child killed by police in Cleveland. The initial 911 call reported a "guy here with a pistol." That is what the police heard. The caller also qualified the initial report by saying that the gun was "probably fake" and the individual was "probably a juvenile." For whatever reason, these caveats never made it to the responding police.[97] They drove up to Tamir Rice in the park where he was playing and within two seconds, one of the officers shot him at point-blank range.

Correct information is critical and can dramatically influence how police act. A University of Colorado experiment with 300 police officers from eighteen different agencies illustrates the point. All officers were told there was a trespass in progress. Some were told that the subject had a gun; the others were told that the individual was talking on a cell phone. The researchers relied on an interactive firearms training simulator to conduct the study, and found something remarkable and disturbing. Only 6 percent of officers who were told the subject had a cell phone shot the individual. By contrast, 62 percent of the officers who were told the subject had a gun shot the individual.[98]

Framing effects—that is, how a situation or individual is characterized—can profoundly influence how others see the situation or individual and, in turn, the approach that they take.[99] When we consider the police, then, we need to focus not only on police-citizen interactions, but also on the "framing" that occurs prior to that interaction.

With that backdrop, we can appreciate how important the 911 system is in police officer decision-making. This system determines if police are dispatched, how quickly they respond, and what they are assuming when they arrive on the scene. What is relayed to the police depends in part on what call-takers are told but is also influenced by the discretion that they exercise. Research conducted by the Vera Institute, for example, found substantial differences in call classifications made by call-takers compared to the classifications made by researchers.[100]

Jessica Gillooly, a research fellow at the Policing Project at the New York University Law School and a former call-taker, conducted research demonstrating that call-taker discretion often leans in the direction of overstating the seriousness of the situation. Gillooly emphasized that call-takers are trained and incentivized to err in that direction:

There's a huge training emphasis that essentially tells call-takers, "You're safer and better off by sending a police over-response." The big fear is that you don't send a big enough or serious enough response and something bad happens.[101]

Independent evidence backs this assessment. For example, it is estimated that between 20 and 40 percent of the crimes dispatched by call-takers are subsequently downgraded by police when they arrive at the scene.[102]

A comprehensive assessment of the 911 research literature by the Vera Institute concluded that we really do not know much about the 911 system, call-maker discretion, and the impacts—good, bad, or indifferent—that these have on public safety or justice outcomes. It also concluded that little was known about how calls are processed; how call-takers, dispatchers, and other 911 personnel are trained or supervised; and the effectiveness of any training.

Without such information, we are left in a similar and now all-too-familiar place: evidence of design and implementation flaws that undermine police effectiveness. There is, at the same time, the concern that the 911 system contributes to mission creep in what we ask of the police. If a call does not involve a fire or a need for an emergency medical system (EMS) response, it will likely go to the police, whether it is within the traditional scope of police responsibilities (crime) or not. Absent other options, the police tend to be the go-to default. That includes cases involving suicide and mental health crises, situations that not only fall outside the purview of preventing or reducing crime but also require even more specialized training than most officers can or do receive.

Problem 14: Police Use of Time

Our reliance on the police, both in terms of volume of requests for service and the variety of activities we expect them to perform, is quite revealing. Research shows that it is common for public safety call centers to receive between one and two calls for service per person in a given jurisdiction annually.[103]

Many research reports and media stories document how police use their time. The *Los Angeles Times* found that since 2010, there were 18 million calls for service in Los Angeles, and fewer than 8 percent were for violent crime.[104] The *New York Times* compiled calls for service data from ten different cities and found that about 1 percent of calls were for serious violent crime. The *Times* analysis also found that police in New Orleans spent 4 percent of their time on serious violent crime. The estimates were similar for Montgomery County, Maryland, and Sacramento, California.[105]

A more comprehensive analysis was conducted by Cynthia Lum, Christopher Koper, and Xiaoyun Wu.[106] Their research analyzed over four million 911 calls across nine different jurisdictions and classified the calls into one of fourteen categories: administrative and non-crime events; alarms; vice; disorder, including disturbing the peace, graffiti, and public intoxication; domestic related; follow-ups; mental; medical; missing persons; violent crime; property crime; suspicious persons/vehicles; traffic; and nonviolent interpersonal disputes.

Lum and colleagues found that the most common types of calls for service on average were traffic (17 percent), disorder (16 percent), suspicious persons/vehicles (13 percent), and follow-up calls (11 percent). Calls for violent crimes constituted 6.4 percent of all calls for service, and 10 percent were for property crimes.

The authors then estimated the percentage of total call time spent on each call category, providing an estimate of the relative time burden for each. The highest was traffic (18 percent), property crime (15 percent), and disorder (12 percent). Violent crimes comprised just over 9 percent of all call time spent.

Finally, the Lum and colleagues' analysis looked at call outcomes. It is quite rare for police to actually make an arrest or issue a citation. Between 2 and 8 percent of calls resulted in an arrest or a citation, and traffic citations accounted for the bulk of these outcomes. Lum and colleagues concluded:

> For a large majority of calls for service on average and across particular event types, officers rarely made an arrest and infrequently wrote an official report. Most of the time (between 62% and 83% of calls received) they are likely providing assistance, advice or peacekeeping functions, and took no official action . . . beyond responding to the call.[107]

Thinking about police use of time serves as a starting point for (1) determining what police actually do and how much time is devoted to each type of activity, and (2) rethinking the roles and responsibilities of the police. Indeed, it forces us to rethink the goals of policing. And it leads, we argue, to clear evidence of the design flaws we enumerated earlier. Misuse and ineffective use of employee time is essentially guaranteed when organizations suffer from ambiguity about their goals and from mission creep.

Later in the book, we present solutions that we argue can position the police to more effectively promote public safety, but that require reforming not just how we approach policing but also how we approach public safety writ large. As this discussion highlights, one obvious starting point consists of allocating police time to be focused exclusively, or near exclusively, on crime prevention and reduction efforts. That requires, however, identifying ways for other government or societal institutions to address the myriad other matters to which police presently attend. Reforming policing is not, it should be evident, a matter of focusing only on the police but also, and simultaneously, on institutions outside of the police.

Problem 15: Police Ill-Equipped to Manage the Consequences of Mass Reentry

This is not a book on mass incarceration, but we would be remiss in not highlighting the consequences of the marked growth in prisons, and thus prisoner reentry, on policing.[108] Each year, over 600,000 individuals from prisons are released into the community. And, on any given day, there are about 870,000 individuals on parole.[109] Based on research on the consequences of incarceration, we know that many of these individuals may be at a higher—not lower—risk of reoffending. Why? Because incarceration can be criminogenic.[110]

These individuals return to communities and may be at more risk of offending and, in general, are higher risk than the average person. In addition, their withdrawal from and return to communities may contribute to higher crime rates in these areas.[111] But the problem goes beyond mass incarceration. It involves what might be termed mass corrections. The police do not just work in communities where individuals released from prison go, they work in communities that have individuals on probation or parole as well.

The police, of course, are the ones most likely to encounter these individuals, and their most likely response will be an arrest. What else can they do? They do not have the mandate, funding, or training to address the diverse issues and needs of the correctional system population, nor are they readily equipped to empower communities in ways that can reduce the potential harms that correctional system populations and punitive crime policies may create.

Problem 16: Police Officers' Attitudes about Their Jobs

The current climate of policing, in particular the high-profile killings of minorities by police, has led officers to report that policing is more difficult than in the past. The Pew Research Center survey of police shows that 86 percent believe their job is harder.[112] The vast majority (93 percent) express concern about their personal safety.

The Pew survey paints a divided picture of police officers and their reactions to their job. Over half say their work makes them feel proud, 50 percent say their job often frustrates them, and 56 percent say it has made them more callous. Those who have become more callous also are more likely to be angry or frustrated with their jobs.

Although the vast majority of officers are strongly committed to making their department successful and three-quarters are satisfied with their jobs, they are less sanguine about their departmental leadership. Only 30 percent expressed support for the direction that their agency leadership was taking.

They also expressed significant reservations about resources. Nearly all believed that they have too few officers to adequately police their jurisdiction.

Just as importantly, police officers believe that the public does not understand the dangers, risks, and challenges involved in policing. Nearly 90 percent stated that the public does not understand these aspects of the police role.

Despite this bleak picture, recent Department of Labor statistics provide a more optimistic one. Nationally, 6 percent of workers left the workforce, while local police agencies lost just 1 percent of workers.[113] Remaining in a job does not, of course, mean that one likes it or feels safe or appreciated. It is possible, for example, that police benefits suffice to keep officers on the force, but do not offset the concerns and fears that officers feel.

The relevance should be clear. As a society, we want people to enjoy their work. Beyond that more benevolent stance is a selfish interest—if the police are to be effective in promoting public safety, it likely helps if they enjoy their work, feel appreciated for it, and feel that they have adequate training and resources to be effective. All of these factors in turn should result in better police-citizen interactions, resulting in more cooperation with and help from citizens, discretionary decision-making that is just, and improved public perceptions of the police.

Problem 17: Public Attitudes about Policing

For the police to be effective—indeed, for any organization or group to be effective in preventing, reducing, and responding to crime—citizen cooperation is essential. How, then, does the public view the police?

Gallup has been tracking public confidence in the police for nearly three decades. A 2020 poll—conducted in the aftermath of the killings of Breonna Taylor and George Floyd, and nationwide protests—recorded for the first time ever that public confidence in the police fell below 50 percent. In just one year, confidence in police dropped five percentage points, from 53 percent to 48 percent.[114] Clear racial and ethnic differences in police confidence can be identified. One in five Black respondents stated that they had a great deal or quite a lot of confidence in police. By contrast, over half (56 percent) of white respondents felt that way.[115]

Public concerns about equitable treatment constitute a parallel concern. For example, 45 percent of registered voters in a 2021 Hill-Harris poll stated that relations between police and communities of color have gotten worse.[116] A *USA Today/Ipsos* poll revealed that only one in five Americans believe that the police treat everyone equally. That represents a double-digit decline compared to a *USA Today/Pew Research Center* poll in 2014, when 32 percent said the police treat all Americans equally.[117]

A 2020 AP-NORC survey found that nearly one-half of Americans believe that police violence against the public is an extremely or very serious problem. That represents an increase of sixteen percentage points since 2015. Among Black respondents, it was 83 percent and for whites, 39 percent. Moreover, the majority of Americans, including majorities of white and Black adults, believed that police who cause injury or death to civilians in the course of their job are treated too leniently.[118] Sixty-nine percent of respondents reported that police departments are not holding officers accountable when they engage in misconduct.[119]

A national CATO poll focused on police competence or effectiveness reveals additional racial and ethnic differences. Forty percent of Blacks and 50 percent of Hispanics said that the police are effective in enforcing the law, responding quickly to a call for service, and protecting them from crime. By contrast, 60 percent of white Americans hold this belief. There is also a political divide—5 percent of independents and Democrats believe the police are effective compared to 70 percent of Republicans.[120] A *Washington Post/Ipsos* poll found that the vast majority (91 percent) of Blacks between 18 and 34 years old consider how the police treat Blacks as one of the most important issues that influence their voting.

Nevertheless, few whites and people of color support abolishing police. Abolition is more strongly related to age—one-third of people 18 to 34 support abolition of police compared to 4 percent of those 65 and over.[121] More generally, despite a variety of concerns—including eroding trust and confidence in the police, the view that the police do not treat everyone fairly, and the belief that police violence is a growing problem—most Americans, including large percentages of Blacks, want a greater police presence in their neighborhoods and support hiring more police.[122]

Let us step back, then, and consider public safety. Public concerns about excessive use of force, lack of confidence and trust, lack of fairness, and lack of accountability—these all stand as important policy concerns in their own right. In a democracy, citizens are supposed to feel that they live in, well, a democracy, not a police state. They are supposed to feel that everyone is equal, and that the criminal justice system and police treat them, and their concerns, equitably. Shortfalls along any of these dimensions warrant addressing in and of themselves.

They matter, moreover, for preventing and reducing crime. All of these dimensions speak to public views about police legitimacy.[123] When the public views the police as legitimate, they are more wiling to obey the law, assist the police, and work with them in an ongoing collaborative manner to make their communities safer.[124] It is not an understatement that any effective public safety strategy will require increasing public perception of police legitimacy, a task that likely will be especially difficult in areas with the highest crime rates because these are areas where mistrust of the police, and of the criminal justice system more broadly, may be the greatest.

Critical Problems in Policing—Lack of Research, Monitoring, and Oversight

Finally, we turn briefly to a focus on a perhaps mundane but no less critical set of problems in contemporary American policing—the lack of research, monitoring, and oversight of a wide spectrum of policing activities. Without these, there is little that can be done to effectively improve policing or, by extension, public safety.

Problem 18: Little Systematic Reliance on Research

Operating any organization or agency without research is akin to steering a ship in the night without a map, compass, and data on one's position in the ocean. A similar problem plagues much of criminal justice.[125] Policies, programs, practices, decisions, and more are made with little systematic research on the need for them, their implementation, their effectiveness, or their cost-efficiency. That is problematic in general, and no less for policing.

We have already touched on this problem. For example, how do we know whether to hire more police? The only way to do so is to clearly define the goals of policing, identify precisely how policing may achieve these goals, and what exactly officers must do. The problem is much broader, however. To be effective, police departments must be able to document the extent to which they and officers are guided by theoretically and empirically supported practices. They must ensure that officers act in a manner that flows directly from their training. Departments must ensure that appropriate supervision occurs. They also must document their impacts. How much credit, for example, can they claim for any reduction in crime? How willing are citizens to contact or work with them? How efficient are they?

To answer these types of questions requires research infrastructure. That includes databases for calls to the police. But it requires much more. For example, we ideally would have surveys of citizens to more accurately identify the prevalence of and trends in crime, to gauge citizen willingness to cooperate with the police, to learn about citizen experiences with police use of force, and more. We ideally would have surveys of the police as well to learn about their experiences, departmental culture, their compliance with and knowledge of certain protocols, and still other dimensions.[126] We also need staff with the expertise to analyze data and to leverage it in ways that permit evaluation of the impacts of different initiatives.[127] With such data and research capacity, police agencies—and governing bodies that oversee public safety efforts—can evaluate the need for and implementation and effectiveness of different strategies.[128]

The fact remains, however, that policing occurs without the requisite data or infrastructure for systematic, regular reliance on research. Instead, piecemeal evaluations and analyses occur. These can be helpful. They provide indicators of what might be working well, or not. But they do not provide ongoing guidance about the need for implementation or assessment of the effectiveness of specific policies, interventions, practices, and the like.

So, what happens when a new reform is introduced? Typically, we learn almost nothing about the quality of implementation or its intended or unintended impacts. That includes potential adverse effects on aspects of policing that were not the target of the intervention. Consider the now widely prevalent practice of placing police in schools. Does it reduce crime in schools? Does it adversely affect student willingness to report crime or to cooperate with the police? How does it affect student engagement in academics? A narrowly focused study might examine trends in student arrests, but that would miss other relevant impacts.[129]

Problem 19: Accountability and the "Black Box" of Policing

We have discussed the challenges and problems associated with discretion in police officer decision-making. The problems run deeper. Police agencies may engage in practices that are illegal or abusive, and that are both enabled and hidden from view by organizational culture. The problem also cuts the other way. Many police departments may be quite effective, yet without empirical research to document that, we are left to rest on claims of effectiveness. Citizen review boards can only go so far in detecting problems or documenting success. One of their primary barriers will be the lack of relevant data for monitoring decision-making, identifying fraud, or assessing adherence to training or professional protocols.

When lawmakers or the public call for accountability, they cannot follow through without relevant empirical measures of performance, outcomes, adherence to rules, and so on. Put differently, policing occurs in the functional equivalent of a "black box." Lots may be happening in that box, some good and some bad, but we cannot credibly or accurately document it without relevant data and analysis. That opens the door to anecdotal accounts to buttress claims of effectiveness or ineffectiveness and appropriate or inappropriate decision-making.

Most departments do not operate under court-ordered oversight. Consider, then, that even when such oversight exists, it is difficult for police agencies to do what they are supposed to do. As Ronald Weitzer has highlighted, even when reforms are initiated, social scientists know just how hard it is to make them "stick"—institutionalizing them in training, codes of conduct, performance evaluations, and rewards and punishments, and being embraced in the police subculture. . . . The record is mixed for departments that have undergone a Justice Department pattern-or-practice investigation and then introduced the mandated reforms.[130]

That is the situation with oversight, so one can only imagine the situation where no or limited oversight exists. And, it should be emphasized, even with court or Justice Department oversight, we frequently find that we lack relevant data for accurately and completely assessing agency performance. Illuminating the "black box" of policing is not "extra," it is not "research for research's sake." It is essential to creating accountability and improving public safety efforts.

Conclusion

A litany of problems. That is the state of contemporary American policing. The public deserves better. So, too, do the police. Creating a safer society is not rocket science. A starting point to improving public safety begins with acknowledging problems and, as we discuss in the next chapter, how we got to this place. We do recognize that many bright spots exist on the policing landscape. Yet, we recognize, too, the perils of giving them too much attention. When the ship is sinking, taking time to appreciate the craftsmanship that went into making the masts will not take one very far, except to the bottom of the ocean. Our end goal is not, however, to be negative. Nor is it to offer solutions to every problem identified above. It simply is to begin with an honest appraisal, one that can provide insight into where we can go from here. On that count, we are optimistic. As we will argue in later chapters, there is in fact much that can be done to improve policing.

3

How We Got Here

Policing That Does Not Prioritize Public Safety

THE PURPOSE OF THIS CHAPTER is to look at the historical influences that have led to the state of policing in the United States today. As we know from what we discussed in Chapters 1 and 2, there is much wrong with the American criminal justice system, which obviously includes policing. Our effort here is to understand generally how contemporary policing got to this point. What historical circumstances contributed to the evolution of modern policing? We are not trying to account for all of the problems and dysfunctions discussed in Chapter 2. Rather we look back to distant and more recent American history to explain the big picture of policing—for example, the expansion of law enforcement, the militarization of local police, the modern police culture, and the increasing responsibilities placed on police, among others. In short, what are the significant events and circumstances that have influenced the practice and administration of local policing?

Our discussion will, by necessity, be broad. Presently, there are approximately one million state and local law enforcement officers in the United States, working in nearly 18,000 local police agencies. The agencies consist of municipal police, sheriff's offices, and special jurisdiction police organizations, such as school districts, colleges and universities, public transit systems, and government offices. Some of these agencies have jurisdiction over large metropolitan areas, but the majority (70 percent) serve communities of fewer than 10,000 population. About one-half of all local law enforcement agencies in the United States have fewer than ten officers.[1] There is, then, substantial variation in the structure and organization of policing nationally. Yet, common threads can be seen in how they have developed over time and their focus today. For that reason, we discuss significant influences that have shaped law enforcement in general. We discuss the longer-term origins of policing in America, then turn to more recent events of the past fifty to sixty years that played a critical role in bringing us to where we stand today.

Historical Origins of Policing

The creation of the modern police force in America is by no means a linear story. Parts of what became our formal police force evolved in response to particular challenges the nation faced at various times and places. In the beginning, a sheriff, constable, and night watch system existed in major U.S. cities. They patrolled and reacted to various forms of disorder. In the South, militias and watch groups merged to create slave patrols, born out of concerns about resistance and slave uprisings. They functioned primarily to respond to slaves' defiance, escape, and other forms of noncompliance. The western frontier had volunteer vigilante groups as well as the U.S. Army, which operated as a quasi-police force, responding to uprisings and defiance by Native American tribes in the post–Civil War era.

Between the 1790s and 1830s, U.S. cities saw large urban growth that led to disorder and demanded a more formal police system. Riots escalated in the 1830s over the influx of Irish and German immigrants. And disorder and violence emerged because of the Abolitionist movement, economic and political instability, and other sources of insecurity and volatility. Local militia took the lead in responding to these conditions. Because of the varied mechanisms of policing that existed and Americans' historical objection to standing armies, debates ensued over the existence, role, and structure of a formal domestic police force that would function to quell the enduring disorder and violence.[2]

The first American police forces were officially established in Boston in 1838 and in New York in 1845 by their local governments.[3] However, Lepore argues that to say American urban policing began here undermines the role slavery played in the origin of American police.[4] Threats of slave rebellions were a major incentive to create a larger, more formal police force to replace slave patrols and continue to control the Black population in the United States.

Less than ten years prior to the creation of the Boston police, an abolitionist named David Walker, whose father had been enslaved, sought to publish a book calling for a violent rebellion; local and state authorities resisted it by limiting distribution of Walker's book and through arrest. The governor of North Carolina wrote to his state's senators in 1835 in response to Walker's call to fight against oppression and for equal rights. He wrote, "I beg you will lay this matter before the police of your town and invite their prompt attention to the necessity of arresting the circulation of the book." By police, he meant slave patrols, given that no formal police force existed at the time. Shortly after, North Carolina established a statewide "patrol committee."[5]

By the 1890s, U.S. cities were establishing their first urban police systems. The approach to American urban policing differed from the British model. In America, local city governments commissioned police forces. By contrast, the London police were highly centralized and relied on this centralization as a source of institutional legitimacy and power.[6] Centralization allowed the British authorities to set high standards for hiring. In the United States, however, one needed only a political connection.[7] A decentralized system meant that the first U.S. police forces were authorized by political factions, wards, and neighborhood leaders.[8] The early years of the police varied from city to city and from North to South, dependent on the controlling political party and varying along many dimensions, including required training, regulations, enforcement, police-citizen relationships, and police behavior.

This situation led to corruption and political patronage, given that police officers relied on and answered to the municipal government official or political party's ward boss that hired them.[9] The corruption in police departments in the nineteenth century was unmitigated, endemic, and a product of the political corruption occurring more broadly in America. Patronage played a key role in police employment. That meant that police administrators frequently turned a blind eye to the frequently criminal activities of political bosses.[10]

Concurrently, between 1840 and 1920, the "police" of the western frontier (i.e., the U.S. Army, mobs, vigilantes, and law officers like the Texas Rangers) lynched hundreds of Mexicans and Mexican Americans and killed thousands more, in Texas and in territories that would become California, Arizona, Nevada, Utah, Colorado, and New Mexico. Chinese immigrants were targeted and lynched in Los Angeles. In the 1870s and 1880s, the U.S. Army engaged in more than one thousand combat operations against Native peoples. At the same time, volunteer-based vigilante groups, some numbering in the thousands, arrested, tried, and hanged "criminals," who typically were minorities that these groups self-determined to be "criminal."[11]

At the end of the nineteenth century, Progressives pushed for better leadership and clear standards for policing. Most of their ideas did not come to fruition, and they were unable to separate police departments from major political machines. However, the short-lived programs and few changes they did make helped end the more obvious, blatant corruption and political patronage.

Starting in 1910, more successful reform came when a group of police chiefs established the idea of administrative professionalism, giving them more managerial authority and effectively ending the political patronage system. Berkeley, California, police chief August Vollmer was the major innovator of this movement. He established the practice of recruiting college students, using automobiles to patrol, performing extensive tests to select applicants, using forensic scientists to solve cases, and relying on lie detector tests. Vollmer sought to fashion domestic police like the U.S. military. A U.S. Army veteran himself, he believed that domestic policing could be informed by looking to the military. Vollmer explained: "Ever since Spanish-American War days, I've studied military tactics and used them to good effect in rounding up crooks. . . . After all we're conducting a war, a war against the enemies of society."[12] Other police chiefs soon began basing their police trainings on their own military experience and war manuals.

The combination of a military-modeled police force and a police force consisting of mostly army veterans established the origins of the kind of force we see today.[13] Vollmer's prodigy student, O. W. Wilson, would go on to be just as influential, initiating one-officer cars and founding the first professional school of criminology.

On the surface, this wave of professionalism, which persisted into subsequent decades, shifted police departments away from "political operatives" to highly efficient, military-fashioned, businesslike public servants with much more autonomy. Although the professional movement did away with a good bit of corruption, it had consequences that endure to the present. These include a situation in which the police came to operate more independently, with little substantive oversight, and with a culture that contributed both to this independence and to separation from the very communities that they were charged with protecting.

It is upon this early foundation that the pivotal events of the 1960s emerged and contributed directly to modern American policing. Indeed, many societal changes in this era grounded much of the subsequent evolution of crime policies and policing.

As we have discussed, modern policing crystallized in the 1800s as a way of maintaining public order, with concerns—especially among business leaders and white citizens—that putatively "dangerous" groups, such as minorities, the poor, and immigrants, posed the most direct threat.[14] Policing emerged as an intrinsically political activity. Politicians appointed law enforcement leaders and relied on the police to support their efforts. This led to the 1929 Wickersham Commission and attendant efforts to create barriers that would inhibit political influence and professionalize policing.[15] Yet, policing remained a politicized and politically charged activity, one that arguably was furthered by professionalization efforts, such as those that Vollmer and others pioneered, that led to an increased emphasis on crime control and "disorder" and a decreased emphasis on social service.[16] Politics and punishment thus emerged hand-in-hand as policing evolved, while prevention took a backseat.[17]

For our purposes, these can be viewed as "design" problems that went largely unaddressed (or were ineffectively addressed) up to and through the 1960s and beyond. The goals of policing, such as combating "disorder," were vague. "Disorder," for example, can be interpreted in a myriad of ways, from excessive noise to riots. It in turn can be used to justify almost any action. At the same time, by politicizing and bureaucratizing policing, a separation between communities and government-authorized agents of social control emerged. This separation enabled the view of certain groups or entire communities as "criminal" or "other," and simultaneously facilitated a focus on reactive, punishment-oriented responses rather than ones that prioritized prevention.

In the 1960s, these tensions escalated and led to a near-exclusive and much-expanded focus on retribution. The latter can be seen in the policies that arose in subsequent decades, including sentencing reforms, typically with a focus on more certain punishment and longer terms of supervision or incarceration; the War on Drugs; the expansion of criminal codes that in turn have led to an ever increasing number of acts that count as crimes; exponential growth in prison capacity and correctional control; and, not least, a punishment-focused policy-making process that has relegated crime prevention to an afterthought.

Changes in policing both reflected and have played a fundamental role in this evolution of crime policy and the contemporary landscape of criminal justice. Most prominently, modern American policing has grown dramatically over the past six decades. Spending on state and local law enforcement has risen substantially. Between 1960 and 2019, state and local spending (adjusted for inflation) increased by nearly 700 percent. The inflation-adjusted per capita spending on state and local law enforcement increased by a staggering 325 percent.[18] Today, the cost of policing is roughly $115 billion per year.[19]

Not surprisingly, the number of police officers increased by over 50 percent between 1980 and 2019.[20] The U.S. population increased as well, so it is appropriate to also look at changes in the numbers of police per capita. Piecing data together from different sources, we were able to compile a time series of police per capita from 1981 to 2016. The rates are per 1,000 population. The bottom line is that over this period, per capita rates of sworn officers increased for most of the series. The rate in 1981 was 2.03. It peaked in the 2001–8 period (around 2.50) and then declined slightly. These changes represent roughly a 20 percent increase in the number of police over this time period.[21] They unquestionably and logically led to more enforcement of laws, more arrests, more convictions, and more punishment. And to the litany of problems that we detailed in the previous chapter.

What did not happen? A steady or increased focus on crime prevention; on working consistently and effectively with local communities; on serving diverse, disadvantaged, and disenfranchised populations; or on acting in ways that foster trust in the criminal justice or correctional systems.

Contributors to the Expansion of Policing as a
Reactive, Control-Oriented Institution

The question at hand is why did law enforcement expenditures and employment increase over this period? Put differently, what justified the large-scale expansion of police? And not just the police in general but the police as a largely reactive institution that is used as an instrument of control and punishment rather than community empowerment and crime prevention? Why did policing not evolve in a way that prioritized public safety and justice? One obvious place to look is crime.

Crime

From 1960 to 1994, based on reports to the police, violent crime increased to unprecedented levels, rising from 161 to 714 per 100,000 people.[22] A brief downturn occurred in the early 1980s before spiking upward in the late 1980s and peaking in the early 1990s. Thereafter, and beginning just prior to the 1994 Crime Act, crime rates steadily declined.[23] The crime decline of the 1990s brought us historically low crime rates comparable to rates in the early 1970s.

If the expansion of policing was a policy response to the threat of crime, then the evidence presented above, based on police report data, partially fits that argument. However, as crime declined and cities became safer, there was no commensurate decrease in policing. Instead, investment in more police and in expanded police responsibilities continued to increase. Since the beginning of the 1990s crime decline, per capita inflation-adjusted spending on police increased by approximately 125 percent.[24]

The continued and expanded investment in policing is more extreme when we consider actual crime based on data from the National Crime Victimization Survey (NCVS) rather than reported crime. The latter may be influenced by the number of police, willingness to report crimes, and other factors. By contrast, the NCVS is based on random samples and asks individuals if they have experienced various types of crimes, regardless of whether they reported them. Based on the NCVS data, the rate of violent crime from 1973 to 1994, for example, was relatively stable. It trended downward somewhat from around 1980 to 1986, and then from 1986 to 1994 back up to where it had been in 1980. From 1993 onward, violent crime declined rapidly.

It is this latter period where trends identified in the Uniform Crime Reports (UCR) and NCVS converge. For property crime, the story between the two during the previous decades differs even more. Based on the NCVS, property crime declined steadily from 1974 throughout the 1970s, 1980s, 1990s, and thereafter.[25] That remains one of the largely unrecognized facts that stand in contrast to the several-decade commitment to retributive policies. Granted, property crime does not garner the same concern as violent crime. It is, however, a central justification used by policymakers to justify tough-on-crime responses. If they had proceeded from the more accurate source of information about property crime, they would have held steady or decreased their investment in policing.

This is a pattern observed more generally in the U.S. criminal justice system. In the 1960s and again in the 1980s, a ramp-up of tough-on-crime responses occurred in response to concerns about increased violent and property crime. It occurred as well in response to generalized concerns about actual or perceived civil disorder. In both periods, as the problems dissipated, the criminal justice system continued to grow. Crime alone does not account for that phenomenon, not for criminal justice as a whole or for policing in particular. Obviously, there are other factors that need to be considered to better understand how policing evolved over time.

Civil Disorder and the Johnson Presidency

Barry Goldwater was the first presidential candidate to try to leverage law and order in a campaign. Lyndon B. Johnson's campaign claimed that his War on Poverty in fact was a war against crime. This framing of how to approach crime helped to counter Goldwater's law-and-order approach, and in 1964 ushered Johnson into the White House.

Despite Johnson's rhetoric about the broader effects of his War on Poverty—that is, that it reduced crime and disorder—he was quickly confronted with a dramatic rise in crime and an unprecedented wave of urban riots. These events were to alter Johnson's nearly exclusive focus on the Great Society and War on Poverty as solutions to crime and disorder. Although Richard Nixon is largely credited with launching the wars on crime and drugs, as early as March of 1965, Johnson unequivocally declared that addressing crime and disorder was paramount:

> No right is more elemental to our society than the right to personal security and no right needs more urgent protection. Crime will not wait while we pull it up by the roots [a reference to the War on Poverty's focus on the root causes of crime]. We must arrest and reverse the trend toward lawlessness.[26]

Critical to the decisions of the Johnson administration and Congress were increasing crime rates and the riots that swept across the United States, beginning in the Watts neighborhood of Los Angeles in August of 1965 and affecting essentially every city of any size (generally 100,000 or more) during the period 1965 through 1968. An estimated 425 significant race-related civil disorders occurred during the 1965–68 period.[27] Some were more severe than others, with a notable clustering of civil disorders in late spring and summer of 1968, after the assassination of Martin Luther King. Although the severity of these disorders varied in terms of the number killed and injured, number arrested, and amount of property damage, a common denominator for many of them was that a negative encounter with the police triggered the event.

On the heels of the Watts riot, Congress passed the Law Enforcement Assistance Act. Congress envisioned that local police constituted the front line in a domestic battle in urban minority neighborhoods and viewed law enforcement as the main mechanism to deter future civil disorder. As Elizabeth Hinton, a leading expert, states,

> Johnson intended police departments to be the primary beneficiaries of the newly available funds because he saw urban policemen as the "frontline soldier" of the national law enforcement program. "We are today fighting a war within our own boundaries," the president believed.[28]

The funding to local police departments was administered through the Office of Law Enforcement Assistance (OLEA), with two goals. The first was to increase police presence and police patrols in minority neighborhoods. The second was to enhance the weapons arsenal and protective gear of police departments in preparation for more riots. These included armored vehicles, automatic weapons, bulletproof vests, and helicopters.

Although the Johnson administration was expanding the size and capabilities of local law enforcement to fight a war on crime and disorder, it continued fighting a war on poverty through the Great Society program. Efforts to enhance education, employment, housing, and social welfare were supported by liberal policymakers and members of Congress.

It became evident that crime continued to increase and that the government could not effectively quell the riots, especially during the peak period after Martin Luther King's assassination. Against that backdrop, Johnson signed the Omnibus Crime Control and Safe Streets Act of 1968. The Safe Streets Act further added funding for law enforcement through the Law Enforcement Assistance Administration (LEAA) within the Department of Justice. The legacy of the LEAA included the disbursement of federal funding to over 80,000 law enforcement crime control projects.

By way of perspective, between 1964 and 1970 federal funding to local police increased by 2,900 percent.[29] This was precedent-setting in scale and in establishing the direct involvement of the federal government in local law enforcement.

This change amounted to a tidal force in steering national and local public policy. With crime and disorder posing substantial public safety and political threats, the Johnson administration shifted attention away from a "regulating the poor" and a liberal social reform approach through Great Society social welfare programs.[30] Its new emphasis? Funding law enforcement, not only to address crime but also to divert attention away from seemingly failed welfare policies. Hinton has described this seismic political, social, and economic shift:

> As the federal government increased its investment in fighting crime and pulled back from social welfare programs, law enforcement continued to try to fill the void left behind by the many promising War on Poverty programs that were shuttered during the second half of the 1960s.[31]

With the eventual dissolution of the War on Poverty, the federal government declared the criminal justice system and especially law enforcement to be the path forward for dealing with crime and disorder. Although Johnson did not put the final nails into the coffin of the Great Society and the War on Poverty, he certainly set the stage for subsequent administrations to continue efforts to expand the police, the front line in managing the crime and disorder that seemingly were becoming fixtures in the urban landscape.

Tough on Crime

The past fifty years have been characterized by a nearly relentless penchant for punishment and retribution. Any number of metrics will suffice. These include growth in the prison and jail populations, incarceration rates, numbers and rates of individuals under correctional control, capital investment in the expansion of prison and jail capacity, changes to sentencing laws resulting in a broad movement toward determinate sentencing with mandatory sentences and mandatory minimums as the hallmarks, truth-in-sentencing laws, excessive use of pretrial detention, and prosecutors' efforts to maximize conviction charges and sentences in plea deals.[32]

All of these trends, including the politicizing of crime and punishment, have perpetuated tough-on-crime policies in the federal system, the fifty state systems, and most of the 3,100-plus county criminal justice systems in the United States. Tough on crime has driven the dramatic changes to statutes, criminal justice policies, procedures, and culture, as well as funding. Moreover, tough on crime has pervaded political campaigns ("Vote for me, I'll lock 'em up and throw away the key"), legislative deliberations and lawmaking (e.g., sentencing and parole statutes), prosecutors' charging decisions and plea agreements, judges' bail and sentencing decisions, corrections officials' actions (e.g., parole and probation revocations), and certainly policing.

Law enforcement is the front line of the criminal justice system. Tough-on-crime policies, laws, and culture have influenced policing in part by promoting the crime-fighting role of police. At the same time, major U.S. Supreme Court decisions have given police more crime-fighting tools and discretion to initiate what in the past would have been viewed as invasive and counter-democratic actions.

Take, for example, search and seizure, one of law enforcement's key investigatory activities. Over several decades, the U.S. Supreme Court has relaxed many restrictions on the search-and-seizure capabilities of police. Stop and frisk (*Terry v. Ohio*) is illustrative, as are warrantless searches of vehicles (*Carroll v. United States*); searches of "open fields" such as fields, wooded areas, and vacant lots (*Hester v. United States*); plain-view searches (*Harris v. United States*); searches of public schools (*New Jersey v. T.L.O.*); and the narrowing of the exclusionary rule by arguing the good faith exception (*United States v. Leon*). Moreover, *Ker v. California* established the two reasons a police officer can enter a premises without announcing himself: if it is "suspected" that evidence is being destroyed and/or it is "suspected" that an individual is armed. Ker effectively neutered the Castle Doctrine and laid the groundwork for essentially removing the concept from the Fourth Amendment.

From the 1960s, then, to the present, we can see not only a shift toward increasingly control-oriented and punitive criminal justice policy, but also an increased reliance on police as the front line in what has come to be viewed as an ongoing war on crime. The police constitute the vanguard of tough-on-crime activities. In that capacity, they hold special importance because they typically are the face of criminal justice for many citizens. And what these citizens— disadvantaged groups in particular—see is not a member of their community or individuals or agencies aligned with their interests, but instead agents that in many respects may appear to them as the equivalent of a military presence or occupation.

The 1994 Crime Bill

By the time Bill Clinton hit the campaign trail for the 1992 presidency, the Republican Party had enjoyed a thirty-year vice grip on tough-on-crime policies. Barry Goldwater launched the idea in 1964, Nixon began implementation, and Reagan, more than anyone else, made it a reality.

By the early 1990s, the Democratic Party, especially at the national level, decided that crime control was too politically important to continue sitting on the sidelines. Time and time again, Republicans were portrayed as tough,

Democrats as soft. That wedge had substantial electoral consequences. At the same time, the Clinton administration came into office in 1992, after a steady increase in violent crime, murder in particular, since the late 1980s. Politically and on substantive grounds, then, impetus existed for taking action.

The Clinton campaign was determined to gain political equity and to address crime by pursuing a decidedly different approach than what Democrats previously had promoted. The New Democrats, as Clinton-Gore branded themselves, included tough-on-crime policies that came straight out of the Republican playbook. Among the most prominent examples of the pivot is the Violent Crime Control and Law Enforcement Act, also known as the 1994 Crime Bill. The bill implemented more federal mandatory sentences and led to the adoption in forty-two states of truth-in-sentencing laws, such as requiring that individuals who commit a violent crime serve at least 85 percent of their sentence. These sentencing changes mirrored federal initiatives, such as the Sentencing Reform Act of 1984, implemented under Reagan.

Most relevant for our discussion here was the provision for funding 100,000 new local police officers. Communities across the country felt the impact immediately. Between 1990 and 1999, the number of police on the streets increased by roughly 30 percent.[33]

The impact of the Crime Bill remains debated and difficult to assess. The long-term decline in crime had already begun, not only in the United States but in Canada and every Western European country. Clinton claimed that the Crime Bill, including the 100,000 additional police on the streets, led to the decline, but the reality is more complex. For example, none of our Western allies pursued tough-on-crime policies, including adding significant numbers of police. Many states varied in these policies, yet nearly all experienced the substantial declines that occurred. Conservatives could argue that the decline stemmed from twelve years of get-tough policies under Republican rule, prior to the Clinton administration. That, though, does not square with the steady decline in property crime that continued from the 1970s through subsequent decades.

Our point here is simple—the 1994 Crime Bill added further momentum to the expansion of local law enforcement. It did so by prioritizing policing as a critical component in addressing crime and by providing dramatically increased funding for more police. In this respect, the bill extended the movement that began in the 1960s to push the police increasingly to center stage in efforts to reduce crime and to signal that social order constituted a political priority.

The War on Drugs

When Richard Nixon declared drugs public enemy no. 1 in 1971, he set in motion a series of statutory, procedural, policy, and funding changes that have had profound impacts on the lives of tens of millions of individuals,

minorities, communities and neighborhoods, and the criminal justice system. By identifying the criminal justice system as the set of agencies and
institutions that are responsible for this problem, he defined drugs as a
criminal matter, not a public health problem. That has been the enduring
approach to this day.

But Nixon may have had other things in mind when he declared a War on
Drugs. Nixon's aide John Ehrlichman stated in a 2016 interview:

> We knew we couldn't make it illegal to be either against the [Vietnam] war
> or black, but by getting the public to associate the hippies with marijuana and
> blacks with heroin, and then criminalizing both heavily, we could disrupt those
> communities. We could arrest their leaders, raid their homes, break up their
> meetings and vilify them night after night on the evening news. Did we know
> we were lying about the drugs? Of course we did.[34]

Whether subsequent administrations sought to implement Nixon's policies about Blacks, the result is that the continuing War on Drugs has selec-
tively targeted minorities. Although whites and minorities engage in drug law
violations (e.g., possession and dealing) at similar rates, the odds of a Black
person being arrested for a drug crime is 2.8 to 5.5 times greater than a white
person's, relative to population.[35]

The year 2021 was the fiftieth anniversary of the War on Drugs. Some sobering facts stood in the way of celebration. The United States spent over $1
trillion on this war, and since 1995 nearly 40 million arrests were made, the
vast majority of which were for possession. Those 40 million arrests equate
to the entire population of California, or the combined populations of the
twenty-nine most populous cities in the United States, starting with New
York and going all the way down to Louisville, Kentucky.

In 2019, there were 495,800 arrests for Part 1 violent crimes and 1,074,300
arrests for Part 1 property crimes. In that same year, there were 1,558,900
drug arrests, or essentially as many drug arrests as arrests for serious violent
and property crime. Forty percent of those drug arrests were for marijuana,
and the vast majority of marijuana arrests were for possession.[36]

Drug arrests have been on an upward trajectory since 1980. Total drug arrests have increased by almost 300 percent since 1980. In 2020, 87 percent of
all drug arrests were for possession of, not selling, drugs.[37]

Today, drug law violations are the single most common reason someone
is arrested in the United States. Strikingly, marijuana represents the most
common drug involved in those arrests, a pattern that has persisted to the
present.[38] Statistics on the War on Drugs reveal that the war ultimately has
targeted the end user rather than the higher-level producers and distributors,
and that there has been an enduring focus on marijuana.

The implications for understanding the effects of the War on Drugs on American policing are clear. Just as the War on Drugs provided individuals to help fill increasing numbers of prison beds over the past fifty years, it also provided a rationale and motivation to expand policing. Consider the fact that law enforcement stands as the front line in this war and that drug violations are the most common reason for an arrest.

A study conducted in New York City highlights the amount of officer time involved in making a misdemeanor-level marijuana arrest. The researchers found that the amount of time varied between 2 and 3 hours and 4 and 5 hours to process a misdemeanor marijuana possession suspect. They then used 2.5 hours of officer time as a conservative estimate to extrapolate how much police time went into the marijuana possession arrests over a six-year period. During that period, there were 440,000 marijuana possession arrests. The researchers estimated that the arrests required over one million hours of officer time. As they note, "That is equivalent of having 31 police officers working eight hours a day, 365 days a year for 11 years, making only marijuana possession arrests."[39]

With drug use on the rise[40] and five-year rearrest rates of individuals released from prison at almost 80 percent, there exists a nearly endless supply of drug law violators for police to arrest. The cycle continues—arrest, prosecute, convict, punish, repeat. That approach runs counter to the public health approach to drug problems that previously existed, if only in part. This shift has been well documented and led some judges, such as United States District Judge Lois Forer, to resign from their positions rather than treat public health problems as criminal affairs.[41] Despite documentation of the problems associated with this approach, a get-tough approach to drugs prevails and has placed the police in the position of facing a much wider population of individuals to arrest. And it has made them the face of policies that reflect and can contribute to stark racial, ethnic, and class divides in American criminal justice and in society at large.

Mission Creep: Dumping More and More Responsibilities on Police

The police have become a dumping ground for ever more responsibilities, with unrealistic expectations for what they can achieve. David Brown, the former chief of police of Dallas and currently the superintendent of the Chicago Police Department, makes the point very well:

> We're asking cops to do too much in this country. We are. Every societal failure, we put off on the cops to solve. Not enough mental health funding, let the cops handle it. Here in Dallas, we have a loose dog problem. Let's have the cops chase loose dogs. Schools fail. Let's give it to the cops. That's too much to ask. Policing was never meant to solve all of those problems.[42]

We have seen the police role evolve over time—without any clear master plan and without any clarity or consistency in the goals we expect of policing—in response to a wide variety of problems that local, state, and federal officials cannot, do not want to, or do not know how to resolve. Chief Brown commented on mental health, loose dogs, and schools as examples, but those represent the tip of the iceberg. Each year, more and more social, economic, or public health problems are dumped on the police to manage.

The consequences of this constant expansion go to the heart of the dysfunctionality of policing and criminal justice more broadly. And they highlight the failure to develop a coherent systemic approach to crime prevention. There is, for example, the failure to adequately fund education, mental health and substance abuse treatment, social services, medical care, and affordable housing. There is, too, the failure to successfully address poverty—although the poverty rate has fallen over time, especially between 1960 and 1975, there are approximately 40 million individuals in the United States living in poverty.[43]

Absent institutions that can address these problems, someone must step up. Or, more precisely, the police are assigned to fill any and all gaps. As former police officer and now legal scholar at the University of South Carolina Seth Stoughton puts it,

> When I was an officer, I got calls about dead animals, ungovernable children who refused to go to school, people who hadn't gotten their welfare checks, adults who hadn't heard from their elderly relatives, families who needed to be informed of a death, broken-down cars, you name it. Everything that isn't dealt with by some other institution automatically defaults to the police to take care of.[44]

Arthur Rizer, a researcher at R Street, a research and policy organization, highlights this same issue and what should be different:

> I want to make policing prestigious again—not the prestige of power, but the prestige of respect. But in order to do that, we need to stop underfunding everything else and leaving the police holding a bag of shit.[45]

No organization, and no individual within an organization, can be successful if the organization's goals are vague and constantly change, if the organization has to assume ever more responsibilities, and if those responsibilities cannot be realistically addressed by that organization.

An illustration of this problem can be seen in Austin, Texas, where Kelly lives. Several years ago, the Austin City Council voted to remove bans on where homeless individuals can camp in the city. Hundreds of tents and assorted belongings quickly appeared in public areas. The city council sought to simultaneously expand affordable, supportive housing capacity but failed to do so, thus contributing to more homeless camps and public frustration at the inability of the city to assist the individuals and to address the problem.

In May 2021, a referendum was put forth that would ban camping in most of the locations where the homeless were camping. Who, though, was to be responsible for enforcing the ban? The Austin Police Department (APD). A plan arose to create four phases for enforcing the ban. Phase 1 would involve the APD issuing verbal warnings to those camping in prohibited areas. In Phase 2, the APD would issue written warnings and citations. In Phase 3, it would initiate arrests and begin to clear out encampments. And Phase 4 would continue with the APD making arrests and clearing out encampments. Timeline? All this work would occur in four months.

Rather than creating or utilizing existing social service personnel to address homelessness and the larger issue of affordable housing, the city decided that criminalizing legal camping was needed and appropriate and would be effective. Never mind that research shows that a significant proportion of the homeless have mental health problems, situations that are usually better served by social services than police. Never mind that the police have other duties and responsibilities. Never mind that displacement—with individuals uprooted from one area simply moving to another—could be fully anticipated. There are many complicated policy issues, but this is not one of them. When we fail to address root problems and load an institution with unrealistic expectations, and when we underfund their ability to try to meet them, there should be no mystery that the end result will be failure and tragedy.

This type of approach to societal problems—including problems rooted in social inequalities—is part and parcel of how policing has been shaped in recent decades. The police serve as the go-to agency for a wide variety of society's ills and inequities. Yet, as Chief Brown and many others have stated, the police are not trained, equipped, or funded to adequately address the variety of problems that are dumped on them.

The problem is worse—profound consequences arise because of these policy choices. We can see that in, for example, a focus on individuals with mental illness. The Treatment Advocacy Center conducted research that shows that the risk of being killed by police is sixteen times higher for a person with a mental illness who is approached by police than someone who does not have a mental illness. The research also shows that between one-quarter and one-half of fatal law enforcement encounters involve an individual with a mental illness.[46] Poor policy kills.

The editorial board of the *Washington Post* used an interesting and appropriate analogy to illustrate the futility of this policy of relying on the police for more than is reasonable or realistic.[47] The board suggested that we think of public safety the same way we think about public health. The health of the population cannot rely on hospitals alone. Rather, a broad public health approach—including primary care physicians, public clinics, health education, and emphasis on prevention, a toxin-free environment, systems to protect and vaccinate individuals during a pandemic, and more—is needed. Relying on the police for many inappropriate matters has distracted society and law enforcement from developing and implementing more effective tools for reducing recidivism, preventing crime, and enhancing public safety.

911 and Reactive Policing

In 1968, AT&T designated 911 as the emergency number for police, fire, or medical assistance. By the end of the twentieth century, the vast majority of the population and geographic areas of the United States had a 911 call system. The 911 systems evolved over time with significant technological advancements such as computer-aided dispatch, automated caller location, and telephone number identification.

Each year, 911 systems receive around 240 million calls. Most of these calls are not for serious violent crimes. They sometimes may require a police response, and those that involve violence or some type of crime clearly do.

How have 911 systems shaped the nature of local policing? The Vera Institute has conducted a considerable amount of research on 911 systems and policing. The evidence indicates that the majority of police time is spent responding to 911 calls:

> Front line police officers spend a substantial amount of their time reactively responding to 911 calls. Though the vast majority of calls for service (CFS) are unrelated to serious emergencies or crimes in progress, police are often the de facto responders, which makes responding to emergency communications a critical aspect of the day-to-day responsibilities officers are tasked with.[48]

This technological change that began in the 1960s thus directly influenced how the police spend their time, and it leads the police to spend that time in a largely reactive mode. Indeed, this 911-driven, reactive model has largely defined modern policing. And, ironically, it has diverted attention away from crime prevention or even crime! As the Vera study indicates, many of the 911 calls for service for police either do not involve crime or do not involve serious crime.

The calls constitute yet another pathway by which a wide variety of situations default to the police to solve. What is perhaps the most critical consequence? Time responding to 911 calls is time that the police cannot devote to proactive efforts, including crime prevention, problem-solving policing, and community policing, as but a few examples.

Broken Windows

In 1982, George Kelling and James Q. Wilson published an article in *The Atlantic* called "Broken Windows: The Police and Neighborhood Safety." Their idea was novel—a broken window left unrepaired leads to additional broken windows, in turn leading to the deterioration of public space. They combined the physical disorder of an area (graffiti, abandoned vehicles and buildings, litter, human waste, closed businesses) with what they called incivilities or minor, petty offending by individuals in these deteriorated areas. The logic was simple—physical disorder sends a message that no one is watching or cares, thus encouraging petty or nuisance crimes or behaviors. The kicker? These areas of physical disorder and petty, public order offending will eventually lead to more serious crime.

This idea caught on and resulted in a new set of demands on law enforcement called broken windows policing. It required police to arrest individuals engaged in petty, quality-of-life crimes. The goal? Manage disorder and incivility by expanding police power and the scope and scale of arrests.

The New York City Police Department, under Mayor Giuliani and Chief Bratton, implemented an aggressive, zero-tolerance order maintenance arrest policy that required officers to arrest those involved in minor, public order offenses. Other cities soon adopted the approach, leading to a substantial addition to the portfolio of responsibilities among local policing agencies nationwide.

As serious crimes declined in the 1990s, arrests for them also declined. Today, an estimated 5 percent of police arrests involve serious violent crime.[49] What happened? As arrests for serious crimes declined, arrests for low-level drug offenses, quality-of-life crimes, and a variety of other minor misdemeanors increased, a result of the War on Drugs and aggressive expansion and implementation of broken windows policing.

Despite the logical appeal of the broken windows idea, scientific evidence shows that physical disorder and petty offending do not lead to more serious crimes, and aggressive arrest policies of petty crimes do not lead to reductions in crime.[50] Nevertheless, broken windows policing added a significant set of responsibilities—addressing disorder and quality-of-life offenses—to the increasing list of police responsibilities. It is possible that broken windows approaches, if guided by a coherent theoretical foundation and a targeted set of well-implemented activities targeting theoretically relevant mechanisms, might be useful and effective in some contexts,[51] but the evidence for this possibility is weak and there are other approaches that hold much more promise and that enjoy a stronger level of theoretical and empirical support.[52]

The Warrior Cop

The developments of the 1960s, including the devolution of increasingly reactive approaches to crime and disorder, created the groundwork for a para-military approach to policing. Several decades later, it has become normative to see police dressed in riot gear and heavily armored vehicles, and employing tear gas and high-powered weapons. The police departments in most jurisdictions in the United States have at least some, if not a considerable amount of, surplus military equipment. The deployment of this equipment, often used to serve a drug-related warrant, creates—understandably—the perception that the police have, over time, become increasingly militarized, or what many have labeled "warrior cops." That perception exists not only in the public mind but also in how many officers view their chosen vocation.

The first special weapons and tactics (SWAT) team is attributed to the Los Angeles Police Department's Chief Daryl Gates in the 1960s, as a military-style capability for events like the Watts riot, the Whitman mass shooting on the University of Texas campus, and other situations where the police responded ineffectively. Gates in fact consulted with the military in the course of developing the SWAT concept.[53] Other police departments soon followed suit, spurred on and defended based on the race riots that occurred during the rest of the 1960s, increasing violent crime, campus protests over the Vietnam War, Nixon's successful law-and-order presidential campaign, and his subsequent declaration of a War on Drugs.[54]

Access to military equipment undergirds the creation of a "warrior cop" culture. This takes us back to President Lyndon Johnson. The 1968 Omnibus Crime Control and Safe Streets Act led to the creation of the LEAA, which in turn laid the groundwork for funding local police and the growth of SWAT teams nationwide. Local departments received items such as emergency radios, body armor, face shields, and heavy-duty weapons like grenade launchers.[55]

Don Santarelli was appointed director of LEAA in 1971. Radley Balko, in his influential book *Rise of the Warrior Cop*, writes of the concerns Santarelli expressed about the increasing militarization of the police:

> Some of the police chiefs he worked with had an increasingly gung-ho mentality. . . . It seemed like every police department in the country wanted a piece. That wasn't so unusual. But it was what they wanted that Santarelli found concerning. "They didn't value education or training. They valued hardware." The city of Birmingham asked him for an armored personnel carrier. Other chiefs wanted tanks. Los Angeles asked him for a submarine, "Anything the police chiefs could dream up to make themselves look more fearsome, they wanted."[56]

Federal funding for LEAA ended in 1982, but many police departments were well on their way toward militarization. President Reagan's 1986

Anti-Drug Abuse Act gave SWAT units greater importance in fighting the War on Drugs. In the early 1980s, SWAT teams were used roughly 3,000 times per year. By the 1990s, their deployment increased to 45,000. The vast majority (76 percent) of these deployments involved drug raids.[57] Here, then, we can see the synergy of law enforcement expansion, criminalization of drug use, and greater reliance on police for addressing even the most minor public order problems come into play. They not only led to more policing that penetrates all aspects of society but also created more opportunities for a "warrior cop" culture to surface in a more public way, justified in no small part by sustained get-tough rhetoric from politicians on both sides of the political aisle.

Further support for a "warrior cop" approach to policing came from the Reagan administration's efforts to propel tough-on-crime policies with the 1984 Omnibus Crime Act. A new provision in the bill included asset forfeiture, which allowed federal agencies and local police to share assets seized in the course of drug investigations. Drug investigations thus became a source of revenue for police departments that assisted federal agents in such cases. Balko observes that asset forfeiture played a significant role in militarization of police: "These forfeiture policies would soon help fund the explosion of SWAT teams across the country—forging yet another tie between the escalating drug war and hypermilitarized policing."[58]

In 1989, George H. W. Bush signed the National Defense Authorization Act, which authorized surplus military equipment from the Department of Defense (DOD) to be given to local law enforcement. It constituted yet another step in the direction of supporting and expanding a "warrior cop" culture. The big push came in 1997 when the Clinton administration launched the 1033 Program which transferred $7.5 billion in surplus DOD equipment to over 8,000 local police departments. Items included tanks, armored vehicles, M16 rifles, radios, silencers, and shields. The scale of military transfers was historically unprecedented. Between 1997 and 1999, the 1033 Program resulted in $727 million worth of military equipment being transferred to police in all fifty states.[59]

Still another push toward militarization of police came after the 9/11 terrorist attacks. The wars in Iraq and Afghanistan stemmed from them, but a domestic response also resulted. The Department of Homeland Security (DHS) distributed over $34 billion in terrorism grants. However, the stage was set for using this money for the War on Drugs. The Bush administration carried out a TV and print-ad campaign claiming that casual drug users financially supported the terrorist organizations that carried out the attacks. That gave local police the moral license to use DHS funding to further expand caches of military equipment and use them mainly for drug raids.[60]

The inception of the militarization of local police initially arose as a response to the 1960s riots and protests. Over time, the War on Drugs played a fundamental role in transferring DOD military equipment to police. Asset forfeiture laws then added substantial funds to police budgets to enhance the military footprint. Today, SWAT teams are ubiquitous. According to an article by the American Bar Association, nearly 90 percent of cities with populations over 25,000 have SWAT units.[61]

The militarization of police is not, though, just about equipment. It is about police culture, training, and socialization. It is the de-emphasis of problem-solving and de-escalation approaches to crime. Balko speaks, for example, of the battlefield mentality of many police. We will return to this issue later but for now, consider the observations of Joseph McNamara, the former chief of the Kansas City, Missouri, and San Jose, California, police departments, in an op-ed in the *Wall Street Journal*:

> Simply put, the police culture in our country has changed. An emphasis on "officer safety" and paramilitary training pervades today's policing, in contrast to the older culture, which held that cops didn't shoot until they were about to be shot or stabbed. Police in large cities formerly carried revolvers holding six .38-caliber rounds. Nowadays, police carry semi-automatic pistols with 16 high-caliber rounds, shotguns and military assault rifles, weapons once relegated to SWAT teams facing extraordinary circumstances. Concern about such fire-power in densely populated areas hitting innocent citizens has given way to an attitude that the police are fighting a war against drugs and crime and must be heavily armed.[62]

Conclusion

Our goal in this chapter has been to identify the major factors that have shaped contemporary American policing. Like the rest of the criminal justice system, policing has grown substantially over the past sixty years, in terms of numbers of officers as well as expenditures. As we and others have argued, the expansion of criminal justice arose initially as a response to high crime in the 1960s and 1970s, as well as the massive wave of riots and campus protests that swept across the nation between 1964 and 1970. These events are directly implicated in the rise of tough on crime, the preeminent set of policies, statutes, procedures, and expenditures at all levels of government that had a very simple goal—more punishment for more people.

The War on Drugs, broken windows policing, and the continual dumping of more and more responsibilities on police greatly broadened the scope of police work and dramatically expanded the police presence in communities across the country. In addition, it amplified the roles and responsibilities of the police—not so much by design as by default. The police stand at the front line in the War on Drugs and at the same time serve as the agents responsible for enforcing quality-of-life offenses. Policies that target drugs and panhandling have had profound consequences for what policing looks like. Stop and frisk, the enormous number of low-level misdemeanor arrests, and the fact that the majority of drug arrests are for simple marijuana possession constitute but a few of the most obvious examples of expanded police responsibilities that have watered down the focus on serious and violent crime and diverted attention from systematic and comprehensive approaches to crime prevention.

One of the main contributors to this situation has been the ongoing failure at all levels of government to adequately fund public health, affordable housing, and public schools, and then leaving it up to the police to address the inevitable consequences. Illustrative of this situation is the chronically insufficient webs of support for preventing and responding to mental illness. That has led the police to become the frontline responders to situations involving persons with mental illness, the outcomes of which all too often end badly. Similarly, putting the police in charge of managing homelessness, which frequently involves substance and mental health issues, is not a solution but often a revolving door into the municipal justice system. The police contribute, then, to a system that fails to address root causes of social problems.

Police presence in public schools is also emblematic of problems that run deep in our communities as well as our schools. In recent decades, it has become commonplace to put police in schools, something that rarely occurred in the past. As can be expected, the trends in "regular" policing can be found in schools—confusion about the purpose of placing police in an educational setting, and increased reliance on punitive responses to instances of minor misconduct. Obviously, some schools experience substantial violence, but placing police in schools does not in any clear way address that problem. And in low-crime schools officers who may view their role in a more "warrior cop" mode invites criminalization of behaviors that historically would be viewed as minor misconduct.[63]

Congress, state legislatures, and city, town, and county governments have been front and center in promoting and funding tough-on-crime agendas, and local police have often been on the receiving end of tremendous infusions of financial support. As we discussed above, much of that funding has been used to support the militarization of local policing. It also has been devoted to the failed War on Drugs.

Where does that leave us? Militarized police forces that serve to reinforce the tough-on-crime mantra of criminal justice policy for over fifty years. What is symbolically tougher than armored personnel carriers, automatic weapons, and police decked out head-to-toe in protective gear? To be fair, there are circumstances where such use of force is necessary, but they are rare.

The problem quite clearly does not lie with policing alone. What we have today is a criminal justice system designed to be almost entirely reactive. The engine of the criminal justice system does not start until somebody commits a crime, the crime is reported through the 911 system, police respond, and make an arrest. The 911 system dictates that most police work comes from responding to calls. The courts then deal with the cases that the police bring to it. What can they do? Little except to punish.

Missed in this approach is the fact that a reactive criminal justice system does little to prevent crime and enhance public safety. To make matters considerably worse, the actions that the police take after they catch someone who has committed a crime does little to reduce the likelihood of reoffending. Indeed, experiences that individuals have once they become enmeshed in the system serve to all-too-frequently increase recidivism. Worse still, all the efforts of the criminal justice system make it seem that we are making significant progress. However, they divert attention—like a magician's use of one hand to draw the eye away from the trickery under way in the other—from an almost complete failure to adopt policies and approaches that could prevent crime and reduce recidivism. In short, the U.S. criminal justice system is criminogenic. And to make matters worse, it is engendering mistrust among large swaths of the population.

4

A Clean Slate

What Would an Effective Public Safety Approach Look Like?

O NE WAY TO GAIN INSIGHT into the profound flaws in our current approach to policing—and more broadly to crime—is to imagine what an effective public safety approach would look like. What if we started with a clean slate?

Imagine the following. We land in a society—call it Anywhere—with several million people. No institutions or agencies exist to take charge of public safety. We, though, have been hired to take on that responsibility. Our official title? Director of Public Safety.

If we adopt a rosy view of human nature, the job will be easy because we can assume that there will be no or minimal crime. Conversely, if we adopt a Hobbesian view of the world, we can expect that crime will run rampant unless we take extreme action.

Let us instead sidestep philosophical debates about human nature and adopt the straightforward assumption that crime occurs. Let us further assume that crime may be somewhat checked by societal values, norms, and varying levels of community cohesiveness, but that a need will exist to prevent or reduce crime through governmental intervention.

How does this society differ from contemporary American communities? For starters, we begin with a recognition that communities contribute to public safety. They therefore have a central role to play in preventing crime. Second, we encounter none of the institutions, such as the police or corrections, typically associated with public safety. Third, we are being asked to take charge of public safety. No contemporary agencies in America have that role. Each one, such as the police or courts, play only a small part, and none face the mandate to coordinate all efforts to address crime. Fourth, and by extension, we are not held back by the past. We are free to create a comprehensive and systematic approach to public safety rather than one aimed at fixing this or that aspect of the law, policing, courts, prisons, and so on.

Might we end up reinventing the wheel? That is, might we simply end up creating sentencing laws, police departments, courts, and prisons? It is possible, but doubtful. Any rational approach to public safety would prioritize prevention, crime reduction, and the causes of both. Such an approach would not likely lead to reinventing the approaches currently used in contemporary America. Why? These are almost entirely reactive, largely ignore the causes of crime, and do not work.

This basic insight can be lost in the endless politicization of crime and the focus on piecemeal criminal justice reform. If we cannot keep this insight front and center, then, much like Sisyphus's endless attempts to reach the mountaintop, we will be doomed to failure. We will make ever increasing investments in approaches that barely make a dent in crime, can worsen it, can contribute to injustice and inequality, and, not surprisingly, leave citizens dissatisfied, disenchanted, and, quite understandably, angry.

Let us think through what an effective approach to public safety would look like if we were not fettered with the institutionalization of poorly designed approaches to public safety. In so doing, we can and will discover that in many respects the solutions are at once simple, yet groundbreaking. We will discover, too, that, as currently designed, contemporary policing simply is not well-designed to promote public safety. But we also will discover that opportunities exist to reinvent policing to better create a safer society. We will discover that—if public safety is our priority—any such reinvention will almost assuredly mean that the police constitute but one part of a much larger and comprehensive strategy of effective crime prevention. Not least, we will discover that we need to reinvent our approaches to lawmaking, criminal justice, the courts, and corrections. Even more than that, we will need to reinvent our approach to public safety writ large. Such an approach will require rising above, rather than being driven by, these institutions.

Our thought experiment will lay the groundwork for subsequent chapters. This is purposeful. Before going too far into the weeds, we think it is important that all of us—we (the authors), you (the reader), the public, policymakers and practitioners, and researchers—have a clear vision for thinking about public safety. With it, we will be better able to appreciate the problems in contemporary policing identified in Chapter 3. And we will be better able to anticipate how best to reform traditional policing (which we discuss in Chapter 5), and how to reinvent and adopt new ways of doing policing (which we discuss in Chapter 6).

Establish Clear Goals: Crime Prevention and Public Safety

We land in Anywhere and receive our charge as the Director of Public Safety: make society safer. What likely would be, or should be, our first step?

In policy development and evaluation, the first step is to identify goals.[1] What exactly do we want? Less crime.

That seems obvious. Observe, though, that this clarity does not exist in contemporary criminal justice or corrections. Something gets in the way. Many things, in fact, get in the way. One of the most important is that we lose sight of this fundamental goal. Policies, programs, practices, interventions, and the like proliferate, yet have little clear connection to public safety.

The opposite should happen. These efforts all should *directly* tie back to public safety. Every aspect of them should be designed to achieve that goal, much like every part of a race car serves to make it go faster.

Before moving on, let us be a bit more specific. We want public safety, and by that we mean not just "less crime." *We want as little crime as possible.* Accordingly, we want both to respond to crime when it happens and to prevent it.

Consider two communities, "A" and "B." In community A, 100 crimes happen. In 20 of them, we catch the individuals who committed crimes and then punish or intervene with them in some way. The other 80 individuals who committed crimes get away. For simplicity's sake, we will assume one individual per crime.

Imagine that community A uses a highly effective program that reduces recidivism by 50 percent. Community A thus ends up with 90 crimes the next year—80 that are committed by the 80 individuals who never got caught and 10 that are committed by those for whom the intervention did not work. In short, there is a 10 percent reduction in crime.

Community B, which has an identical population and identical group of 100 individuals who committed crimes, relies on a program for the 20 caught individuals. Let us assume that their intervention program is not quite as effective as community A's. Perhaps it reduces recidivism only by 20 percent. But community B also has a prevention program—which implements services targeting at-risk groups and areas—and it reduces reported new crimes by 10 percent. Keeping the math simple, we will again assume one individual per crime. Four of the 20 participants do not go on to commit crime (20 individuals × 20 percent), and the prevention initiative leads to 8 fewer crimes (80 individuals × 10 percent). In total, then, community B has 12 fewer crimes for a 12 percent reduction in crime.

The example substantially simplifies matters. Most importantly, it ignores the potential for the crime prevention program to prevent offending among at-risk groups or areas (not just among individuals known to have engaged in crime) or to reduce it among groups already engaged in offending (but not under our supervision) or in areas with higher crime rates. The example thus dramatically understates the extent to which community B's approach is more effective.

Of course, the devil is in the details. Implementing an ineffective prevention program, for example, gains us nothing. Worse, it leads to wasted expenditures and missed opportunities. Community B would not win out in that situation.

The point remains, however, that the community A approach ignores the vast bulk of crime and so can never result in appreciable gains in public safety. Yet, its approach represents how most of America responds to crime. Arrests happen. Convictions happen. People go to prison. But no appreciable reduction in crime occurs. Community B's approach, by contrast, has the potential to substantially improve public safety. It is, though, hardly used.

Our goal? We do not simply want to respond to crime and perhaps reduce it a little bit by targeting individuals known to commit, or to have committed, crime—we want to make the public as safe as possible. That requires both preventing crime *and* reducing it among individuals engaged in crime or in areas with the highest rates of crime. We need, in short, a dual-pronged prevention and intervention approach.

Identify and Monitor the Level and Distribution of Recidivism and Crime

To address any problem, we need to understand its contours: How large is the problem? Where is it located?

That seems simple but, as with much criminal justice policy, often gets ignored. Why? In part, it may be ignorance. Most of us have trouble appreciating the importance of something that we do not understand. In addition, we may become accustomed to certain sources of information and forget or remain unaware of their shortcomings.

In Anywhere, we have no source of information yet, and so have a fresh start. We can create the information that we need. One option might be a system where we wait for citizens to report crimes to us. That would be problematic. Why? Some people may not report anything but the most serious crimes. Some may not trust government agencies and so want nothing to do with them. Others may fear that reporting may create problems for them. Still others may not care. And still others may lie. Relying on reported crime, or on reported crime alone, would be less than ideal. We can and should use it. But we want to augment it to ensure that we more accurately gauge the amount and distribution (location) of crime.

A better option—use surveys. We can poll the public about their involvement in criminal activity and whether they have been victims of crime. This approach turns out to be viable. Indeed, the entire discipline of criminology rests heavily on this idea, one that has been empirically tested. It turns out that people will respond to and accurately complete a well-designed and implemented survey, even one that asks about personal involvement in criminal activity.[2] Surveys can be done poorly or well. When done well, they can provide highly accurate and useful information; the opportunities and advances for doing so are so much greater today, especially with the advent of the internet (which we have in Anywhere).[3]

This step seems simple. It is. But observe that all across the country, local and state law enforcement agencies operate with no self-report survey data. Their only source of information about crime comes from arrests and calls to the police. So, if police bias affects arrests, that will result in apparent—but not real—group differences in crime. Or if some groups or citizens in certain areas are reluctant to call the police, law enforcement agencies will underestimate crime for these groups or areas.

We can and should go several steps further. For example, we will want to monitor changes over time in the *level* and *distribution* of crime. That way, we can determine if crime is rising or falling or if it is shifting to certain areas. Such information can help guide us in targeting our efforts to prevent and reduce crime. It can also help us in evaluating these efforts.

In identifying and monitoring crime, we will want to focus on at least two distinct "levels" of analysis. The first is crime across communities and the second is offending among those individuals who have come into contact with our public safety system. Admittedly, in our clean-slate approach, we have not yet discussed what we will do to prevent or reduce crime. For the time being, though, let us assume that when individuals offend, we do something to help ensure that they do not commit any more crimes. We therefore will need to monitor their offending. By "offending," we mean *actual* criminal activity. Recidivism can refer to "offending." Typically, though, recidivism studies rely on arrest and conviction data. That means that recidivism reflects a combination of actual offending *and* societal responses, such as the resources allocated to arresting individuals. Relying on self-report data can help us ensure that our measure of recidivism, self-reported offending, provides a more accurate gauge of criminal activity alone.

Can we collect such information? Absolutely. In the past, collecting good data typically required substantial investments of time and money. It still does. But with the advent of the internet, online survey capabilities, advanced computing capacity, and numerous statistical and data visualization programs, it is now possible to cost-effectively create, analyze, and present data in an accessible manner. That means that as the Director of Public Safety, we—along with poli-cymakers, the public, and anyone recruited to help with crime prevention and reduction—can work from accurate information about recidivism and crime.

Identify and Monitor the Causes of Recidivism and Crime

If your car stops running, you pay someone to fix it. Or, if you like working on cars, you fix it yourself. Either way, to fix the car requires figuring out why it stopped working. Many possibilities exist—a dead battery, failed starter or fuel pump, dirty or worn spark plugs, a broken alternator drive belt, clogged air or fuel filters, an empty fuel tank. The list goes on. Some of the repairs may be simple and cost little. For example, filling the fuel tank would require no repair, apart from possible towing costs. Others might be complex and cost a great deal. Most of us want the car repaired and at the least cost. We do not want to spend money on repeated unnecessary repairs that fail to correct our problem. For that, we need accurate diagnosis.

The policy arena is no different: If we want to reduce recidivism (i.e., continued offending) among individuals who have come into contact with our criminal justice and correctional system and if we want to reduce crime in communities, we need to understand the causes of them. Fortuitously, we have a large body of theories and empirical research that identifies many of these causes. But—this caveat is important—that work helps more in the abstract when thinking generally about possible solutions. It does not help a great deal in specific instances. Think back to the car. A variety of factors could prevent it from starting. You want to identify the one that prevents your car from starting and then fix it.

Knowledge of the causes of offending among individuals or the causes of crime rates in communities provides sensitizing information. It helps us to think about possible causes. But it is no substitute for on-the-ground iden-tification of the specific causes among the individuals we supervise or the communities whose safety is our responsibility.

What to do? Well, the first thing *not* to do is to spend money on one-time studies or evaluations of particular programs. That, unfortunately, tends to be the approach many localities and states take. They conduct a single study that shows crime increased in some area, then off they run implementing policies of some type or another. Or they simply assume that they know what has caused crime to go up, or why recidivism rates are high, and support a program or change that they feel confident will work. This approach is akin to paying for different repairs on a car based on a mechanic guessing rather than actually examining your car. Or based on your gut instinct that replacing the engine is needed and will solve the problem.

The solution? We need to collect information about the array of factors that can contribute to recidivism (continued offending) or community crime. If poor family support appears to be the most prevalent cause of recidivism among individuals previously in contact with the criminal justice system or under our supervision, then we might target our efforts at that. Similarly, if a lack of community cohesiveness appears to be the primary cause of crime in a community, we might target our efforts to this cause. In reality, we will likely identify a range of factors, with some more prevalent than others. We can weight our responses accordingly.

A small extension of this approach is not only to identify which causes seem most prevalent but also to monitor them over time. That way we can see which ones increase or decrease over time. When we begin implementing policies of various types, we then can assess whether they reduce the causes of recidivism or crime. If they do, great. If they do not, we can take stock of why, tweak the policy, and reevaluate whether it now is effectively addressing the causes.

What do we need to create this information? Research. We have to invest in research if we are to know how to proceed. Few of us would agree to surgery when the physician has no idea what ails us. Lab work, X-rays, physical exams, and more all provide information necessary for knowing how to proceed. We should approach public safety the same way, collecting and analyzing information before determining what policy we think we should adopt. The difference from the medical example is that we need the information on a regular basis, not just for a one-time possible surgical intervention.

Consider for a moment that most of contemporary criminal justice operates with little to no credible research on the causes of offending among those who come into contact with our criminal justice system or are under correctional supervision, or of crime in communities. Different parts of the public safety response "team"—lawmakers, the police, courts, corrections—operate with little systematic research at all. As a result, they end up stabbing in the dark, hoping that this policy or that will make a difference. It is a recipe for failure.

Because there are many causes of offending (at the individual level) and of crime rates (at the community level), any effective crime prevention approach must be comprehensive. It must target the specific causes of offending and crime for particular individuals and communities. With information about these causes, we have a fighting chance to improve public safety.

Use Evidence-Based Strategies to Prevent Offending
and Reduce Recidivism (Individuals)

Address Known Causes of Offending and Recidivism

Public safety requires that we address both offending and recidivism. Offending is criminal behavior that individuals commit, and recidivism is offending committed by individuals currently or previously in contact with the criminal justice system or under correctional supervision. In the former instance, we may not know if the individuals are committing crime. In the latter instance, we have individuals who have had criminal justice or correctional system contact. ("Corrections"—the very term suggests that we identify the problems and fix them. The term is ironic given that little about contemporary corrections involves accurate identification of the causes of recidivism or research-informed approaches to addressing it.[4]) We know that these individuals have committed crime, or at the least had contact with the criminal justice system, and we know for that reason that an elevated risk of continued offending exists.

The distinction between offending and recidivism matters. If we want to make an appreciable dent in crime, we should not let the tail wag the dog. That is to say, we should not wait until someone commits a crime and gets caught before we intervene. We should intervene when we can prevent criminal behavior from happening. Of course, on a caseload of caught and convicted individuals, we will want to take action. And we may want to continue to offer services or interventions for individuals no longer formally under supervision. But that should not be our exclusive focus. We should be focused on preventing crime among individuals in the community who currently commit crime or may do so.

At the same time, we should be clear that our current or past supervision caseloads may present unique challenges. When people grow older, the medical problems multiply and can be trickier to address. Similarly, the individuals who get caught may constitute a more serious group, one for whom we may need different or more comprehensive interventions than what we might use for others who commit crime, or may do so, but have not been identified.

In all instances, we want to address the factors that cause individuals to offend. Research has identified a diverse range of them.[5] Low self-control, strain, weak social bonds, poor social support, and more can play a role. We will want to address the specific causes among the individuals who we have identified as at risk or who are on our supervision caseloads.[6]

In so doing, we will want to focus not only on reducing risk factors but also on enhancing protective factors. Risk factors contribute to the likelihood of offending. By contrast, protective factors impede the influence of risk factors and/or facilitate prosocial outcomes.[7] They can be seen as the inverse of factors known to contribute to offending. For example, higher levels of strain increase the risk of offending, while lower levels decrease it. They are much broader than that, however, and include changes that directly or indirectly impede risk factors or lead to prosocial behavior. For example, increased self-esteem or social competence may not directly reduce offending, but they may buffer the influence of risk factors and so reduce offending and contribute to improved life outcomes, such as academic success.[8]

We will know better than to put all our eggs into one basket, which is to say, we will not subscribe to silver-bullet solutions that imagine that one program or another will solve offending or recidivism. Instead, we will want to target risk and protective factors across multiple domains. For example, when focusing on an at-risk youth population, we would want to target individual, family, peer, school, and community factors.[9]

Fortunately, we will undertake research that can guide our interventions. For example, reliance on validated risk and needs assessments will enable us to know not only which factors to target but also whether our efforts to change these factors result in improvements.

Finally, we will know to be careful about potential harms from our interventions. For example, all of us have faced the problems that attend to labels. For example, calling individuals "offenders" makes it seem like some people are just that, "offenders," while others are not. That may reinforce the very problem we seek to eliminate.

Focus on Three Levels of Prevention

We already know the perils of waiting for problems to occur and then responding. Prevention provides a much better platform for promoting public safety. Stop crime before it happens. Will some people commit crime? Yes. Should we respond? Yes. But not in lieu of a substantial investment in preventing crime from happening in the first place.

What should be our approach to prevention? At least three types exist, are widely used in public health, and can be used in our efforts to promote public safety.

The first is *primary prevention,* in which we implement interventions prior to a problem emerging. For example, we might implement parenting classes that seek to improve the development of self-control in children and, in turn, prevent delinquency.

The second is *secondary prevention,* in which we focus on individuals, groups, or areas where people are at risk of engaging in problematic behavior. For example, we might target youth with poor educational outcomes and then offer services aimed at addressing these risk factors, with the hope that the intervention might not only improve academic performance but also prevent delinquency.

The third is *tertiary prevention*, in which we intervene with individuals, groups, or areas for whom or where problematic behavior already exists. Here, we might target programs at individuals who have been arrested or communities where crime rates have rapidly escalated.

Other conceptualizations and terminologies exist. For example, from the medical field, we might distinguish *universal prevention* (measures that are "desirable for everybody in the population"), *selective prevention* (measures that are "desirable only when an individual is a member of a subgroup of the population whose risk of [developing a problem] is above average"), and *indicated prevention* (measures that are desirable for "persons who, on examination, are found to manifest a risk factor, condition, or abnormality that identifies them, individually, as being at high risk for the future development of a [problem]").[10]

For our purposes, what matters is that prevention is not something that just targets those with a problem. To the contrary, it involves a three-pronged focus—preventive measures before any evidence of a problem exists, preventive measures where there exists a clear risk of a problem developing, and, last, preventive measures where a problem is known to exist.

We will go far if we pursue all three types of prevention. (To avoid confusion, we will present both sets of terms for characterizing types of prevention.) Consider, then, that the vast bulk of all that encompasses criminal justice and corrections focuses only on the last type (i.e., tertiary or indicated prevention). And it does that poorly.

Rely on a Comprehensive Approach

Perhaps our most critical challenge in addressing offending and recidivism will be to devise a comprehensive approach. We will face many obstacles. For example, well-meaning advocates will promote particular programs, even though these programs may not be what we most need.

A familiar theme surfaces here—we will need research to guide us. Which individuals or groups are most likely to offend, which groups who have come into contact with our criminal justice system or are under supervision present the greatest risks, what particular causes should we target, and how can we address as many of the most important ones as possible? Answering these questions requires that we operate with good information. We can and should obtain it. Only then can we devise an approach that comprehensively addresses offending and recidivism.

Use Evidence-Based Strategies to Prevent and Reduce Crime
(Communities)

Address Known Causes of Crime

As with a focus on individuals, we will want to devise policies and interventions that address the known causes of crime rates. It is natural to think of individuals when thinking about crime. And obviously crime rates result from some number of individuals committing offenses of various types. But we risk missing the biggest way to promote public safety if we center our attention only on individuals.

Consider a public health view of the matter. We know that if individuals do not wash their hands, they will be more likely to pick up a disease. If we focus only on individuals, we then might be led to educate those who become sick. For example, we wait for them to enter a doctor's office and then provide them an informational brochure. That, though, means that we miss a tremendous opportunity to prevent the spread of disease in the first place. What do we do? We implement an informational campaign about the importance of hand washing, and we target everyone. That is, we implement a primary (universal) prevention strategy. In devising this strategy, we likely will discover that different communities vary in their acceptance of this information and, in turn, whether to increase their hand washing. Accordingly, we will want to tailor our efforts in ways that consider these community differences.

The issue is much the same when we think about crime. There can be characteristics of communities that increase the risk of criminal activity. For example, communities that have more "collective efficacy" (i.e., areas where residents are more willing and able to look out for and help one another) may have lower crime rates.[11] That characteristic—collective efficacy—does not inhere to any one individual. It reflects a dynamic that inheres to a community.

By addressing the factors that contribute to crime in a community, we can make a much more substantial dent in crime rates. Think of it as a tidal force. We may protect certain beaches if we install seawalls, but if we can affect the tide we can protect many more beaches. Obviously, changing the tide lies outside of the possible. But community change is not—we can implement supports and work with communities in ways that can reduce crime.

Failing to focus on the causes of community crime rates means that we relegate ourselves to small-scale gains in public safety. That point bears emphasis: If we go by the conventional approaches taken to public safety, we will find ourselves trapped in a responsive approach that ultimately leads to a narrow, individual-level focus on recidivism reduction. Should we focus on individuals who commit crime? Yes, but not to the exclusion of a whole-hearted commitment to lowering crime rates. The only way that the latter can occur is if we devise prevention efforts that target communities.

Focus on Three Levels of Prevention

As with a focus on individuals, our prevention efforts with communities can proceed along several levels. We can implement efforts to prevent crime in all communities (i.e., primary, or universal prevention). We can implement efforts to prevent or reduce crime in identified at-risk areas (i.e., secondary, or selective prevention). And we can implement efforts to prevent or reduce crime in high-crime communities (i.e., tertiary, or indicated prevention).

At risk of sounding like a broken record, information will be critical to our efforts. With it, we can implement a three-pronged approach. Without it, we are left with a scattershot approach that almost assuredly will lead us down the road of either no community prevention efforts or ones that focus only on high-crime communities. The latter constitutes an important investment. However, we want to avoid any community from getting to the point where it experiences entrenched and high levels of crime. At that point, change will be much more difficult and expensive, failure will be more likely, and we will be driven to give up on prevention.[12]

What do we then do? In all likelihood, we will turn our focus to the "criminals." Punishing these individuals may satisfy some retributive itch, but our assigned task was to promote public safety. On that count, we will have failed miserably.

Rely on a Comprehensive Approach

Community-focused efforts can become easily politicized or diverted by well-meaning individuals who promote a particular program in which they believe. An effective public safety strategy, though, will require that we devise a comprehensive approach. We will want to ensure that our resources get allocated in ways that avoid duplication and that collectively will most prevent and reduce crime. Once again, this insight may seem simple, but even a cursory glance across the criminal justice landscape will reveal that it does not guide public safety efforts.

What are the particular steps we would take? In subsequent chapters, we will turn to reforms in policing and then, more broadly, in criminal justice that can produce more public safety. For the time being, let us maintain a bird's-eye view. Doing so can help us appreciate the shortfalls of contemporary policing and criminal justice writ large, and where we need to go.

As Director of Public Safety for Anywhere, we will want to employ many strategies to prevent and reduce crime. Among them will be implementation of primary (universal), secondary (selective), and tertiary (indicated) interventions that focus on individuals and communities. Our primary and secondary prevention efforts will be where the greatest returns lie because they will have the potential to influence many more people. Our tertiary (indicated) prevention will help as well, but its contribution to overall public safety will be lower because of the smaller numbers of individuals targeted. Even so, we will want to ensure that we implement robust tertiary prevention because these individuals will be among those most likely to engage in more, and likely higher rates of, criminal activity. Without effective intervention, they will disproportionately contribute to overall crime rates.

We have a moral obligation to address the higher risk of offending among individuals known to have engaged in criminal activity. Failure to take proactive steps to reduce their criminal activity arguably will make us complicit in the predictable victimization that would result. Yet, we also have a moral obligation to ensure that we emphasize primary and secondary prevention efforts as well for the same reason—failure to do so will assuredly result in higher crime rates and more victimization.

Broadly, then, we will need to implement laws, policies, programs, and practices that facilitate different types of prevention. We will need institutions that can help families, schools, and communities. We will need institutions as well that can ensure effective implementation of prevention strategies as well as ones that can respond to crime. These institutions will be responsible primarily for preventing further crime.

In Anywhere, we also will need institutions that secure some requisite level of retribution. They should be separate from our public safety institutions, though. Combining them under the same "roof" (i.e., within the same institution or agency) may be problematic. Why? Competing priorities invariably will result in deprioritizing one goal or the other, as well as contribute to inefficient swings from one priority to the next. Retribution has a place in how we respond to crime, but it has little relevance for public safety. Yes, some deterrent effects result from harsh punishments, but research suggests that it has nominal influence relative to prevention and rehabilitation efforts.[13]

Coordinate All Efforts

Taking charge of public safety will require many institutions and diverse efforts. If we do not proceed carefully, we will end up investing too much here or there, missing entire areas where targeted efforts could yield substantial returns and allowing duplication of efforts. Worse, when viewed in its totality, our efforts likely will fail. And we will have paid for that failure.

We need, therefore, to coordinate all crime prevention and reduction efforts. That will require a centralized approach. It will be no simple task, but can be done. Outside of the United States, there are many countries that operate with a more centralized approach to public safety.[14] Consider, by contrast, the United States. According to the Bureau of Justice Statistics, an estimated 18,000 federal, state, county, and local law enforcement agencies exist in the United States, with the most common type consisting of "the small town police department that employs 10 or fewer officers."[15] That creates tremendous complexity, redundancy, and waste. And observe that these agencies do not have public safety as their primary mandate. By and large, they respond to crime and play little to no role in prevention or crime reduction efforts. Our centralized approach will differ by ensuring that public safety constitutes our central priority and by ensuring implementation of a well-coordinated, comprehensive approach.

Rely on Continuous Research and Assessment

We could trust that virtually anything we do is effective. We could trust philosophical and ideological arguments about why what we do necessarily is effective. Further, we could trust that everything we do magically gets implemented and works as planned.

But this would be ineffective. That should be obvious. Yet, consider that the vast bulk of contemporary policing and criminal justice goes unevaluated.[16] The situation results from a design flaw—namely at local, state, and national levels, government spends next to nothing on research. The spending that does occur constitutes but a small fraction of expenditures on policing, courts, and corrections. Policymakers sometimes call for running government like a business. If it did so, a great deal more would be spent on research. Businesses understand that good information provides the foundation for sound decision-making. They invest substantially in research for this quite pragmatic reason.

In Anywhere, we might do well to follow this practice and build in the infrastructure for creating useful information. One approach would be to follow the evaluation hierarchy. That is, create the capacity for (1) monitoring and assessing the need for and design of policies and practices, (2) assessing and improving implementation, and (3) assessing impact and cost-efficiency.[17] As part of our effort, we will want to be sure to collect information from citizens, including their views about and experiences with our public safety efforts. Our Department of Public Safety exists to protect them. It therefore only makes sense to learn about their views and experiences. What do these different approaches entail? We describe each one below.

Assessing and Improving Policy Design

A first step when devising effective policies and practices consists of assessing the need for them. None of us makes a sizable investment without determining if we really need to do so. We should do the same with our public safety efforts. Of course, crime will be our primary concern. But we will want information on how much crime and where crime is occurring. We want information, too, on its causes so that we can identify what kinds of responses are needed.

A related step then is to design policies, programs, practices, and interventions. View it much like designing a house or a bridge. The best designs will build on knowledge about our goals, knowledge about key materials, and research on how to combine them. The same holds true for policy. We want clarity about the specific goals of particular interventions. We want information about the activities that will be involved. We want information about whether assumptions we make rest on credible empirical grounds. And, not least, we want information about how to implement the policy to good effect. Only then can we expect our policies to work well and improve public safety.

Assessing and Improving Policy Implementation

After developing our policies, practices, or whatever particular intervention we deemed necessary, we implement it. Here, we should take heed of a basic insight from policy studies and from all of our own personal lives—to wit, the gap between ideal and actual practice may be large. The insight surfaces so frequently in policy research that it would be irresponsible to proceed without a mechanism in place to monitor implementation and to identify ways to improve it. So, that is what we will do. We will create the research infrastructure to monitor, assess, and improve policy implementation.

Assessing Policy Impact and Cost-Efficiency

Next, we want to assess whether what we do "works." That is, does it produce the impacts we want? Is it cost-efficient? All else equal, we want the most impact for the least cost. And we want to ensure, in the process, that we minimize unintended harms. The solution for us then will be to build in the capacity to assess policy impact and cost-efficiency. This will entail a substantial investment of resources. Yet, we face an inescapable truth—without good information, we cannot make good decisions. Investing in good information, then, constitutes a central pillar of effective policy.

Assessing Citizen Views and Experiences

We will not want ever to lose sight of the fact that our primary mandate is to improve public safety. For that, we need to continuously monitor levels of crime. We need as well to assess relevant outcomes associated with our various policies and institutions. For example, if we have some modified version of a police department, we will want information on whether officers do their job appropriately. Do they employ use of force when necessary and according to training and regulation? Do they follow best practices for conducting investigations? We also want information on the stresses and challenges associated with policing. These are outcomes that we know attend to policing, and so we will want to monitor and address them.

Of central importance, however, will be citizens' views and experiences. The public constitutes our ultimate "customer." If we perform our job well, the public should be safer. They also should *feel* safer. They should feel respected. And they should feel that any and all public safety measures are implemented in a fair and equitable manner.

Let's take a brief detour. The Bureau of Justice Statistics conducted a study and found that 21 percent of U.S. residents age 16 or older had some type of contact with the police in the past year.[18] The most common type entailed a traffic stop—8.6 percent of residents experienced a traffic stop. That was more than the percentage who reported crime (6.7 percent of residents).

Is this a rational use of police time? Is it the best way to forge relationships with citizens? Not likely. Ask anyone if they liked being pulled over for a traffic stop. Or if they felt it was fair. Why pay large sums of money for humans to enforce speed limits or issue red-light or parking citations when these can be done with cameras and through a variety of environmental designs that promote speed limit and traffic law compliance? How could anyone feel that a speeding violation is fair when all around them they see speeders who received no citations, and when they know that enforcement occurs rarely? Even under the best of circumstances, this most common type of contact with the police hardly provides a solid platform for developing a positive impression of the police or a willingness to work with them to fight crime.[19] Indeed, it creates a context in which citizens and officers may be endangered and where negative impressions of law enforcement result.

We can do better. Through public polling and other data collection strategies, we can learn from the public how they view our public safety efforts. We can learn as well what they think we can do better. It is likely that they can shed light on how we can do so. Collecting information from the public can help hold us accountable. And it shows the public that their views can and do matter. Nowhere in America, though, does that currently happen with any regularity. In Anywhere, it should be central to our public safety efforts.

Conclusion

There are, as we will discuss, many needed reforms to policing. But just focusing on problems in policing will not take us far. The same can be said of our approach to public safety. We need to do better, yet simply responding to problems will not gain us much. A new law, program, or head of corrections—these and other steps typically occur in piecemeal fashion. No clear overarching plan guides their selection. No benefit to public safety occurs. Then, when more crime happens, everyone expresses outrage. Policymakers respond with piecemeal reforms. The cycle continues. And public safety? It becomes a footnote to policy.

This chapter serves to provide a roadmap—a clean slate—that clarifies what we should, and should not, do to promote public safety. This roadmap can help us to avoid the myopic thinking that supports piecemeal change and point us to systemic change that matters. We want to stop the *Titanic* from sinking, not tidy up the chairs on its deck.

First and foremost, any effective approach to public safety will require that our eyes stay constantly focused on our end goal of less crime. To achieve that goal, we need information. More specifically, we need good information about rates of offending among those under supervision and, more generally, of crime in communities. We need good information about the causes of recidivism and crime rates. We need to implement evidence-based strategies that address these causes. We need a comprehensive approach to prevention, including primary (universal), secondary (selective), and tertiary (indicated) prevention strategies that target supervision populations and communities. We need to coordinate our diverse portfolio of efforts to avoid redundancy, to ensure that we target our biggest drivers of crime, and to be cost-efficient. Not least, we need to monitor and assess these efforts. That includes constantly assessing the need for and design of our policies (including programs, practices, interventions, and the like). It includes constantly monitoring, assessing, and improving policy implementation. And it includes constantly monitoring, assessing, and improving cost-efficiency. All the while, we want to collect information on citizen views and experiences for insights about what we can do better and to hold ourselves accountable.

When we think about public safety in this light, it should be clear that the problems in contemporary policing and criminal justice run deeper than what we detailed in Chapters 1, 2, and 3. At bottom, the problems begin and end with a design flaw—our institutions and approaches to public safety operate without any overarching, coordinated plan. They do not prioritize public safety. And, by design, they cannot do much to prevent crime.

This roadmap, though, points to the contours along which we can improve policing and all of our approaches—including the laws on the books, the courts, and the correctional system—to reducing crime. These institutions do not compensate for the lack of a coordinated, well-designed approach to public safety. But they can be substantially improved, and they can be effective if coupled with such an approach. Indeed, without such an approach, none of what currently passes for a public safety institution—the police, courts, and corrections, in particular—can do much to appreciably reduce crime. We need institutional changes that occur alongside of systemic change. They go hand in hand, as we show in discussing how to reform traditional policing (Chapter 5) and how more broadly to reinvent our approaches to policing and public safety (Chapter 6).

5

Reforming Traditional Policing

Eliminating What Doesn't Work and Keeping and Improving What Does Work to Promote Crime Prevention and Public Safety

W E HAVE PRESENTED a considerable amount of evidence in earlier chapters that policing in the United States is—like the rest of the criminal justice system—ineffective, criminogenic, and extraordinarily expensive. The model of American policing that is practiced across the United States today, call it "traditional policing," falls well short of making society safer. That in no small part stems from the fact that contemporary policing in America does not follow a master plan, much less a well-designed one. It evolved over time, shaped by a variety of goals, needs, opportunities, contingencies, pressures, politics, financial considerations, and failures of other institutions.

Therefore, a first step in improving traditional policing requires deciding what components or approaches to eliminate and what to keep and, in the latter instance, identifying needed adjustments to increase their effectiveness. That is what we consider Phase I of a strategy for transforming policing in ways that help it to be more effective at accomplishing traditional policing goals. Phase II, which we present in Chapter 6, is to reinvent policing by prioritizing crime prevention and public safety (which are not primary goals of traditional policing) and adopting a model that is at once comprehensive, systematic, and research-based in its approach. But, first things first: What should be done with traditional policing approaches? More specifically, what should be eliminated and what should be kept, expanded, or done better?

Improve Traditional Policing—What to Eliminate

We begin by identifying practices that many or most police departments engage in that, based on our review of the evidence, are not warranted. Moreover, many of these policies and practices are ineffective, waste police resources, are inappropriate or a poor fit for the police, and, in many instances, counterproductive. We recommend that police departments eliminate these practices. Further below, we recommend practices that should be retained.

Eliminating these practices sounds simple, but it is not. In many instances, doing so will require shifting responsibility to other agencies, such as mental health organizations. That possibility alone highlights a theme to which we will return—any improvement in policing must be accompanied by a broader plan and multi-agency approach for improving public safety. It also will involve allocating significant resources to other governmental agencies as well as non-profit and nongovernmental organizations (NGOs). In others, it will involve eliminating practices that enjoy considerable support from police officers and unions, but which cause considerable negative downstream consequences, such as when individuals are arrested for low-level misdemeanors and then face an array of challenges and disadvantages disproportionate to the offense.

Many organizations accumulate practices over time that may have served a useful purpose, or perhaps did not but nonetheless were retained. In this sense, the task facing police departments is a universal one—now and again, trimming is needed to help an organization stay focused on its mission. Accordingly, we consider these recommendations as a starting point for more clearly defining the roles and responsibilities of traditional policing, as well as using expensive police resources more effectively and cost-efficiently. Perhaps in some cases, some version of the practices might be defensible. That would not alter the fact that contemporary policing is riddled with practices that are not defensible and should be eliminated.

Random, Preventive Patrol, Especially in Large Geographic Areas

Can a police presence serve as an effective deterrent to crime? Yes, sometimes. Whether police patrol or intervention is effective depends in part on the area or place where police are deployed. Crime tends to be concentrated in small geographic areas, like a particular street address, a street intersection, an apartment complex, or a handful of street segments. For example, in the 1980s, Sherman and colleagues studying crime and place in Minneapolis found that 3.5 percent of street addresses accounted for 50 percent of crime calls to police. Weisburd and colleagues expanded this research to multiple cities and confirmed the concentration of crime—5 percent of street segments accounted for 50 percent of crimes.[1]

The problem with random patrols, especially in large geographic areas, is that this fact is ignored. By definition, a random patrol entails placing police in areas at random, irrespective of the likelihood or amount of crime. It is never going to make a significant dent in crime. There is a related issue—spreading patrols over large geographic areas means that one has fewer officers to attend to high-crime areas.[2] We will discuss hot spots policing later, but note for now that contrary to random patrolling, highly targeted patrols in micro-level areas where crime is concentrated can be an effective and efficient use of patrol resources for deterring crime.

Traffic Enforcement

Assessments of how police spend their time indicate that the second most common activity, after responding to noncriminal calls, is traffic control. Between 15 and 20 percent of officers' time is allocated to traffic-related issues.[3] Consider an alternative way of looking at this situation: Of the roughly 50 million people who come into contact with the police in a given year, about half are stopped by the police in a car they were driving or in which they were a passenger. Another 9 million were involved in a traffic accident.[4] The scale of police involvement in traffic control is hard to justify, especially when we consider this question: What exactly does traffic enforcement have to do with addressing crime? The answer: almost nothing. At a minimum, then, police involvement in traffic enforcement precludes them from engaging in activities that might do much more to prevent and address crime. But there are still other problems associated with relying on the police for traffic enforcement.

Police have nearly unfettered discretion in making vehicle stops. Motor vehicle laws cover considerable ground, which gives the police an abundance of opportunities to stop vehicles for as little as not using a turn signal soon enough, a "faulty" license plate, or an expired registration. Discretion in these and other cases has led to concerns about law enforcement's role in traffic control. A central concern? Vehicle stops often serve as a pretext to stop and search a vehicle. Although Henderson County, Texas, which is southeast of Dallas, is not representative of counties nationwide, the fact that Henderson County sheriff's deputies searched 40 percent of vehicles they stopped illustrates the leeway for Fourth Amendment abuse.[5] By way of contrast, the Texas Department of Public Safety, which enforces traffic laws solely on Texas highways, searched approximately 5 percent of vehicles they stopped in 2020.[6]

National data reveal that when vehicle stops result in searches, they turn up contraband in only about one-quarter of these searches, and only 15 percent of the searches uncover contraband that merits arrest. If we measure success in terms of finding contraband or finding sufficient contraband to warrant arrest, the conclusion would have to be that real questions exist about the returns on this expensive and risky activity that can contribute to real or perceived disparities.

The legality of vehicle searches has been routinely affirmed by the U.S. Supreme Court. The Carroll Doctrine gives police broad discretion with warrantless vehicle searches based on the premise that vehicles, unlike buildings, are mobile and can easily flee a jurisdiction. Consent searches, the most common way that police initiate a warrantless search of a vehicle, can readily occur because the Court has held that the police do not need to inform drivers of their right to refuse this type of search. The main concern is, then, not legal but rather pragmatic: What do we gain and what do we risk with vehicle stops and searches?

One clear risk is the potential for racial and ethnic minorities to be differentially targeted for stops and searches. A recent study estimates that Black drivers are 20 percent more likely to be stopped by police than white drivers, relative to their distribution in the population, and nearly twice as likely to be searched than whites, even though Black drivers who were searched were less likely to be in possession of illegal contraband.[7]

Analysis of 24 million traffic stops in North Carolina between 2002 and 2020 found that Blacks comprised about one-half of the stops but comprised only 21 percent of the state's population. Moreover, vehicle stops resulted in arrest only 2 percent of the time and discovery of weapons in 1/10 of 1 percent of the time.[8]

The Stanford Open Policing Project compiled data on roughly 100 million traffic stops across the nation. Analyses conducted by the researchers at Stanford found racial disparities in vehicle stops. Blacks were significantly more likely to be stopped than whites. Hispanic drivers were stopped at about the same rate as whites. However, once stopped, Black and Hispanic drivers were searched at a higher rate than whites. Disparity or discrimination? The Stanford study found that overall, police search Black and Hispanic drivers with less cause or suspicion than white drivers, indicating, according to the researchers, clear evidence of discrimination.[9]

The question at hand is whether the police should be in the business of traffic enforcement. Consider that many violations have little bearing on public safety; often stops are used as a pretext for consent searches that are usually fishing expeditions; the searches are not typically "successful," especially in terms of finding evidence of a crime worthy of arrest; and racial and ethnic disparities and discrimination play a part in stops and searches. Are these efforts really in the interest of public safety? On the face of it, no. And, even when benefits can be identified, the many potential costs cast doubt on the wisdom of this policing activity.

Mears and Lindsey have made a very compelling case for getting law enforcement out of the business of speed limit enforcement, as well as providing a useful framework for thinking about law enforcement and traffic control more broadly. They present evidence that police enforcement of speed limits may be ineffective. Why? Any deterrent effects are likely to be localized and temporary. In addition, there are real risks. Stops create the potential for injury or death to officers. And the discretion officers use with speeding enforcement opens the door to bias and abuse. There is, too, another compelling consideration: Since effective alternatives to speed enforcement exist, why not invest in them, especially if they cost less, could be more effective, and risk fewer potential harms and less disparity in enforcement? And why not do so if it would allow the police to spend time preventing and addressing crime and doing so more effectively? As Mears and Lindsey observed,

> Opportunity costs—whose significance stems from the availability of alternative approaches to reducing speeding [like speed cameras and traffic-calming strategies like speed bumps and rotaries]—underscore the inefficiency of relying on officer-based enforcement. . . . The existence of such alternatives highlights the salience of viewing officer-based enforcement through the prism of opportunity costs. For society, the question is, how might the funds expended on officer-based enforcement be better invested? The lack of a strong empirical foundation to support officer-initiated enforcement, when coupled both with evidence of grounds to anticipate harms [bias and abuse], and with evidence that effective alternatives exist, highlights that the opportunity costs likely are considerable.[10]

The same logic applies to most other law enforcement traffic-related activities. The questionable effectiveness of pretext stops and subsequent searches, combined with racial disparities and discrimination and alternatives to traffic enforcement that we will discuss in just a moment, all point to the opportunity costs associated with police involved in most traffic enforcement. Moreover, what we will recommend for reforming traditional policing and, in Chapter 6, reinventing policing will require a considerable redistribution of police resources, and one area where substantial resources can be reclaimed is traffic enforcement.

Some jurisdictions are pursuing an alternative by deprioritizing low-level traffic violations to reduce the volume of stops. To illustrate, the Berkeley, California, city council voted to end police stops for such minor violations as a broken taillight and an expired license plate or registration. The police could spend time on serious crime, while minor violations like these would be the responsibility of unarmed Department of Transportation staff.[11] A similar approach was proposed in Brooklyn Center, Minnesota. One resolution was to create an unarmed civilian traffic enforcement department that would be responsible for all non-moving traffic violations.[12] Philadelphia pursued a related approach, as illustrated by the Driving Equality Bill, which divided traffic violations into primary and secondary violations. The police would handle primary violations but be prohibited from stopping motorists for secondary violations like a broken taillight, an air freshener hanging from the rearview mirror, or an expired tag.[13] Another example can be seen in Virginia, which passed a statewide ban on police vehicle stops for low-level infractions.[14] All of these and related efforts seek to reduce police involvement in activities that have little relevance for appreciably addressing crime and that can lead to tragic outcomes.

Although a step in the right direction—which is to say, one that may be productive—the problem with these policy changes is that they still keep a large police footprint in traffic enforcement. The restrictions on police involvement in low-level infractions may mitigate some of the problem, but much of it remains. We characterize these modifications to police involvement in traffic stops as a reasonable first step, but do not believe that it should end there. We argue that police should not be involved in traffic enforcement except under quite limited circumstances.

There obviously exist exceptions to the wholesale exit of police from traffic enforcement. Driving while intoxicated (DWI) or driving while under the influence (DWI) might seem to be an example, though even here we would highlight that a wide range of potentially far more effective prevention strategies exist to prevent such behavior. More relevant would be situations involving motor vehicle theft, human trafficking, and major drug distribution. Regardless, the balance of traffic enforcement can be handled by alternative means, such as unarmed civilian traffic enforcement. That is how traffic patrol is handled in the United Kingdom (UK). Traffic and community support officers can issue citations but are unarmed and lack arrest power.[15]

Jordan Woods, a law professor, has proposed removing police from traffic enforcement and transferring the responsibility to non-police public agencies.[16] Woods recommends the creation of agencies staffed by traffic monitors who are responsible for enforcing traffic laws with in-person traffic stops as well as administering automated systems such as speed and red-light cameras. The authority and activities of the monitors would be limited to traffic enforcement. They would not be involved in criminal investigations and would not run warrant checks or criminal background checks of violators they encounter. Although traffic enforcement would not involve the police, traffic monitors could involve the police. For example, they might do so if, in the course of a stop for a traffic violation, it becomes clear that the person is driving a stolen vehicle or is involved in a violent crime. In such situations, the traffic monitor would process the traffic violation and police would handle the criminal matters. Noncompliance with the traffic monitor would also be one of the limited exceptions when police would be called by the monitor.

This transition of traffic control from the police to traffic agencies would be facilitated by reclassifying traffic violations as civil, not criminal, offenses. Traffic violations in many states are, in fact, considered civil infractions and violators go to civil court to resolve cases. However, that is not the case across the board. Traffic violations in Texas, for example, are classified as Class C misdemeanors, which are criminal offenses. In most states, driver's license violations, such as driving with an expired license, are a criminal offense. Reclassifying these as civil infractions would facilitate them being handled by traffic monitors rather than the police. Woods also proposes that traffic agencies handle all aspects of automated traffic enforcement, from determining if a violation occurred to issuing citations.

The main point is that alternatives exist. Mears and Lindsey present a range of ways that speed limit compliance can be obtained or coerced. These include physical road designs, better signage, technological applications that notify drivers when they speed, and so on. Similarly, Woods provides a well-developed framework for transitioning traffic enforcement from the police to an alternative public agency. It would not be an easy transition, especially in light of recent survey data that indicate that the vast majority of police do not support efforts to reduce the role of police in traffic enforcement.[17] A variety of reasons may exist for that view, but they have little to do with a rational, evidence-based, or efficient approach to reducing crime.

Aggressive Policing, Zero-Tolerance Policing, and Broken Windows Policing

Every year, tens of millions of individuals are arrested for low-level misdemeanors, such as disorderly conduct, possession of marijuana, public intoxication, littering, panhandling, camping in prohibited places, and hundreds of other misdemeanor and ordinance violations. Some misdemeanors can be serious. However, the vast majority of individuals arrested annually in the United States have committed or are suspected of committing incivilities, also known as public order or nuisance crimes. Eighty percent of arrests nationwide are for minor misdemeanors and most of those arrests are dismissed— that is, not prosecuted.[18]

These aggressive, zero-tolerance arrest policies are grounded in a logic that is not empirically supported. One example is the notion of broken windows policing, which assumes that low-level crimes, including incivilities or markers of them (e.g., broken windows), will eventually lead to more serious crimes. (A brief pause: During the 1980s, when tough-on-crime criminal justice policies surged, policymakers justified the shift based on increased crime rates. They neglected to recognize or acknowledge that, while violent crime indeed was increasing, property crime had been decreasing for many years and was continuing to do so.[19]) The aggressive, zero-tolerance approach can also be seen in stop-question-frisk or *Terry* stop practices that resulted from the U.S. Supreme Court decision *Terry v. Ohio.*

Although broken windows policing and *Terry* stops may be appealing, the premise of zero-tolerance, aggressive policing—that reducing minor offending will reduce more serious crime—simply is not supported by existing research, as the *National Research Council* concluded:

> There is a widespread perception among police policy makers and the public that enforcement strategies (primarily arrest) applied broadly against offenders committing minor offenses lead to reductions in serious crime. Research does not provide strong support for this proposition.[20]

The results of a more recent meta-analysis of zero-tolerance, aggressive policing of incivilities are consistent with the conclusions of the National Research Council's assessment and those of others[21]—aggressive arrest policies targeting individual disorderly behavior do not produce significant crime reductions.[22]

Arresting individuals for low-level offenses not only does not reduce crime, it can be counterproductive. An analysis by the Vera Institute found that 99 out of every 100 arrests result in the arrestee being booked into jail. The negative consequences of pretrial detention have been well documented and include potential loss of a job, loss of housing, loss of a vehicle, family disruption, mental health problems, and more.[23] Arrests in such instances, therefore, can be criminogenic rather than crime-reducing.

Aggressive policing extends to many other areas, and generally is not well-grounded in theory or research. One example involves reliance on local police to enforce immigration law or to police immigrant communities more intensively.[24] Such efforts accord with what some policymakers and the public view as common sense—somehow immigrants, especially those who enter the country illegally, must be much more engaged in murder, assaults, burglary, and so on. This view ignores the fact that there exists little credible evidence to suggest that immigration flows increase crime or that immigrant groups engage in more crime. As one example, some research suggests that rates of offending may be lower, and that subsequent generations of immigrants eventually end up committing crime at rates commensurate with native citizens.[25] Efforts, therefore, to target immigrants are unlikely to produce appreciable gains in public safety, especially insofar as they commit less crime or, by extension, less serious crime.

As police continue to aggressively arrest individuals who commit low-level offenses and as prosecutors prosecute those cases that are not dismissed, the downstream effects jeopardize public safety. A recent study conducted by the National Bureau of Economic Research demonstrates that individuals who were arrested for low-level misdemeanors but not prosecuted were much less likely (specifically 60 percent less likely) to be rearrested over the subsequent two years compared to those who were convicted.[26] The effects were largest for individuals arrested for the first time. They conclude that avoiding conviction lessens the criminogenic effect of justice system involvement. Moreover, they investigated whether a new non-prosecution policy for low-level offenses increased crime rates, based on the idea that crime could increase if local residents believed there are no consequences for bad behavior. They found no evidence of an increase in crime after the non-prosecution policy was implemented. In fact, the evidence shows a decline in crime overall.

These findings support the policies of reform-oriented district attorneys (DAs) to decline prosecution of low-level misdemeanors such as marijuana possession, minor theft, and other low-level crimes. Unfortunately, these DAs face substantial pushback from police departments, associations, and unions. They argue that such policies will increase crime. On the other hand, Rachael Rollins, the former DA for Suffolk County, Massachusetts, was able to forge a productive relationship with the Boston Police Department and helped to avoid this conflict. The end result? Historically low arrest rates and reductions in crime. Change is possible.

Aggressive, zero-tolerance arrest policies of low-level crimes are not only ineffective in terms of reducing crime, but also have criminogenic consequences that can increase it. On top of that, pragmatic considerations—such as appropriate and efficient police use of time—should be considered. An average misdemeanor arrest takes a police officer two to three hours to process.[27] That is time when the officer could have been undertaking other activities. Put differently, current practices risk contributing to crime through criminogenic influences on those who are arrested and through the opportunity cost of not engaging in effective crime prevention.

Mental Health Calls

The police encounter mental health–related situations every day. But their approach, and their involvement more generally in such situations, is profoundly flawed. The editorial board of the *Washington Post* recently wrote:

> Earlier this year [2020], Daniel T. Prude died after a brutal police encounter when officers responded to a 911 call from Mr. Prude's brother, who was seeking help for his brother's psychosis. Daniel Prude's senseless death emphasized

the tragic reality that too often, a moment of crisis turns into a fatal brush with the law, particularly during a mental health emergency. The obvious illogic and cruelty of using force against a frightened, unarmed individual who poses no risk raises the question: couldn't people in crisis be assisted by someone other than an armed policeman?[28]

In the evolution of policing, one of the strangest and most damaging has been the turn toward relying on the police as the primary responders to mental health calls, most of which do not involve any criminal activity. Why would anyone view the police as the best option for these situations? A simple reason—there has been a failure to adequately fund local, community-based mental health treatment facilities. That leaves the police as the default go-to responders. In many jurisdictions across the country, there simply is no one else to call.

The sociologist Max Weber long ago pointed to the perils of bureaucratization, but also to the benefits. One of those is expertise. When a certain type of situation exists that requires specialized attention, one wants institutions that have the necessary expertise to respond. It should be evident that police training, woefully inadequate in general, does not create a foundation that substitutes for years of education and experience in responding to mental health crises or assisting or managing individuals who have a mental illness.

Relying on the police in these cases simply defies logic. And it creates tragedy. All too often when police respond to a situation involving a mental health issue or crisis, it ends in the death of the individual who has the mental health problem. The *Washington Post* compiled data on fatal police shootings broken out by a number of criteria, including whether the subject who was killed had a mental health problem. Between 2015 and 2022, there were 8,015 police killings of civilians. Twenty-one percent (1,676) of those involved the death of persons with a mental illness.[29] Echoing this analysis, research conducted by the Treatment Advocacy Center revealed that individuals with untreated mental illness are sixteen times more likely to be fatally shot by police compared to others stopped or approached by police.[30] A Brookings study reported that over one in five deaths by the police are directly associated with the victim's disruptive behavior due to mental health or substance-related circumstances. Brookings also reported that individuals in a mental health crisis are much more likely to encounter police than medical professionals, contributing to the jailing annually of an estimated two million individuals with a mental illness.[31]

Although death is the ultimate tragic ending of such calls to the police, there is a more frequent and also tragic outcome—arrest of the individual and booking into jail can trigger decompensation. Simply being in the presence of armed police while in a mental health crisis can result in adverse outcomes, including an escalation of symptoms that itself may lead to more intensive responses that further escalate the situation. Calling the police to a mental health situation typically will not have the preferred result of connecting the individual to emergency psychiatric services or some other treatment alternative. The police typically have a limited repertoire of responses. That, combined with limited mental health treatment resources in many jurisdictions, leads to medically adverse—and avoidable—outcomes.

An aggravating factor in how the police respond to mental health situations is a lack of training in crisis intervention. For example, between January of 2019 and June of 2020, the Washington, DC, police responded to an estimated 36,000 calls for assistance involving someone with a mental health problem. Yet, the vast majority (77 percent) of the Metropolitan Police officers during this period had reportedly received no crisis intervention training.[32]

We will discuss alternatives further below, and here simply will highlight that the police should not be the presumptive first or primary responders to mental health calls and calls involving drug-induced behavior. Just because a number of factors have resulted in the police being the default responders does not mean they are the appropriate responders. The evidence indicates that the immediate and downstream outcomes of such situations simply serve to aggravate already difficult cases.

Police in Schools

In 2016, 42 percent of public schools in the United States had at least one full-time or part-time school police officer or school resource officer (SRO).[33] By 2018, that had increased to 61 percent. By way of comparison, in 2018, about 50 percent of public schools had any capacity for diagnostic mental health assessments for evaluating students' mental health. Only 38 percent reported any availability of treatment for students with mental health problems.[34]

The ACLU investigated the presence of police and the presence of counselors, social workers, psychologists, and nurses in public schools nationwide.[35] The results of their investigation are not surprising, but they certainly are troubling. Citing statistics on increases over time in child suicide (70 percent increase between 2006 and 2016) and the prevalence of adverse childhood experiences (ACEs) among kids under age 18 highlights the need for mental health intervention. Add to that the developmental trajectory of the adolescent and teenage brain and the obvious conclusion is that school-age children and teenagers are at substantial risk for behavioral problems.

The question is how do public schools address behavioral problems of students? The ACLU report highlights that those schools that have more school-based mental health professionals also have improved attendance; fewer suspensions, disciplinary incidents, and expulsions from school; and better academic achievement and graduation rates. Unfortunately, there are millions of students who do not have adequate behavioral health resources in their schools.

But they do have police or SROs, and in increasing numbers over time. In fact, 14 million students are in schools with police but no counselors, nurses, social workers, or psychologists. The ACLU report also found that those schools that do have mental health professionals are substantially under-staffed, with very few states meeting professional standards for the ratios of mental health professionals to students.

There are obvious parallels here with our prior discussion of mental health calls. For whatever reasons, many schools have elected to deal with behavioral problems in schools with police rather than with mental health professionals. Well, one reason is simple—behavioral problems and crime in general have become criminalized and linked to a simplistic formula: Get tough on crime and the world will magically be safer.

Unfortunately, few school police have any specialized training in dealing with behavioral problems. The research is limited, but what is known is that although school police do have some awareness of child and youth devel-opmental issues, they do not appear to use or apply that knowledge in their day-to-day policing in schools. Interestingly, school police reported in inter-views that they would like to receive more formalized, structured training in interacting with and interviewing students.[36] Another study focusing on the Chicago school system found that school police received no specialized train-ing other than knowledge of the Chicago Public Schools Code of Conduct.[37]

Research has identified that a fundamental tension arises when police are in schools.[38] Specifically, are they supposed to support an educational mis-sion or to serve as crime control agents, much like officers on the street? How are administrators, teachers, or students supposed to view the police? Are students supposed to reveal information about their friends, confiding in the police in the police-as-counselor or -mentor role? Or in the police in the traditional officer role? This most likely depends on the specific school police officer and the school's policy, the views of teachers, and even those of the students. Montes and colleagues echo that such variation exists and that the blurring of police roles creates a situation that is confusing and likely to be disruptive to educational and safety goals.[39] There may be benefits to police in school, but there are also substantial risks, with much depending on the alignment of school administrator versus police priorities, and whether these priorities lead to an emphasis on effective or ineffective strategies for promot-ing safety in schools.[40]

What, though, do we know about the benefits and disadvantages of the presence of school resource officers in U.S. public schools? The report card is troubling. The 2017 report, *Handcuffs in Hallways: The State of Policing in Chicago Public Schools,* is based on research conducted by the Sargent Shriver National Center on Poverty Law. The findings are consistent with other major studies of police in schools:

> Research shows that the mere presence of police officers in school increases the likelihood that a student will be referred to law enforcement for adolescent behavior. School-based arrests, which fall more harshly on students of color, put students in direct contact with the justice system. Poor policing within schools therefore puts students on the fast track to the school-to-prison pipeline.[41]

Other research suggests that the presence of SROs increases the severity of the responses to student behavior.[42]

There is a considerable amount of research that demonstrates that contrary to reducing crime in schools, the presence of SROs actually increases crime.[43] In other words, SROs do not make schools safer. Moreover, students in schools with SROs have a higher risk of arrest and referral to the juvenile justice system as a result of the criminalization of behaviors that are traditionally resolved internally, through normal school disciplinary processes.[44]

A recent comprehensive study by Gottfredson and colleagues utilizes a natural experiment to assess the impacts of increasing SRO staffing in the treatment group of schools and not increasing SRO staffing in the control schools. The key findings are sobering and compelling, and suggest that SROs not only may not generate improvements in safety but also may create harms for students and schools:

> The National Association of School Resource Officers (NASRO) states that the primary goal of SROs is making schools and children safer. Our study suggests, to the contrary, that increasing SRO dosage in schools does not reduce school records of any form of school crime. . . . NASRO also denies that SROs contribute to the "school-to-prison-pipeline" because SRO officers are discouraged from arresting students for disciplinary issues that would be handled by teachers and administrators if the SROs were not there. As summarized earlier, the most rigorous prior research indicates instead that SRO presence is related to higher levels of referral of students to law enforcement as well as arrest. Our study . . . did demonstrate that increasing SRO dosage in schools increases the number of exclusionary responses to disciplinary infractions. Exclusionary responses to discipline have serious consequences for students. Aside from the damaging effects on academic success, exclusionary responses to discipline increase the likelihood that youth will become involved with the criminal justice system. SROs, by increasing exclusionary responses to school discipline incidents increase the criminalization of school discipline, and in so doing contribute to the "school-to-prison-pipeline."[45]

Such findings should hardly be surprising. Schools are educational settings, ones where children and adolescents push the boundaries and act out in a myriad of generally minor ways. All their behaviors, though, can look different when viewed through a law enforcement prism. Even with the best training, officers are left with the fact that their primary role is that of responding to crime. Serving as counselor, mentor, friend, and so on is secondary. In addition, there are compelling arguments for harms. What is the message to a student body when teachers seek recourse in the police to respond to general low-level misconduct rather than through traditional school disciplinary measures? One possibility is that it delegitimizes the school and the police, and in so doing contributes to a greater risk of crime.

There are, of course, schools with extremely high levels of crime. They are rare, relative to the universe of schools, and any solutions for them likely have little broader relevance for schools nationwide. And such solutions almost assuredly require responses that go well beyond siting police at schools and making arrests. They would require the same kinds of prevention-oriented efforts needed to address crime in general. That includes targeting resources toward crime prevention. By contrast, investing in more SROs not only will do little, but it will also divert resources away from investments that could be more effective.[46]

This is not to say that police have no business at schools. There are certainly many situations that require a police response. Our argument is that such responses should come from police off campus.

One other issue that warrants discussion is whether SROs prevent mass shootings or protect students from armed threats. An analysis conducted by the *Washington Post* casts considerable doubt on this argument. The evidence shows that out of approximately 200 school shootings nationwide, school police intervened successfully only twice.[47]

Just in the past two years, especially after the murder of George Floyd by a Minneapolis police officer, several jurisdictions have either removed SROs from their schools or significantly reduced their number. These include Alexandria, Virginia, Minneapolis, Seattle, Oakland, Denver, Portland, Oregon, and Los Angeles. Yet, tragedies such as the mass shooting at Robb Elementary School in Uvalde, Texas, in May of 2022, will almost assuredly create pressure to have an increased, not decreased, police presence in schools.

We fully agree that schools can and should take prudent steps to prevent these tragedies. But the evidence does not support the notion that police are the solution. Indeed, the evidence is clear that police presence in schools is, for the most part, ineffective in reducing crime and may be counterproductive. There is also strong evidence that SROs' ability to protect students from armed threats and mass shootings is quite limited.

What should be done? There is a need for a tempered change. Presently, the police may be serving to compensate for a lack of investment in mental health and behavioral services, both in schools and in the community. But there is the need, too, to understand that simplistic, get-tough responses to school shootings will do little to protect children or teachers.[48] A first step forward is to acknowledge that behavioral problems frequently stem from a diverse array of factors. A second is to recognize that any attempt to predict mass shootings in advance is fraught with tremendous error. We should not expect much, if any, return from such efforts.

A logical corollary to these steps is to invest in prevention services that can help reduce the likelihood that given individuals spiral into a place where they decide to shoot anyone, much less to seek widespread death. There is, too, the need to integrate information across different agencies so that individuals who clearly signal that they have problems can be identified and helped. An all-too-common situation across many school shootings is the discovery, after the fact, that not just one but a great many signals were evident across many different people and, more concerning, school, social service, and police agencies. It should be clear that these are not obvious police functions, though under a reinvented model of policing, which we discuss in Chapter 6, the police might have a role in working with schools, communities, and a variety of agencies to prevent school crime and shootings.

Predictive Policing

Predictive policing is the use of historical police data in what are generally proprietary statistical algorithms to predict or forecast the location of future crime and the identity of individuals at high risk of offending. These forecasts are then used to inform police deployment of resources with the goal being the prevention or reduction of crime. They entail two distinct activities, or challenges: accurate predictions of places and people, and implementation of effective prevention strategies.

This approach to crime fighting is proactive relative to the traditional reactive 911 model, and it seems evidence-based. It appears to be scientific because it uses historical crime data and information about individuals who have committed crimes. And it focuses police resources on crime prevention. There are, however, serious questions regarding accuracy of the predictions, whether the police response is appropriate and properly implemented, and whether this approach in fact prevents and reduces crime.

Although many advocates of predictive policing exist—in part because of considerable financial interests in selling the results of the algorithms to police departments—so, too, do critics. Rachel Santos has highlighted one of the most significant problems:

Unlike hot spots policing and problem-oriented policing that have specific processes and practices as well as a foundation of evidence based in research, at this
point in time, predictive policing is simply a label used for a variety of analytical
practices used to direct a variety of police tactics, rather than a comprehensive,
evidence-based policing approach to crime reduction.[49]

Among the criticisms are a lack of transparency and lack of academic rigor
regarding the analytic models used to make predictions. We know little about
the method employed in the prediction models (e.g., what variables are used,
how they are weighted, what estimation techniques are used), the assessment
of the models by independent academic researchers, and the prediction accuracy (e.g., false positives and false negatives or some other measure of statistical reliability and validity). Just because something is analytical does not
mean it is accurate or useful. One would hope that police departments would
be able to know about the efficacy of what they are purchasing, but that does
not often seem to be the case.[50] One of the key reasons? The analytical methods tend to be proprietary, thus precluding researchers from evaluating the
models and assessing their reliability and accuracy.

These issues aside, the success of predictive policing in preventing or reducing crime depends heavily on police departments implementing appropriate
responses or interventions. The jury is out on this issue as well. As Browning and Arrigo conclude, "The overall effectiveness of predictive policing
programs seems to be negligible at worst and modest at best; in other words,
current research on the effectiveness of predictive policing is inconclusive."[51]
As a logical matter, though, how could predictive policing help much if police
departments operate with no consistent and valid source of information on
the prevalence and location of crime or its causes? At its best, any accurate
predictive undertaking might help to raise a flag about a possible problem,
but it does not necessarily shed any light on the causes or solutions. Under
traditional policing, the typical approach is to react, which is to say, make
arrests. Doing so does not address the diverse array of underlying causes of
crime. We should not expect, then, that predictive policing would take us very
far in the direction of crime prevention or reduction.

An additional concern involves the potential for racial bias in the crime
location predictions. Since the algorithms generally build on historic data,
predictions may incorporate racial bias—when it exists—embedded in these
data.[52] The extent of the problem is largely unknown, in part because of data
limitations, but it seems reasonable to conclude, given the history of racial
inequality in America and its criminal justice system, that predictive policing
has a significant potential for bias.[53] At the least, its use would need to be justified based on the extent to which agencies can affirmatively demonstrate that
predictions are highly accurate, help to reduce crime, and do not reinforce or
amplify racial inequalities or disparities for any groups.

Recognition of these types of concerns seems to be taking hold in many jurisdictions around the country, and suggests some movement away from relying on predictive policing. Some early adopters, for example, of predictive policing—Los Angeles; Chicago; Santa Cruz, California; Palo Alto, California; and the state of Utah—have either discontinued or reduced their reliance on it.

Improve Traditional Policing—What the Police Should Do, Do More, and Do Better

Having identified practices that could and should be eliminated, we turn to discussing traditional policing policies and practices that can and do play an important role in reducing crime and enhancing public safety. They are not the only ones, and not all jurisdictions around the country use them or do so well, but they are prominent in police agencies around the country.

Our goal here simply is to identify the benefits of traditional policing and some of the obvious, evidence-based improvements that should be made. We seek to illustrate that many aspects of contemporary policing warrant retaining. We also seek to highlight that even if retained and improved, these activities will not suffice for making appreciable gains in public safety, or justice.

In what follows, we discus the contours of different police activities and why they should be retained. Detailed accounts of them can be found in many other sources, such as the Office of Community Oriented Policing Services, the Center for Problem-Oriented Policing, the Center for Evidence-Based Crime Policy, and the National Academies of Sciences, Engineering, and Medicine, Committee on Proactive Policing, among others.

911 Systems

We begin with the nation's 911 systems. Although not a police activity per se, it has a profound impact on policing. And it is a mainstay of virtually any system for responding when crime occurs. We discuss it for that reason, then, in Chapter 6, and revisit it because of its centrality to any effort to more systematically and effectively improve public safety.

Many experts have labeled 911 call-takers and dispatchers the gatekeepers of the criminal justice system. Although the police themselves initiate a good bit of their contact with the public, the majority of activities in most departments come from calls to 911 systems.[54] How 911 centers interpret, analyze, and act upon these calls directly and profoundly influences policing and public safety.

There are an estimated 240 million or more calls to 911 systems annually in the United States. They go to approximately 6,000 call centers or "Public Safety

Answering Points." Most calls are not crime related.[55] Typically, they are for nuisance complaints, like loud music or late-night parties, homelessness issues, requests for wellness checks of individuals, concerns about suspicious persons or activities, and reports of low-level misdemeanors and city ordinance violations. Only about 1 percent of 911 calls involve in-progress violent crimes.[56]

A Vera Institute analysis of 911 calls in five jurisdictions (Tucson, Detroit, Seattle, New Orleans, and Camden) found that less than 30 percent of calls involved any kind of criminal activity. Only 1.4 percent related to violent crime.[57] A subsequent study by the Center for American Progress and the Law Enforcement Action Partnership investigated 911 calls from eight cities (Detroit, Hartford, Connecticut, Minneapolis, New Orleans, Portland, Oregon, Richmond, California, Seattle, and Tucson) in 2019. The percentage of calls determined to be low priority and non-urgent ranged from a high of 45 percent in Seattle to a low of 23 percent in Hartford. The researchers also estimated the percentage of calls that could be handled by an alternative responder or an administrative alternative other than the police. The answer? A lot. Between 28 and 34 percent of calls were classified as needing a police response in Seattle, Richmond, Portland, and New Orleans. In Minneapolis and Tucson, 45 to 50 percent required a police response, while in Detroit and Hartford, approximately 60 percent required one.

Most jurisdictions have three options for 911 emergencies: fire, EMS, or the police. If a call is not fire- or EMS-related, the dispatcher typically has only two choices, either send the police or do not send anyone. Dispatchers tend to err on the side of sending the police, as Rebecca Neusteter, one of the leading experts of 911 systems in the United States, argues:

> Even though 911 is intended to serve as a hotline for emergencies, most calls have little to do with a public health or safety emergency. Unfortunately, due to the way in which 911 was designed and implemented, it often defaults to a police response to crises that need other forms of support. . . . Building a system of safe, supportive, and community-driven responses to 911 calls is long overdue. America's 911 system must be able to respond to a variety of matters in tailored ways, rather than default to the police.[58]

This default places a tremendous burden on police in terms of time and workload, and creates substantial inefficiency for them. It also leads to mission creep—that is, the practice of dumping more and more responsibilities on police for a real or perceived lack of viable alternatives, an issue that we discussed in Chapter 3. The problem compromises modern policing. Consider a recent analysis of the Seattle 911 call center—the researchers estimated that roughly one-half of calls do not require a response by armed, sworn police officers. They proposed, reasonably, that in the future, alternative, non-sworn individuals should respond to nearly half of calls received.[59]

Much of what plagues the criminal justice system—especially law enforcement, prosecutors, and judges—arises from faulty decision-making.[60] Incorrect decisions can and do originate from lack of information, incorrect information, bias, and more. For example, Gillooly argues that police responses can be influenced by priming and anchoring bias. Priming is a subliminal or overt influence on behavior:

> Police responses are likely linked to dispatch decisions because of a psychological phenomenon known as anchoring bias . . . a phenomenon whereby people make estimates in the face of uncertainty by adjusting from an initial value or starting point. Because different starting points yield different estimates, which are biased toward the initial values, high initial values will result in high end values. If police are primed for a high-priority encounter, then, based on anchoring bias, they will be more likely to perceive of the incident in those terms upon arrival.[61]

Accuracy of information, either from the caller or the call-taker, directly influences how police respond to situations. Although several studies show that once police arrive on the scene, they downgrade between 20 and 40 percent of calls from what the call-taker initially indicated,[62] priming and anchoring bias can work against making such adjustments. This can have tragic consequences. Consider the killing of 12-year-old Tamir Rice in a public park in Cleveland. Soon after exiting the patrol car, the officer shot and killed Rice. Why? It started with a 911 call. The caller stated that there was a black male with a gun in a park, then reported that the person was probably a juvenile and the gun a fake. The latter clarifying information never made it to the responding police officer. Information that the police receive, or do not receive, can affect their decisions and actions.

In response to the Tamir Rice killing, a criminologist and former police officer, Paul Taylor, conducted an experiment to test the effects of information on police actions. We discussed the experiment in Chapter 2, but the design and findings warrant revisiting. Taylor recruited 300 officers from eighteen different police departments and used an interactive firearms training simulator. He presented the officers with a possible trespass-in-progress scenario. Some of the participants were told that the subject appeared to be holding a cell phone. The others were told he appeared to be holding a gun. Then the simulator played out two situations. In some, the subject pulled a cell phone out of his pocket and started to film the police; in the others, he pulled out a gun and pointed it at the police. A striking difference emerged. In the cell phone situation, 6 percent who were told the subject had a cell phone shot him in the simulation. Over 60 percent who were told he had a gun shot him, even though he pulled a cell phone out of his pocket.[63] The conclusion? Information relayed by dispatch plays a critical role in the officer's understanding of the situation and, in turn, their responses.

A study conducted by the Pew Charitable Trusts focused on how 911 call centers manage behavioral health calls. Based on a non-representative sample of thirty-seven agencies, out of 233 call centers, the research explored how dispatchers interpreted behavioral health calls, their options for responding, and resources available in the jurisdiction for addressing behavioral health situations. What they learned—few call centers have call-takers or dispatchers trained in how to deal with behavioral health situations, including how to assess call information and how to dispatch responses. Moreover, most of those responding indicated that they had limited options in their jurisdictions for dealing with behavioral crisis situations, and some stated that they did not have any specialized resources for mental health crises.[64]

There is no question that 911 call centers play an essential role in public safety, but a pressing need exists to improve the accuracy of information collected and then how that information is processed and relayed to others. Unfortunately, there exist few standards or requirements for call-handling and dispatch procedures.[65] One result is the greater likelihood of police over-response and another is mis-response.

Such concerns have been highlighted in other research. For example, the Vera Institute conducted a study of 911 calls to develop estimates of errors or discrepancies in information coding. Researchers listened to actual 911 call recordings and coded the information. They then compared their codes to those of the actual 911 call-takers. The codes differed in about one-half of the cases. The primary source of the discrepancy stemmed from the incident type coding.[66] It turns out that call-takers differ systematically in classifying the same type of incidents as high priority.[67]

Here, again, the solution is not to dispense with 911 call centers. It also is not to continue current practices. Reliance on 911 call systems should be retained, but also improved. Criteria-based dispatching (CBD) is one promising improvement. CBD has been used successfully for many years by medical and fire dispatchers. It provides a structured set of automated, standardized questions and prompts that assist in systematically gathering accurate information.[68] It mirrors how public opinion data are collected in a telephone survey—a structured, computerized script guides the questioning, with prompts to enhance clarity of opinions. Presently, CBD is being piloted in several cities.

The Vera assessment as well as the work by Gillooly and others point to one simple improvement—better training and better pay. These and other accounts indicate that call-takers and dispatchers receive insufficient training and salaries that are too low and incommensurate with their responsibilities. As the Vera report emphasized, dispatchers are "often among the lowest paid and least well-trained representatives of the public safety system."[69] Many problems in life stem from a weak foundation, and that is no less true of our 911 system. Precisely for that reason, we return to it in Chapter 6 and identify the central role of improvements to 911 call centers that will be necessary to improve not only police responses but public safety more generally.

Hot Spots Policing

Crime in urban areas clusters in small, micro-geographic areas.[70] Concentrating police resources in these hot spots can increase deterrence and reduce criminal opportunity through increased guardianship, with less crime as a result. That is the underlying logic and theory of hot spots policing, which serves as an alternative to random patrol in larger geographic areas.

Meta-analyses of the effects of hot spots policing demonstrate that focusing police resources on micro-geographic areas can significantly reduce crime. One conducted by Braga and colleagues examined seventy-eight tests from sixty-five eligible studies and "revealed a small but statistically significant mean effect size favoring the effects of hot spot policing in reducing crime in treatment places relative to control places."[71] They highlighted that an updated meta-analysis showed moderately larger crime reduction effects for hot spots policing that includes problem-oriented policing interventions. Lum and Koper also found that hot spot interventions that incorporated a problem-oriented approach had stronger crime reduction effects.[72] Other reviews have identified crime reduction effects, though not always; in addition, when the effects are statistically significant, the reported magnitude is sometimes small or modest in size.[73] The effectiveness of hot spots policing depends on a number of factors, including the types of interventions employed by a particular agency. So, on average, some gains come from hot spots policing.

In general, if our goal with hot spots policing is short-term suppression of crime, then using it to identify hot spots and then employing aggressive arrests in that area may be helpful. However, any effects typically will be short-lived.[74] And there are a number of considerations that must be taken into account.

One is that research has not provided compelling evidence about the intensity (i.e., how many police deployed) or dosage (i.e., for how long) required to obtain a reduction in crime. Displacement represents another important consideration. It involves the relocation of offending (spatial displacement) or changing the timing of offending (temporal displacement), which derive from perceived criminal opportunity and risk. If a police presence raises the risk, individuals who might engage in crime decide to relocate or to delay offending.

Evidence about displacement effects is mixed. Many evaluations of hot spots policing do not measure displacement. Fewer than one-half of studies in a recent meta-analysis reported any assessment of displacement.[75] Thus, in these cases, we simply do not know if displacement occurred. Several other studies show significant spatial displacement, especially in drug enforcement interventions.[76] However, other studies report limited to no displacement effects.[77] The bottom line? Displacement cannot be dismissed as a potential harmful outcome of place-based interventions. The evidence on proximate displacement is at best inconclusive, and evidence on more distant displacement is essentially nonexistent.

One of the key issues in hot spots policing concerns the correct identification of hot spots. Innovations in geographic information technology have provided police departments with the ability to identify and map hot spots in real time. Crime mapping software, for example, can be used to identify where crimes cluster, which ones occur more frequently, the timing of criminal activity, and more. Although predictive policing can be used to forecast crime, the concerns that we raised earlier lead us to question the wisdom of using it over what can be provided with conventional mapping technology and alternative geographic analytic approaches.

In his critique of hot spots policing, Rosenbaum highlights a critical point: "Identifying a hot spot is not the same as understanding it."[78] Any policy intervention's effectiveness hinges on the ability to understand what produces a problem, and then targeting the causes. Without such information, we face a red flag waving in the wind, but with no understanding of what to do. Rosenbaum highlights, for example, that the location of crime can be understood in terms of rational choice, routine activity, crime pattern, and social disorganization theories. "But hot spots policing, in practice, is not so sophisticated and reflects a basic deterrence model."[79] That is, once a hot spot is identified, the presumption is that ineffective deterrence caused it. Accordingly, more deterrence-based intervention should occur. The problem with this approach is simple: By not understanding a hot spot, and the variety of criminogenic conditions that cause it, the police cannot implement interventions that target these conditions.[80]

In short, better mapping approaches are needed. One possibility is risk terrain modeling (RTM), a mapping-based diagnostic and prediction methodology that uses sociodemographic and environmental characteristics of places to forecast crime risk. The approach identifies aspects of an area that may be crime generators or attractors.[81] The identification of those characteristics of the area can inform interventions by the police as well as other stakeholders. As Marchment and Gill state,

RTM reliably identifies problematic features that exacerbate the likelihood of future crimes in a given geographic area. The detection of these areas helps prioritize efficient police patrols and other preventive and deterrent measures. In this way, RTM guides efficient resource allocation. It not only identifies potential hot spots but provides a reason for why they are hot in the first place.[82]

A recent meta-analysis of RTM supports the conclusion that it can be an effective forecasting method. For example, based on the twenty-five studies that met the inclusion criteria, the meta-analysis showed that roughly one-half of future crimes occurred in the top 10 percent of what are called risk cells, identified using a grid that divides the geographical terrain of places. Not only is RTA a useful predictive tool, it is easily accessible to police departments and crime analysts, and it may provide a straightforward way to roll in information about potential crime-causing factors that can lead to a wider array of interventions.

Hot spots policing is, then, a viable and valuable approach to reducing crime. Coupling it with RTM can enhance its value by allowing for identification of existing or potential hot spots, and for identification of criminogenic conditions that could or should be targeted for deterrence-based and other types of interventions. We shall return to hot spots, RTM, and crime prevention in the next chapter on reinventing policing.

Problem-Oriented Policing

In 1979, Herman Goldstein argued that policing as it was practiced did not effectively enhance public safety. The standard 911 reactive model largely failed to prevent crime. Policing was too focused on the means of policing—response time and number of arrests—rather than the end goals of crime prevention and public safety.

He therefore offered a different approach, one that amounted to a paradigm change for local policing. It shifted the focus away from a reactive, incident-driven model to one that put police in a better position to engage in crime prevention. He called it problem-oriented policing (POP).

This new approach focused on identifying and understanding problems that caused crime in the community or neighborhood or on the street corner. And it went beyond a focus on crime. Goldstein argued that the police should also be involved in addressing social and physical disorder. He made the case that the roles and responsibilities of the police should expand and so, too, should the tools and resources they use to address crime and disorder.

At the same time, he emphasized that the police cannot go it alone, or, rather, they cannot do so and be effective in making the public safer. The police need to collaborate with a variety of governmental and nongovernmental organizations and agencies, as well as community members. Collectively, such groups can provide an array of responses and resources that do not involve enforcing the law, but that might benefit from cooperation and collaboration with the police. As Lum and Nagin state,

> Much of problem-oriented policing is based on the premise that crime can be averted by changing malleable features of the social or physical environment or people's routines that contribute to criminal opportunities. Changes might include improving lighting, closing problem bars, increasing closed circuit television surveillance, or adjusting spatial and temporal patterns of police patrol. . . . These approaches require the police to play a role in understanding the causes and nature of criminal opportunities at places and then engage in "opportunity mitigation."[83]

The opportunity mitigation strategies include situational crime prevention, crime prevention through environmental design (CPTED), and hot spot interventions. Lum and Koper suggest that POP may be particularly effective when coupled with hot spots policing. Targeted enforcement in micro places allows officers to engage in specific scanning, analysis, response, and assessment, known as the "SARA" model. Strategies specific to the unique area then can be used, and include situational crime prevention (e.g., improved lighting and use of closed-circuit television, or CCTV) as well as efforts to target disorder and other criminogenic circumstances in the area. The evaluation evidence is clear that hot spots policing in conjunction with problem-oriented interventions produces greater crime reduction dividends compared to traditional patrol and enforcement alone. Research also shows that hot spots policing with problem-solving strategies produces larger and longer-lasting effects on violent crime than directed patrol.[84]

Problem-oriented policing can involve a wide array of stakeholders. These can include non–law enforcement agencies and organizations that can help design and implement changes to the social and physical environment. Examples are property owners, business owners, neighborhood associations, regulatory agencies, zoning and code enforcement, and public health officials, among many others. The point is that POP is not just policing but can and frequently does involve the collaboration of many governmental and private entities as well as communities.

Although POP is generally accepted among law enforcement agencies, and has received considerable support from national policing groups, federal agencies, and the Police Executive Research Forum, it would be an exaggeration to claim that it constitutes common practice across the 18,000 police agencies in the United States. Data from 2013 indicate that about one-third of police departments actively encourage officers to engage in problem-solving efforts.[85] Moreover, in those places where the police use it, the extent and quality of implementation varies greatly.

Two major meta-analyses have assessed the effectiveness of problem-oriented policing and found that it can be effective at reducing crime. The most recent meta-analysis by Hinkle and colleagues was published as a Campbell Collaboration Systematic Review in 2020. The findings are based on thirty-four qualifying studies and reveal that POP strategies on average led to a 34 percent reduction in crime and disorder in treatment areas compared to control sites.

An important caveat is one that confronts most policy—there can be a substantial disjuncture between how problem-oriented policing should occur and how it actually unfolds, as Braga and Weisburd have emphasized. The disjuncture leads to what they call shallow problem-solving. It is characterized by partial implementation, such as efforts of limited scope and simplistic analysis or responses. Even so, Braga and Weisburd conclude that shallow POP, when it focuses on high-risk places and people, may be sufficient:

> It is time for police practitioners and policy makers to set aside the fantasy of street-level problem-oriented policing and embrace the reality of what they can expect from the beat officer in the development of crime prevention plans at the street level.[86]

Many challenges confront any effort to implement a comprehensive problem-oriented policing program. One is that POP is counter to the long-term traditional reactive policing model. Second, it requires more time, effort, resources, and training than traditional policing approaches. Third, police culture as well as police associations and unions can be substantial barriers to change. Yet, the research evidence supporting POP is compelling and suggests that this approach to policing should be expanded. Shallow POP, though, represents a minimum bar. We argue for setting the bar much higher, a point to which we return in the next chapter.

Community Policing

One of the most widely embraced modifications to the standard model of reactive policing is community policing, or community-oriented policing (COP). Kelly attended a COP conference in the mid-1990s that was sponsored by the Department of Justice, Office of Community Oriented Policing Services (COPS). The head of the office opened the conference by asking two questions of the 500 or so police officials and administrators in attendance.

The first question was "How many of your departments practice community policing?" Every hand in the room went up. The next question: "Who can tell us what community policing is?" Not one hand went up.

The concept of community policing meant different things to different people. It did so then, and it does so now. The COPS office has provided the following definition:

> Community policing is a philosophy that promotes organizational strategies, which support the systematic use of partnerships and problem-solving techniques to proactively address the immediate conditions that give rise to public safety issues such as crime, disorder, and fear of crime.[87]

Whatever the definition used, a common feature of community policing is the collaboration of police with those in the community—individuals, groups, organizations, and agencies—to undertake a variety of crime prevention and reduction activities. The key components typically include: (a) local citizens playing a central role in identifying concerns about crime, disorder, and public safety; (b) the decentralization of decision-making, allowing the police to better understand and address problems in smaller geographic areas; and (c) problem-solving that aims to identify the nature and scope of crime-related problems and solutions to mitigate them.

In theory, crime prevention is a primary goal of community policing. By successfully reducing community problems, the approach can enhance collective efficacy and, in turn, public safety. The primary prevention strategies include deterrence and opportunity reduction through efforts like increased guardianship, situational crime prevention, and crime prevention through environmental design. Success thus requires a heavy dose of problem-oriented policing.

Although historically popular, full implementation of COP has proven difficult. Most prominent is the pressure on police to prioritize the standard model of reacting to crime after it has occurred, and then the police culture that promotes that approach. Another is the long-term mission creep that has characterized local law enforcement, placing more and more demands on time and resources, and limiting policing options like COP. Among other things, September 11, 2001, placed increased responsibility on local police for the War on Terror.[88] The increased militarization of policing also works against more citizen-centric crime prevention efforts. Survey research of police leaders reported that a majority of those surveyed found it very or extremely difficult to secure the resources necessary to properly implement COP. Roughly 40 percent stated that pushback from line officers also made deployment of COP difficult.[89]

Community-oriented policing is logical and seems like common sense. What, though, do we know about its effectiveness? A recent randomized field experiment tested the effects of positive, individual level, non-enforcement interaction between police and the public on attitudes toward police.[90] The results clearly show that even a single positive, non-enforcement contact enhances perceptions about the police, including legitimacy and willingness to cooperate with the police. Importantly, the effects were sustained over time and included individuals who were inclined not to trust and not to cooperate with the police.

A summary of existing research on community policing outcomes published in 2017 confirms and extends the findings cited above.[91] The review found that when properly implemented, community policing can reduce fear of crime as well as improve perceptions of police as a legitimate authority, resulting in greater compliance with requests from police and obeying police orders. A meta-analysis of community policing by Gill and colleagues relied on twenty-five studies consisting of thirty-seven independent evaluations that qualified for inclusion. The analyses revealed that COP does produce positive benefits, specifically positive effects on citizen satisfaction with the police, citizen perceptions of police legitimacy, and perceptions of disorder.[92] Unfortunately, little consistent evidence surfaced of direct effects on reductions in crime and the fear of crime. (One important limitation in the research to date is that many different versions of community policing are practiced across the thousands of police departments in the United States.[93] It means that we cannot safely generalize results from one study to the next.)

Gill and colleagues highlight that a community-oriented policing approach nonetheless could have indirect effects that reduce crime. It may, for example, improve the ability to undertake effective problem-oriented policing:

> Rather than examining the direct impact of COP on crime, [we should ask] what crime control benefits are derived from strategies and tactics implemented in a community-oriented context? We know from prior research that problem-oriented policing, regardless of community involvement, is effective for crime prevention. . . . If we consider the potential mechanisms by which crime prevention might be achieved directly through COP, it makes sense that a systematic process of collaborative problem solving should be more effective than the police simply talking to citizens.[94]

Lum and Koper, Skogan, and others make similar arguments. Successful community policing efforts, in this view, can enhance community trust, collaboration, and cooperation. These changes, in turn, may facilitate problem-solving efforts and other crime prevention strategies.[95] Skogan notes that community policing may increase the effectiveness of the police through a greater willingness of citizens and residents to provide intelligence to the police. Skogan also suggests that community policing may "rebuild the social and organizational fabric of neighborhoods that previously had been given up for lost, enabling residents to contribute to maintaining order in their community" through strengthening collective efficacy.[96]

For these reasons, community policing constitutes an obvious strategy to continue. Any effort to address criminogenic factors in communities, or to assist individuals at risk of crime and who reside in these communities, requires knowledge about the communities. It requires the cooperation of the individuals, businesses, and organizations with a vested interest in preventing and reducing crime. The notion that the police could independently know what contributes to crime in particular communities and, from the "top down," impose solutions defies common sense. Communities must be involved.

Therein, though, lies a critical challenge—engaging communities in anything can be difficult, all the more so if someone is an outsider and if that outsider has the force of law on their side. And it is even more difficult if the people there mistrust you. So, community policing should continue, but it must be accompanied by increased support for proper implementation and deployment. The need exists. Many police departments make no or little effort to implement community policing, and those that have it frequently do so poorly.

Proactive Policing

The National Academies of Sciences Committee on Proactive Policing defines such policing in the following way:

> "Proactive policing" is used to refer to all policing strategies that have as one of their goals the prevention or reduction of crime and disorder and that are not reactive in terms of focusing primarily on uncovering ongoing crime or on investigating or responding to crimes once they have occurred. Specifically, the elements of proactivity include the emphasis on prevention, mobilizing resources based on police initiative, and targeting the broader underlying forces at work that may be driving crime and disorder.[97]

A variety of police initiatives fall under the umbrella of proactive policing.[98] The National Academies report identified four primary models or approaches to proactive policing: (1) place-based such as hot spot deterrence interventions; (2) problem-oriented or problem-solving where police attempt to determine the underlying causes and correlates of crimes and identify solutions specific to the causes; (3) person-centered approaches, such as focused deterrence and stop and frisk; and (4) community-based initiatives that focus on collaborations with community members and organizations in identifying policing problems and the role of the community in enhancing public safety (e.g., community policing and broken windows policing). Such initiatives are often implemented by individual officers on the street or special units.

Proactive policing occurs outside of responding to 911 calls for service. It can involve officer discretion or police units assigned, for example, to hot spot interventions, directive patrol, community policing, or problem-oriented initiatives, among others.

The National Academies assessment concludes that sufficient scientific evidence exists to warrant the implementation of at least some proactive policing practices. These include place-based initiatives in high crime areas and person-centric initiatives that focus on individuals with a high risk of offending, as well as efforts at problem-solving to discover and mitigate underlying criminogenic circumstances. The assessment concludes, too, that there is less support for community-based approaches but that the evidence is encouraging. What explains the seeming discrepancy? The former (i.e., place-based and person-centric initiatives) consist of more narrowly defined activities, whereas community-based approaches consist of a variety of activities that constitute a broader undertaking. The latter approaches can result in insufficient levels of implementation or low-quality implementation, and thus limited impacts on crime. To do it "right" requires an investment in well-trained officers and intensive, sustained efforts to work with community citizens, groups, businesses, and organizations, and to do so in ways that overcome mistrust. In short, doing it "right" requires much more investment than exists with most community-based policing of any kind.

The good news? When implemented, and when implemented well, proactive strategies can be effective at reducing crime. The bad news? Proactive policing initiatives in practice tend to be limited in frequency and scope and suffer from poor implementation. Recent research by Lum, Koper, Wu, and colleagues investigated these issues. In terms of frequency, the research shows that across four jurisdictions studied, officer-initiated activity varied between 35 and 42 percent of recorded CAD events.[99] However, the authors emphasize that these percentages do not mean that officers spend one-third or so of their time engaged in proactive policing. Why? Many of the cases classified as officer-initiated arise in response to speeding or other driving infractions, or to responding to a request from a person on the street. Moreover, ride-along observational data indicate that the actual percentage of uncommitted time that is proactive policing lies in the 20 to 25 percent range.

Put simply, a significant disconnect exists between what proactive policing can, when done well, achieve and the reality of day-to-day law enforcement. For example, Lum and colleagues note that when proactive policing is used, the strategies primarily fall on the familiar—traffic stops and generalized place-based patrols of short duration. Moreover, the patrols do not routinely rely on crime analysis.[100]

Proactive policing does not appear to be routine in most police departments. It varies in design and implementation across departments as well as across shifts and supervisors within the same department. In addition, police officers typically receive limited training and guidance on proactive policing.[101] Yet, based on the evidence of the effectiveness of proactive policing, it constitutes a sensible investment. To be effective, though, departments will need to devote more attention and resources to training, guidance, and incentives to patrol officers as well as creating special units devoted to proactive policing.

Police Recruiting and Training

Chapter 2 provided a compelling indictment of police training in the United States. The problems include not only the relatively limited number of hours of academy training but also the priorities of the curricula. For example, problems include too much time spent on firearm skills, defensive tactics, and patrol procedures, and too little time allocated to "soft skills" like de-escalation, problem-solving, mediation and conflict management, stress prevention, and community building. In fact, the majority of police departments in the United States rely on a paramilitary or boot camp approach. That stress-based approach involves imposing intense psychological and physical stress. A small minority of academies use a less militaristic approach.[102]

Recruiting is also an important issue. Educational requirements play a significant role in the types of people who apply to be officers. Very few departments require a college degree, even though research shows that officers with college degrees are significantly less likely to be aggressive or to use force and have authoritarian attitudes, and they are more likely to use de-escalation tactics and be aware of social and cultural issues in their jurisdictions.[103] Officers with college degrees prefer community policing approaches, while officers with high school degrees prefer aggressive enforcement of the law.[104] Moreover, significant numbers of police come from the military; indeed, departments recruit such individuals. These recruits may have a more aggressive approach from the start, and be less willing to embrace "soft skills" or policing that would require the use of them.

The best available evidence indicates that training academies do not routinely cover much at all regarding community policing, problem-oriented policing, and other crime prevention strategies. Lum and Koper observe:

Training (like many aspects of policing) continues to reflect the vice grip of the standard policing model. Thus, while the research may point to the importance of proactivity and crime prevention for effectively dealing with crime, academies emphasize learning about procedures and the law, processes related to detaining and arresting individuals (including use of force and weapons training) and reacting to crimes that have already occurred.[105]

Training not only sets the stage for what officers do, it also sets the stage for how they do it. The socialization process that begins at the academy and becomes more pronounced during field training establishes and reinforces in new officers the culture of the department.

Training, therefore, must be increased and improved. One place to start? National standards that require substantial increases in the length of academy training. There should be curriculum standards that require training in the traditional elements of policing (such as firearms training, self-defense, driving, arrest, and control). However, the standards should require academy and field training that focuses on and prioritizes the skills necessary for effective community-oriented policing and problem-oriented policing. These include creativity, problem-solving, critical thinking, communication skills, and enhanced emotional intelligence.[106] De-escalation training is critical as well. Some studies indicate that it may substantially reduce serious force events and do so through spillover effects that influence how entire police departments approach highly charged or potentially threatening situations or encounters.[107]

Police Culture: Transitioning from Warrior to Guardian

Fundamental changes to police training, including academy training, field training, and in-service training, are critical for a variety of reasons. Among the most important is training that changes police culture.

The police as warriors or crime fighters was and remains a failed policy. Force must be used in a limited number of situations, and so officers must be trained in its use. But we know that the vast majority of police time does not involve violent situations, much less ones that require a "warrior" response. The warrior or crime fighter culture does not help in these cases. In fact, especially in comparison to a guardian culture, it can be counterproductive:

Positive police contact facilitates public confidence. People tell good cops what is going on in their neighborhoods and work with them to keep it safe. They view cops as part of their community. The guardian operates as part of the community, demonstrating empathy and employing procedural justice principles during interactions. The behavior of the warrior cop, on the other hand, leads to the perception of an occupying force, detached and separated from the community, missing opportunities to build trust and confidence based on positive interactions.[108]

The military-based police training that creates warriors and crime fighters evolved from the tough-on-crime era. It has been ineffective, save for temporary incapacitation effects and possible, though largely unquantified and unknown, deterrent effects. Even so, the warrior culture is widespread and engrained in modern policing. Academy and in-service training contribute substantially to the warrior culture. The not-so-subtle "life or death" and "survive the shift" thinking permeates many police departments and reinforces a crime-fighting, tough, warrior mentality.

A nationally representative survey of almost 8,000 police by the Pew Research Center found that a majority of the officers surveyed endorsed being aggressive and, in particular, that "in certain areas of the city it is more useful for an officer to be aggressive than to be courteous."[109] Younger officers endorse this view more. Over two-thirds of officers under age 35 believe aggression is more effective. The survey also found that a majority of police (56 percent) have become more callous toward citizens since becoming police officers.[110] In turn, being callous leads officers to endorse the use of aggressive or physically harsh tactics (66 percent).[111]

Most departments track performance with arrest or clearance rates. Police culture thus defines success as reacting to crimes and making arrests. Measures of performance do not include metrics associated with community policing or problem-solving policing. Activities other than crime fighting (to the extent that they exist in a particular department) tend not to be routinely captured in performance metrics, which signals a clear de-prioritization of them.

One of the most, if not *the* most, difficult things to change in any organization is culture. Organizational culture embodies values, expectations, beliefs, perceptions, goals, and behaviors, and sets the social and psychological environment for everything an organization does. Changing police culture will require changing recruiting (including requiring a college degree and dramatically increasing the number of female recruits), academy training, field training, and in-service training, among other things. It will require a dramatically revamped curriculum that has as its core evidence-based tactics and strategies. These evidence-based practices—like problem-oriented policing, community policing, and proactive policing—can prevent crime and make communities safer, in turn, reducing the risk to police and reducing the need for the warrior, crime-fighting mentality. They can help, too, in establishing police legitimacy.

The legitimacy crisis that policing finds itself in arguably stems from failures in recruiting and training, and the sustained promotion in many jurisdictions of the warrior, crime-fighting culture. Scholars have written, for example, about the "Blue Code of Silence"—entailing loyalty among police officers to one another first and foremost—that is "embedded in police subculture" and that promotes criminal activity among the police, an unwillingness to report such activity or any misconduct, and opposition to accountability.[112]

Making fundamental changes to training and culture—and breaking the code of silence—may be difficult, but it is both possible and essential for helping to change how the public, and minority communities in particular, perceive the police. Greater trust in police, in turn, translates into an improved ability to detect crime, identify its causes, and engage communities in helping to prevent it. Greater trust can translate, too, into improved perceptions of justice.

Cultural change is difficult, no doubt, but it can happen. Consider the example of LEED from Seattle, Washington. LEED was developed in 2011 by Sue Rahr, the King County (Seattle) sheriff at the time. The acronym stands for Listen and Explain with Equity and Dignity. Officers receive training to listen carefully, explain what decision has been made and what is going to happen, and then explain why that decision was made so that equity is transparent and so that, when the interaction is over, participants feel that their dignity remains intact. As Rahr and Rice conclude,

> Positive police contact facilitates public confidence. People tell good cops what is going on in their neighborhood and work with them to keep it safe. They view cops as part of their community—one of the key distinguishing characteristics between cops with a guardian mindset and cops who operate with a warrior mindset. The guardian operates as part of the community, demonstrating empathy and employing procedural justice principles during interactions. The behavior of the warrior cop, on the other hand, leads to the perception of an occupying force, detached, and separated from the community, missing opportunities to build trust and confidence based on positive interactions.[113]

There assuredly will always be a need for the police to use force. But the evidence clearly shows that most police activity does not involve serious crime or violent crime. And one need not subscribe to a warrior culture to use force effectively or appropriately. Much more needed, and commensurate with most police activity, is a culture that emphasizes collaboration with communities to prevent and reduce crime. It is in the interest of police officers and departments to adopt the guardian model if they want to be effective at enhancing police legitimacy, trust, crime prevention, and public safety.

Conclusion

One approach to organizational change is to start entirely from scratch. We do not believe that is warranted. Indeed, it would be counterproductive. Far more effective, in our view, is to eliminate many tasks that, over the years, have fallen to the police. It is fair to say that we simply ask too much of them and that, in many instances, the ask simply does not make sense. Do we really need to have officers whose main charge is public safety engaged in issuing speeding tickets? We don't. That function can fall to other agencies, and free up the police to restrict their focus to preventing and, secondarily, responding to crime. We argue, therefore, for eliminating many of the tasks that simply do not logically align with that goal or that can be better undertaken by other government agencies or institutions.

In addition to this step, there is the obvious next one—retain, expand, and improve those traditional policing activities that research says can be effective. Hot spots policing, problem-oriented policing, and community policing, for example, can prevent and reduce crime, and they can improve citizens' perceptions of safety and trust in the criminal justice system. These efforts should not be adopted willy-nilly, and attention must be given to implementation. When done poorly, none of these or other approaches can be effective. They may even worsen matters. So, as with most complex matters, care and attention to details are essential to ensure that traditional policing approaches not only can be effective but also, in actual practice, are. More, though, is needed. And so we turn to what that entails.

6

Reinventing Policing within a System That Prioritizes Crime Prevention and Public Safety

I N THE PREVIOUS CHAPTER, we identified evidence-based improvements to traditional policing, changes that we believe are necessary and can be effective. In this chapter, we turn to a more radical approach—the reinvention of policing—that is complementary to these changes but also goes well beyond them. We have made the point that there really are no agencies, departments, or organizations in charge of public safety, crime prevention, and recidivism reduction. We have many of the pieces in place that could go into a systematic crime prevention and recidivism reduction effort, but nobody is in charge of organizing these pieces or aligning them to achieve these goals. For that reason, we propose a model that begins with addressing that gap. There must be a lead agency charged with overseeing and coordinating efforts to promote public safety.[1]

What, then, would be the role of the police? They would work with other agencies and communities to prevent and respond to crime. They would co-produce public safety. How can they do that if burdened with other responsibilities? They can't, not under current practices. As we discussed in Chapter 5, that needs to change. And it can by eliminating responsibilities that have snowballed over many decades, diverting the police from a central focus on preventing and effectively responding to crime.

For at least sixty years, there have been efforts to fundamentally change policing, though calls for reform have waxed and waned over that period. The Kerner Commission highlighted the role of police in triggering and perpetuating the riots of the 1960s, and the Walker Commission concluded that the police participated in a riot in Chicago at the 1968 Democratic National

Convention. However, concerns over these and other examples of police misconduct fell by the wayside as crime rates climbed and tough on crime became the call to action for American criminal justice. For police, that meant aggressive crime fighting, expanded search and seizure, stop and frisk, no-knock warrants, SWAT teams, and more. It led to the era of the warrior cop. The War on Drugs reinforced this trend, and escalated in the 1980s in part due to growing concerns about crack cocaine and the rapid rise in violence. The push to arrest our way to public safety continued even as crime rates declined through the 1990s and first two decades of the 2000s. And, throughout, it ignored that property crime rates had been on the decline throughout the 1970s and the entire get-tough era.

In recent years, renewed demands for police reform have emerged in response to the deaths of citizens, typically young and unarmed Black males, usually by white police officers. Body-worn cameras and citizen video-taping of interactions have highlighted instances of clearly egregious police misconduct, and with it the understanding that such instances in the past went unacknowledged or unaddressed. The good news is that the evidence has generated substantial interest in reforming policing. The bad news is that the debates about policing, like much criminal justice policy, continue to be politicized in ways that divert attention from the need for a comprehensive, thoughtful, and evidence-based approach to changing our methods not only of policing but also for public safety and justice.[2] One side, for example, calls for eliminating the police, apparently failing to recognize that citizens want police presence and involvement, especially in many high-crime communities. They do not want discriminatory, unresponsive, or ineffective policing, but they do want help in creating safe communities for themselves and their children. Then there is the other side that calls for becoming even more entrenched in a get-tough approach that has, for decades, failed. Worse, it has done a disservice to society and, it should be said, to the people who serve in law enforcement and generally do so out of a genuine desire to help others.

Concerns about policing have led many scholars, media outlets, think tanks, nonprofit organizations, candidates for elected office, and a variety of advocacy organizations and criminal justice agencies to call for police reform. We briefly review what currently is the substance of these calls for reform. We agree with the logic and evidence for many of these recommendations but argue that they fall far short of what will be needed to improve—to an appreciable degree and in a lasting manner—public safety.

The goal for this chapter is to lay out what we believe is a more productive strategy of change that essentially reinvents policing in America. The reinvention of policing is based in part on adopting new goals. These include a focus first and foremost on public safety, and doing so by enhancing trust and legitimacy and preventing crime by the traditional method of deterrence, but importantly also preventing crime by addressing the underlying individual-level and community-level causes of crime. A fundamental difference exists between traditional crime prevention, which emphasizes deterrence and opportunity reduction, and a model of crime prevention that addresses the criminogenic circumstances and situations known to cause crime. Extraordinarily high recidivism rates and persistently high crime rates that concentrate in select communities highlight the futility of traditional crime prevention approaches. We cannot appreciably prevent crime without addressing its underlying causes.

We begin with an overview of police reforms that have been proposed or implemented in jurisdictions throughout the United States, many in the aftermath of the killing of George Floyd and the protests that followed. We then turn to police reforms proposed by policymakers and many academics, and argue that many of the reforms are reasonable and may have some benefits but cannot appreciably achieve public safety goals. This discussion, in turn, provides the foundation for identifying how to reinvent policing and for presenting a new model for how police can be more effective in making society safer. We recognize that the new model will confront numerous barriers, and so we discuss them and incentives that can help break policing out of its traditional, response-oriented approach to one that has a chance of preventing crime and improving justice.

Contemporary and Proposed Police Reforms

Cell phone videos of police use of force and the death of civilians during interactions with the police have raised profound concerns about how law enforcement goes about their work. A turning point occurred during the 9 minutes and 29 seconds on May 25, 2000, in which Derek Chauvin kneeled on George Floyd's neck, in seeming indifference to what he was doing. Floyd died and a jury convicted Chauvin of murder. A video of this event—and what it captured—led to national outrage and protests across the country on a scale not seen since the 1960s riots. It led, too, to the Black Lives Matter movement and heightened awareness about critical problems in contemporary policing. Change was necessary, and city and state elected officials began writing legislation. Within nine months, thirty-six states introduced over 700 reform bills.[3]

Defunding police was one of the most popular reforms. Cities that "defunded the police" include, among others, Los Angeles; Austin,Texas; Norman, Oklahoma; Northampton, Maryland; Burlington, Vermont; Minneapolis; New York City; Chicago; Portland, Oregon; Baltimore; Milwaukee; and

Philadelphia. The defunding did not mean elimination of the police entirely, as some critics wanted. Rather, budget cuts were introduced that typically amounted to a small percentage of the police budget; these funds were shifted to public services. Even so, the cuts went against the trend of constantly expanding the size of police agencies. And they signaled a broader pattern. According to the Police Executive Research Forum, which conducted a survey of their member departments, 48 percent experienced or anticipated a budget cut that targeted such areas as hiring and training.[4] The calls to defund the police exposed a profound mistrust of the police, especially among minority communities, which may be most likely to experience "warrior-style" policing and seemingly proactive policing efforts that may actually reinforce structural racism.[5] They also exposed substantial confusion about what, after the cuts, the police should do, and who exactly would take up the responsibilities or tasks that the police addressed prior to the cuts.

Other popular reforms centered on increasing police accountability. Changes were quickly enacted in many states and cities, including Akron, Ohio, Philadelphia, Colorado, Massachusetts, Illinois, Washington, New York, and Virginia. Many states and cities, for example, have required body cameras and banned choke holds, neck restraints, and no-knock warrants.[6]

In many respects, these and other changes reflect democracy in action—citizens expressed outrage, and legislatures and city councils took action. But they also reflect an incoherent big-picture vision for what the police should be doing. Banning choke holds, neck restraints, and no-knock warrants are important and necessary changes to police use of force. Increasing police accountability is critical. In many places, especially minority neighborhoods, the police lack legitimacy. Citizens do not trust them, and a vicious circle can ensue. Mistrust makes it harder for the police to do their jobs. For that reason, addressing the mistrust must happen to create legitimacy and enable the police to effectively help communities.[7] The police are the face of government in relation to public safety. Accountability can serve to deter misconduct, create greater trust and legitimacy, and, in turn, improve police-community relations.

None of these changes reflects a clear vision, though, for policing or a coherent, systematic strategy for improving policing and public safety. Put differently, the reforms are too narrow and disorganized. The Police Executive Research Forum captures the issue as one of relying on superficial changes, with little attention to more substantial improvements, and instead focusing on a "check-the-box type of exercise":

> Ban chokeholds—check. Restrict no-knock warrants—check. Establish a civilian oversight panel—check. These and other changes are well-meaning and important. But it feels as if they are only scratching the surface and not getting to the deeper, more fundamental changes that are actually needed.[8]

This problem arises for many reasons. One is that policymakers typically pursue a reform that targets a particular type of problem, and then they move on to other priorities. Left behind is any coherent or systematic strategy. Crises rarely make for sound policy, especially when there is no clear vision for the larger-scale changes needed to avoid not only such crises but also the larger problem of crime and our approach to it.

Similar problems attend to efforts to defund the police. It was and remains a confused strategy and runs counter to what most Americans say that they want.[9] From a crime prevention standpoint, it is, we believe, clear that there must be improved funding of social services and efforts to strengthen communities. Federal, state, and local governments need to fund mental health and substance abuse treatment, interventions for individuals with neurodevelopmental and neurocognitive impairments, affordable supportive housing, improvements to public education and the juvenile justice system, social supports for those living in poverty, assistance to disadvantaged communities, and more. But for the police—or any institution charged with crime prevention and responding to and addressing crime—it is, we argue, more funding that is needed. Not, we should emphasize, funding for warrior-culture policing, but for a reinvented approach to policing that occurs within a broader context of systemic change in how society and government prevent crime and improve public safety.

We now turn to recommendations for police reform made by leading academics, think tanks, and research as well as advocacy organizations, starting with the American Civil Liberties Union (ACLU). In their proposal, Vision for 21st Century Policing, the ACLU recommends a myriad of changes to policing.[10] These include establishing standards for use of force that dramatically limit when police can use lethal force; prohibiting police from controlling a range of low-level, non-serious offenses, in turn reducing much of the interaction of police with the public that sometimes results in violence and lethal force; defunding police departments and reinvesting funds in Black and Brown communities; and using alternatives to police such as crisis intervention teams.

The Brookings Institution has identified needed short-term, medium-term, and long-term reforms.[11] Short-term changes include eliminating qualified immunity so that police misconduct can be prosecuted and developing national standards for police training and de-escalation. Medium-term changes include focusing on officer wellness, especially mental health. Finally, longer-term goals involve restructuring union contracts so that they do not interfere with the ability to hold officers accountable when they engage in misconduct, as well as changing from a warrior and us-versus-them culture to one that promotes prevention and community involvement.

The Texas Public Policy Foundation's Right on Crime has developed what they characterize as a conservative agenda for police reform. To wit:

"Conservative reforms retain deference to the traditions and customs of law enforcement, while seeking to improve it in at least three areas: Liberty, public safety and police/community relations."[12] Specific recommendations include demilitarizing the police by moving the police role away from that of a soldier; emphasizing the reciprocal relation between community and police and allowing the community a voice in how they are policed; and enhanced training with a particular emphasis on physical fitness, which the organization argues may reduce the use of force.

A conference sponsored by Carnegie Mellon on reimagining public safety consisted of a variety of participants, including leading academics and police policy experts. They identified areas that should be reformed, noting the problem of mission creep that requires the police to deal with the consequences of mental illness, drug abuse, trauma, homelessness, and poverty, issues that the police are not trained to handle. Experts highlighted the need for better police training, and moving away from a boot camp style approach. And they called for promoting a guardian role for the police rather than a warrior role.[13]

Human Rights Watch made fourteen recommendations aimed at reducing the role of police in certain circumstances. These included ending police involvement in mental health situations, removing police from schools, and reducing aggressive stop and search. They also recommended establishing independent oversight agencies and eliminating legal immunity for police misconduct.[14]

The Vera Institute proposed a variety of changes to the role of police, with a focus on how such changes could reduce mass incarceration. Proposals included alternatives to law enforcement and arrest (e.g., diversion programs); reengineering 911 systems to appropriately divert calls from the police to resources better equipped to handle certain problems (e.g., mental health crises, minor traffic incidents); statutory changes that decriminalize minor offenses; and incentivizing police to use alternatives to crime-fighting tactics.[15]

Another think tank, the Advancement Project, identified five areas of reform to local policing: enhancing accountability, controlling excessive use of force and discriminatory stop and frisk, ending broken windows policing, and improving police training.[16]

Stoughton, Noble, and Alpert—representing a mix of scholarly expertise and in-the-field front-line and leadership experience—in an essay in *The Atlantic* call for changes at the federal, state, and local level that can help reform policing. At the federal level, they recommend eliminating qualified immunity, better nationwide data collection on policing (e.g., use-of-force incidents), and federal support for better police training and local policy initiatives. State-level initiatives include increased guidance on use of force, improved state certification of officers that requires additional training on violence de-escalation and mental health training, and addressing over-criminalization by reducing the number of behaviors classified as criminal. Local-level initiatives include improved accountability systems, better alignment of training programs with best practices, increased transparency after high-profile incidents like lethal force, and promoting professionalism as a centerpiece of the police culture.[17]

The Police Executive Research Forum has a long list of recommended reforms. These include banning choke holds, restricting no-knock warrants, prohibiting officers from placing a knee on a suspect's back, requiring body-worn cameras and penalizing officers who do not turn them on, weakening qualified immunity, developing new use-of-force standards, requiring de-escalation training, and developing a database of officers who have been fired, among others.[18]

The President's Task Force on 21st Century Policing developed recommendations under six pillars: (1) building trust and legitimacy; (2) policy and oversight; (3) technology and social media; (4) community policing and crime reduction; (5) training and education; and (6) officer wellness and safety. The task force's recommendations per pillar include the following:[19]

1. Building Trust and Legitimacy
   - Move from a warrior to guardian mindset.
   - Adopt procedural justice as the guiding policy principle.
   - Develop a culture of transparency and accountability.
   - Increase nonenforcement interactions and activities with communities.
2. Policy and Oversight
   - Collaborate with the community in developing crime policies.
   - Establish clear policies regarding use of force and train in de-escalation.
   - Conduct periodic policy reviews.
3. Technology and Social Media
   - Develop national standards for the use of technology and social media.
   - Use should focus on engaging and communicating with the public.
4. Community Policing and Crime Reduction
   - Community policing should be a guiding philosophy.
   - The police should focus on coproduction of public safety through collaboration between police and the community in identifying problems and solutions.
5. Training and Education
   - Federal government should support development of training standards.

- Establish training hubs that include academies and universities.
- Develop a national postgraduate institute for senior executives to prepare them to lead agencies.

6. Officer Wellness and Safety
   - Agencies should promote wellness and safety throughout the organization.
   - Officers should be provided with first-aid kits.
   - Departments should require that officers wear seat belts and bullet-proof vests.

In 2017, Lum and Nagin wrote an essay, "Reinventing American Policing." Two principles guided their recommendations for reinventing policing: (1) prioritizing crime prevention over arrests, and (2) recognizing that public responses to what the police do matter. The legitimacy of the police, including citizen trust and confidence, is part of an important feedback loop that involves the public assisting the police in crime prevention efforts. Lum and Nagin emphasize that police training and socialization should support the primary goal of making arrests, but also of crime prevention and maintaining good community relations. Crime prevention would entail deterrence and opportunity reduction, whereby police serve as sentinels or guardians of potential targets, in turn diminishing opportunities for offending.

Lum and Nagin discuss several policing strategies that facilitate deterrence and opportunity reduction. These include proactive strategies, such as hot spots policing and problem-solving or problem-oriented policing, with tactics such as situational crime prevention and crime prevention through environmental design. As they put it, "These approaches require the police to play a role in understanding the causes and nature of criminal opportunities at places and then engage in 'opportunity mitigation.' Such activities involve adjusting the levels or types of guardianship in a particular location or changing aspects of the environment, sometimes with the help of residents."[20]

There is, in short, clear common ground in the police reform recommendations from various policing experts, academics, conferences, task forces, presidential commissions, and think tanks. Almost all of them call for better training, including enhanced standards for training; greater police accountability; changing police culture from a warrior to a collaborator or guardian orientation; reducing police responsibility for responding to low-level offenses; controlling excessive use of force; and limiting or eliminating immunity for police misconduct.

So, what more is needed? These recommendations go a long way toward identifying how policing can be improved. Yet, most of them do not directly address public safety. Rather, they focus on process, procedure, and accountability, and are centered largely around harm reduction. They constitute critical parts of any attempt to improve policing, but they do not entail the prioritization of crime prevention. Exceptions certainly exist. Lum and Nagin's call for prevention and incorporating public views is a case in point.[21] Their call provides a critical jumping-off point for how policing can, and in our view should, be reinvented.

Reinventing American Policing to Accomplish Public Safety

The persistent failure to achieve public safety and to reduce crime, victimization, and recidivism stand out in the proverbial Bill of Indictment of the American criminal justice system. The long-term experiment with being tough on crime—predicated on the theory that we can threaten (general deterrence) and arrest and punish (specific deterrence) bad behavior out of people—has been a massive failure that has come at extraordinary expense, both financial and otherwise. There is no doubt that the police and tough-on-crime policies can be effective under certain conditions and to a limited extent. Incarceration can provide an incapacitation benefit, and thus can prevent some crime. But writ large, this approach has fallen well short of rational policy. And it contradicts policymaker calls for government accountability and evidence-based policy. It has not, for example, drawn on theory and research on the causes of crime at individual or community levels and it has not accurately reflected public opinion.

This book grew out of a simple observation—no one is in charge of crime prevention, no one is in charge of recidivism reduction, and no one, more generally, is in charge of public safety.[22] The police try to do some of it, prosecutors try to do some of it, judges try to do some of it, and corrections officials try to do some of it. But there is no one in charge.

Moreover, at local and state levels, one must look long and hard to find a coherent plan for promoting crime prevention by addressing the underlying individual- and community-level circumstances that contribute to crime. As the Kerner Commission concluded over fifty years ago, "The current criminal justice system was not designed to eliminate the conditions in which most crime breeds."[23] That observation remains painfully true today.

Our goal is to contribute to efforts to change this situation and to do so through a particular focus on the front end of the criminal justice system. We each have written extensively about the courts and the correctional system as well as opportunities for improving them.[24] But these institutions are ill-equipped and -positioned to drive or lead crime prevention efforts. For example, many accounts of criminal justice reform focus on diversion and treatment. However, these practices occur after a crime has occurred, after the police are called, and after an arrest is made. Usually, it is post-arrest (and often post-conviction) that decisions about alternative dispositions or probation occur. Judicious use of diversion and investment in rehabilitation make sense, are supported by research, and are needed.[25] They simply do not take us far in preventing crime. Put differently, relying on the courts and correctional systems to prevent crime is akin to relying on hospitals to prevent medical problems. They are not suited to that task. To prevent medical problems, one needs a broad-based public health approach.

Similarly, with crime, we need a systematic and comprehensive approach to addressing the causes of crime and, when crime occurs, to responding in a productive manner that reduces crime and does so in ways that foster justice and minimize injustice. Diversion and rehabilitation are important parts of such an approach. So, too, are deterrence-based and opportunity-reduction strategies. However, they represent piecemeal efforts, at best, to prevent crime. We need an approach that pivots and places crime prevention front and center.

Defining Crime Prevention

Recall from Chapter 4 that we discussed three types of prevention: (1) primary (universal) prevention, which relies on interventions to prevent crime from happening; (2) secondary (selective) prevention, which targets interventions at individuals or groups that are at above-average risk of offending or communities where an above-average risk of increased crime exists; and (3) tertiary (indicated) prevention, which targets interventions at individuals who already have committed crime and are at high risk of committing more, and at communities with the highest crime rates. Traditional approaches to policing have not systematically engaged in any of these three prevention approaches.

The main exception is deterrence-based, opportunity-reduction policing. When the police make arrests or concentrate their efforts in high-crime areas, that can be seen as a form of tertiary (indicated) prevention. It amounts to a response to crime and thus creates the potential for specific deterrence. General deterrence may result as well. But the effect is not likely universal, as the efforts are delimited to specific areas. There is little else that the police do that systematically entails secondary (selective) prevention—that is, efforts to help individuals or communities with elevated risks of offending or crime. And there is almost nothing that they do that amounts to primary (universal) prevention. For example, the police do not undertake activities that target all individuals or communities. A primary (universal) approach might be efficient, given that the probability of offending or higher crime is not randomly distributed among individuals or communities. At the same time, primary (universal) approaches have the potential to "lift all boats" and, in aggregate, create higher levels of public safety. They also have the potential to be observed by all members of society, and so create the potential for increased perceptions of safety. That matters because when groups are actually safe, but do not perceive themselves that way, they may call for actions that may not be warranted.

We argue that prevention should target all three levels. As we discuss further below, primary (universal) prevention is needed through a comprehensive, systematic approach. The police can and should play a critical role in this approach. But they cannot substitute for a situation where no lead agency or institution exists whose sole purpose is to guide and coordinate efforts to improve public safety. It is this agency, not the police, that can prioritize all three types of prevention. The police, though, can be essential in crime prevention that targets the underlying individual-level and community-level criminogenic causes of crime.[26] When they do so with individuals at risk of offending or communities at risk of experiencing increased crime, they engage in a form of secondary (selective) prevention. When they do so with individuals who have committed crime or work in communities already experiencing dramatic increases in crime, they engage in a form of tertiary (indicated) prevention.

Both forms of prevention are important, but it is essential to recognize that tertiary (indicated) prevention risks waiting until problems arise. In these cases, it makes sense to intervene. When crimes happen, the police need to respond and arrests typically need to occur. These actions can be a form of tertiary (indicated) prevention.

The far more effective approach for the police is to prevent the problems in the first place. Primary (universal) prevention is the most effective approach to create public safety, but it requires large-scale changes to society. As we discuss below, some steps in that direction can be taken by relying on a lead agency whose charge it is to create, guide, and coordinate efforts to promote public safety through diverse strategies. For the police, though, the most realistic forms of prevention that they can undertake entail secondary (selective) or tertiary (indicated) prevention. These, therefore, will be our main focus. For simplicity's sake, however, we will just refer to prevention.

The Case for Crime Prevention

We have documented here and in other places that there is little about the traditional crime control response of the American criminal justice system that either prevents or reduces crime. Although incarceration may provide some modest incapacitation effect, recidivism rates tell a story of a punitive system that fails to reduce recidivism and enhance public safety. Combine that track record with the cost and we have a stunning public policy failure.

That does not mean we shutter prisons, send prosecutors and judges home, and tell the police to quit responding to 911 calls. We need prisons and prosecutors and judges and probation departments and police. There are people who do bad things; justice requires punishment of some type. We need police to respond to serious situations and to attempt to reduce criminal opportunity and deter offending. But responding to crime in these ways should not substitute for crime prevention. As Brandon Welsh and David Farrington have argued, "What is really needed is a crime policy that strikes a greater balance between prevention and control."[27] Importantly, they highlighted that the police can play a role in prevention, but observed that, as typically practiced, policing can simply make matters worse: "Policing may indeed represent a better alternative than the present practice of mass incarceration in the United States, but it is often another form of crime control dealing with offenders after the fact."[28]

Our public safety efforts are completely off balance. We focus public safety funding almost exclusively on law enforcement, the courts, and corrections, with little attention to prevention. That has led to decade after decade of federal, state, and local governments failing to address many of the key individual- and community-level circumstances that cause crime or contribute to involvement in the criminal justice system. Mental health is a glaring example. Its contribution to crime may be tenuous, but it is correlated with criminal justice involvement, in part because the police end up as the go-to response organization in situations that involve individuals with a mental illness. Other examples include failures to address poverty, poor parenting, substance abuse, and inadequate public education, among many others. Failing to take these steps constitutes a missed opportunity at large-scale secondary (selective) intervention—that is, intervening with individuals at an elevated risk of offending and areas at an elevated risk of experiencing increased crime.

Despite what seems like wishful thinking by elected officials and policymakers, the justice system cannot punish away mental illness, executive dysfunction, and other neurodevelopmental impairments; substance abuse; the negative effects of poverty and ACEs; and poor educational outcomes. Rather than trying to actually mitigate these crime-related factors, we have simply put the burden on police, prosecutors, judges, and corrections officials to manage the consequences. It is no secret that the criminal justice system, as currently designed, is not equipped to address these factors. They lack the mandate to do so and the tools.

Individual-Level Criminogenic Circumstances

Many individuals enter the justice system with complex comorbidities. ACEs, which include abuse, neglect, violence, having a family member attempt or commit suicide, and being in a household with mental health and substance abuse problems, can have profound consequences for health (e.g., higher risk of heart disease, cancer, and alcohol and drug abuse) as well as criminal involvement, including arrest, conviction, and incarceration.[29] ACEs and many other circumstances, conditions, impairments, disorders, and deficits that underlie criminality—for example, poverty, unemployment, ADHD, impulsivity, low intelligence, low educational attainment, neurodevelopmental impairments, drug abuse, lack of parental supervision and poor parenting, child abuse, and family disruption[30]—underscore the need to view public safety through a much broader and more sophisticated lens. Deterrence alone cannot work.

The evidence base for the effectiveness of crime prevention has been building for decades. Whether interventions target a variety of individual-level issues—youth development, neurodevelopmental impairments, parenting and family dynamics, mental illness, substance use disorders, and many other criminogenic factors—the evidence consistently points to the efficacy of mental health treatment, substance abuse treatment, and interventions for neurodevelopmental and neurocognitive impairments.[31] The Washington State Institute for Public Policy has taken the lead in identifying the effectiveness and cost-benefit of a variety of crime prevention interventions.[32] These include child welfare, pre-K to 12 education, children's mental health, adult mental health, substance abuse, and general prevention (for children and adolescents) programs. Other research bolsters these findings and the logic of early intervention. For example, Piquero and Jennings found that parent training has a significant effect on child and adolescent delinquency and antisocial behavior.[33] More broadly, Lösel and Bender reported positive effects from meta-analyses of cognitive behavioral therapy, child social skills training, and parent training programs on antisocial behavior in children.[34]

Farrington and colleagues assessed fifty systematic reviews of primary, community-based prevention programs targeting delinquency, aggression, and bullying. The results are compelling:

> These programs are defined as community-based programs designed to prevent antisocial behavior, targeted on children and adolescents, and aiming to change individual, family, or school risk factors. Only evaluations that reported effects on the outcomes of delinquency, offending, violence, aggression, or bullying were included. In total, fifty systematic reviews were assessed: five general reviews, 11 reviews of individually focused interventions, nine reviews of family-based programs, and 25 reviews of school-based programs. Every summary odds ratio effect size was greater than one, indicating that all types of programs are effective. The median effect size was 1.46, which corresponds to a decrease in aggression of about one-quarter.[35]

Our goal here is not to provide an exhaustive inventory of prevention programs and strategies targeting individual-level criminogenic circumstances.
Rather, it is to highlight that we have, and have had for decades, evidence-
based options for preventing and reducing offending.

An example of a framework for guiding use of individual-level prevention programs is the Sequential Intercept Model, or SIM.[36] It was developed
to identify the variety of touch points or intercept points where individuals
could be diverted to mental health treatment before or as they enter and are
processed in the criminal justice system. For our purposes, Intercept 0 and
Intercept 1 are the most relevant for crime prevention. Intercept 0 consists of
community services that can be accessed before any criminal justice involvement. For example, Assertive Community Treatment is a service delivery
model that provides community-based mental health treatment directly to
consumers. Intercept 1 is law enforcement. Here, much of the emphasis
centers on avoiding criminal justice involvement by diverting persons with a
mental illness prior to arrest. LEAD and CAHOOTS (discussed below) exem-
plify Intercept 1 diversions.

The framework can extend beyond mental health. Expanded intercept
points could address many of the individual-level circumstances linked to
criminality, such as housing, trauma, physical health, parental training,
educational deficits, and neurocognitive impairments. One approach is to
front-load this effort to the community and to emphasize pre-arrest diversion by police. Doing so would involve a variety of community-based access
points and outreach efforts as well as coordinating with local police to use
community-based resources. By way of example, Screening, Brief Interview
and Referral to Treatment (SBIRT) is designed to identify people at risk of
substance abuse and occurs in places like emergency departments, doctors'
and dentists' offices, and other health care providers. The increasingly common mental health screener that is administered during visits to primary care
and other physicians' offices is another example. A similar approach could be
expanded to include other public health and criminality risk factors and other
touch points or intercepts as well.

Neighborhood- or Community-Level Criminogenic Circumstances

There are well-established neighborhood- and community-level causes of
crime. Variation in crime, especially violent crime, is linked to poverty or
disadvantage, residential segregation, lack of collective efficacy, disorder, and
lack of informal social control, among others.

The foundational work by Sampson and colleagues—and their focus on
collective efficacy—has shaped our understanding of how selected neighbor-

hood characteristics predict the location of crime.[37] Whether focusing on neighborhoods or much smaller micro-geographies within neighborhoods, characteristics such as concentrated disadvantage, residential instability, and immigration concentration account for much of the variation in residents' mutual trust, social cohesion, and willingness to intervene in the interest of the community good (i.e., collective efficacy). The hypothesis posed by Sampson and others was that collective efficacy can mitigate criminogenic influences of concentrated disadvantage and residential instability by creating the neighborhood capacity to engage in collective problem-solving and to exercise informal social control. In so doing, it can reduce the likelihood of future violent crime:

> Together, three dimensions of neighborhood stratification—concentrated disadvantage, immigration concentration and residential stability—explained 70% of the neighborhood variation in collective efficacy. Collective efficacy in turn mediated a substantial portion of the association of residential stability and disadvantage with multiple measures of violence, which is consistent with a major theme in neighborhood theories of social organization.[38]

Subsequent research has demonstrated that collective efficacy can influence the "street efficacy" of residents—that is, the ability to avoid violence and develop strategies to remain safe in their environment. Sharkey discovered that youth who live in areas with low collective efficacy in turn have lower street efficacy. Youth with higher street efficacy are able to better avoid violence and delinquent peers.[39]

The troubling reality is that violence, disorder, collective efficacy, poverty, and segregation are "reciprocally related in a kind of feedback loop."[40] The conditions that cause violence are also perpetuated by violence. As long as these feedback loops exist, we will continue to have this self-fulfilling prophecy of highly segregated, poor, high-crime communities that lack the collective efficacy and informal social control that can help break that cycle.

Collective efficacy has dominated the community-level criminology literature for well over twenty years. There is little doubt that the lack of mutual trust, social cohesion, and informal social control facilitates crime. Indeed, Sampson and Raudenbush have maintained that community development may be more successful in reducing crime than police interventions. Such a focus, which is echoed by a large literature on community-level factors that contribute to crime,[41] is an argument for secondary (selective) crime prevention.

Given the importance of collective efficacy for understanding crime, it is remarkable how little discussion and research there has been on strategies for building collective efficacy. We could identify only a few research papers that discuss the relationship between neighborhood or community development, collective efficacy, and crime. Some research has been undertaken in social work, sociology, and the broader criminological literature, but it is largely an underdeveloped area. One exception is the role police can play in facilitating the development of social cohesion and informal social control.

Sharkey and colleagues investigated the role of community nonprofit organizations on the crime decline of the 1990s. They wrote: "Strong social theory on community life suggests that local organizations are a core component of the informal networks that are essential to generating social cohesion and informal social control, thus limiting violence."[42] Their analysis reveals a significant relationship between the number of local nonprofits and declines in crime in cities across the United States.

A more micro-focused analysis found support for enhanced collective efficacy due to a community intervention that provided training to residents in a variety of strategies, including relationship building with neighbors, identifying norms and values related to prevention of youth violence, youth leadership development, collaboration, and restorative intervention strategies. The researchers commented: "These findings support prior research that demonstrates the importance of interventions that facilitate social cohesion, community engagement and prosocial behaviors, which can contribute to safer neighborhood environments."[43] Other research indicates that participation in neighborhood associations and organizations and developing social ties can enhance collective efficacy.[44] Studies have found a positive relationship between civic engagement and collective efficacy as well.[45]

Research has also targeted interventions in smaller geographic areas within communities or neighborhoods. The logic is that the concentration of effort in micro-geographies such as crime hot spots is more efficient and probably better leverages intervention resources. Telep and Hibdon studied two hot spot interventions by the Seattle Neighborhood Group (SNG), a community-based nonprofit that has been in existence for over thirty years. The SNG's activities at these two hot spots included community building, increasing informal social control, and opportunity blocking. The results of their analysis identify that community-based, non-police-led community-building and crime prevention in hot spots is a promising strategy.[46]

Disorder is another place-based characteristic that influences crime. Physical disorder refers to the condition of the environment—graffiti; abandoned or boarded-up buildings; litter; abandoned, stripped cars; broken streetlights; unmowed vacant lots with litter and junk; syringes and condoms on the ground; abandoned shopping carts; garbage-strewn streets, sidewalks, and alleys; vandalism; and other visible signs of disorder. Social disorder can include loitering, panhandling, public urination, and other low-level misdemeanors.

Wesley Skogan has done considerable work on disorder and has detailed its impact on individuals, micro-geographies, and neighborhoods. The consequences are varied but they involve avoidance of disordered places, resulting in residential and commercial instability and vacancies, decline in community social life and trust among neighbors, and erosion of social ties, in turn weakening informal social control. Skogan has summarized the evidence:

> Research indicates disorder has a strong, negative effect on many factors that discourage crime, ranging from neighborhood solidarity and civic engagement to investment and stability. Disorder undermines the processes by which communities ordinarily maintain social control and preserve their character. Disorder also generates fear, and another very large body of research has documented that fear of crime has an independent, destabilizing effect on neighborhoods. From this vantage point, disorder causes crime via a set of very well understood, mediating causal mechanisms that have been the subject of a half-century or more of criminological research.[47]

There are a variety of ways to mitigate neighborhood-level disorder. Place-based strategies include reducing physical disorder[48] as well as increasing the amount of green space and trees and revitalizing vacant lots.[49] For example, Moyer and colleagues conducted a randomized control trial of vacant lots in Philadelphia over a two-year period.[50] The question was whether restoring vacant lots, as compared to control sites, reduces crime. Two treatments (a greening intervention and a less-intense trash cleanup and mowing) and a control with no intervention were examined. Both interventions significantly reduced shootings compared to the control, with no evidence of displacement.

The Clean and Green program is a neighbor-driven maintenance, cleanup, and greening of vacant lots initiative. Street segments with vacant lots maintained by the Clean and Green program had a 40 percent reduction in violent crimes compared to controls that did not have the maintenance program.[51] Another randomized control trial investigated the effect of restoration of vacant lots in neighborhoods below the poverty line on crime, fear of crime, and perceptions of safety as well as use of outdoor space for relaxing and socializing. There were significant reductions in gun violence, burglary, vandalism, and nuisance crimes and significant reductions in perceived crime and concerns about personal safety.[52] A quasi-experimental study of the effects of remediation of abandoned buildings and vacant lots in poor neighborhoods found significant reductions in firearm violence.[53]

The case for crime prevention is based in part on the failure of tough-on-crime policies to effectively and cost-efficiently reduce crime and recidivism. There is little about arrest, prosecution, conviction, and punishment, especially incarceration, that remedies individual-level criminogenic circumstances.

Moreover, criminal justice involvement does nothing to mitigate community-level factors such as concentrated poverty, residential instability, lack of collective efficacy, and lack of informal social control.

But the case for crime prevention does not require that tough-on-crime approaches have failed. Instead, it requires clear and convincing theoretical and empirical research on the causes of crime, and credible studies that identify beneficial effects of neighborhood and community interventions. That evidence exists. When it is coupled with the logic of addressing not just one or two causes of crime (e.g., insufficient fear, per deterrence-based approaches) but of addressing a myriad of causes, it represents an obvious priority. It should be clear, then, that it is time for a major public safety policy shift that pursues crime prevention in a comprehensive and systematic manner, and that makes prevention the guiding focus of policing.

Crime Prevention Strategies by Law Enforcement in the United States

Although crime prevention is not a policy priority among police departments in the United States, many departments have implemented prevention, or prevention-like, initiatives that attend to specific situations. These most typically are (1) diversion of persons with a mental illness; (2) diversion of juveniles; and (3) diversion of adults who commit low-level or first-time offenses. All three amount to a blend of secondary (selective) and tertiary (indicated) prevention. They are secondary in that the targeted groups might be viewed as not yet, or not really, "criminal," and are tertiary in that these groups in fact have already committed crimes.

It is clear that investment in diversion is limited. A national survey in 2018 shows that about one-third of police or sheriffs' agencies that responded indicated that they participate in diversion practices. One in five reported that they have a formal diversion program. Of those with a formal diversion program, those serving juveniles were the most common (nearly 90 percent), followed by diversion for persons with a mental illness (41 percent) and those who have committed a crime for the first time (40 percent).[54] The decision to divert an individual is made by the responding or supervising officer. In a minority of cases, the decision arises from a collaborative process. Just over one-quarter (27 percent) of diversion decisions occur prior to arrest. A nearly equal percent (28 percent) of diversion decisions occur after arrest, and the rest occur at booking or later.[55] To illustrate what diversion efforts can entail, we turn to examples of police-led programs and some that arise independently of the police.

The Crisis Intervention Team, or CIT, constitutes the most common type of police-led diversion. It was developed in Memphis, Tennessee, in the late 1980s and expanded rapidly. The CIT model proceeds from the premise that specially trained police officers should be the first responders in situations involving an individual with a mental illness. Police typically get alerted to such a situation through a 911 call dispatched to the CIT. Its efficacy hinges in part, then, on the 911 dispatchers recognizing that a call involves a mental health situation.

The model requires specialized training for a select group of police officers. It entails educating officers about mental illness, how to recognize when someone may be having a mental health crisis, how to de-escalate situations, and when and how to divert the individual to treatment. Training typically entails participating in a forty-hour training course that includes live scenario-based exercises and presentations from behavioral health experts, community stakeholders, people who have experience with mental illness, advocacy groups, and officials from treatment facilities.

Research shows that officers who have undergone the CIT training have greater knowledge of mental illness and treatment, can more easily recognize when someone has a mental health problem, have a better understanding and empathy for persons with a mental illness, are less likely to stigmatize mental illness, possess better de-escalation skills, are better able to help a person who is suicidal or in psychosis, and understand that in many situations use of force is counterproductive. Evidence also indicates that CIT results in stronger benefits for officers who volunteer compared to those who were assigned to CIT. The limited evaluation research to date shows that CIT generates improved outcomes relative to comparison groups. In particular, CIT-trained officers are more likely to divert and transport to treatment than to arrest and jail someone with a mental illness who has committed a low-level offense.[56]

Another police diversion program is Law Enforcement Assisted Diversion, or LEAD. Launched in 2011 in Seattle, LEAD is a pre-arrest or post-arrest diversion program for individuals who commit low-level drug crimes, prostitution, or crime that stems from poverty. LEAD is used as an alternative to arrest, jail, and prosecution of individuals who engage in low-severity crimes and who also have behavioral health problems. Police officers working with LEAD exercise discretion at the point of contact in determining whether to divert individuals to the program. Referrals serve to connect individuals to "a trauma-informed, intensive case management program where the individual receives a wide range of support services, often including transitional and permanent housing and/or drug treatment."[57] In so doing, LEAD aims to reduce harm to the individual and prevent crime by addressing underlying criminogenic circumstances, such as mental illness, addiction, and homelessness. Governed by a larger coalition called the Policy Coordinating Group, LEAD operates within a network of law enforcement, behavioral health providers, and prosecutors as well as community groups.

LEAD has generated a considerable amount of attention in its relatively short lifespan. As of 2021, there were fifty-two jurisdictions with LEAD or LEAD-like programs in operation. They vary in size from Los Angeles; Atlanta; Denver; and Houston to Rio Arriba, New Mexico; Findlay, Ohio; Burien, Washington; and Waynesville, North Carolina. In addition, seventeen jurisdictions were in the process of developing or launching a LEAD program.

Evaluation research on LEAD programs shows promising results. LEAD can successfully connect participants to needed social services and mental health and substance abuse treatment, in turn leading to positive behavioral health outcomes. LEAD appears to be well received by both participants and providers and shows significant cost savings for the criminal justice system. Evaluations of the Seattle LEAD program show that participants are 58 percent less likely to be arrested compared to individuals who went through the criminal justice system in the traditional way (i.e., arrest, prosecution, conviction, punishment).[58] Other research indicates that participation in LEAD, as compared to usual processing, results in a significant increase in income or benefits, employment or vocational training, and permanent housing; less time in jail; and a lower likelihood of being incarcerated.[59]

One challenge that attends to use of LEAD involves police exercising discretion. Although many officers understand the importance of diversion, others may not embrace it and, thus, may be reluctant to divert individuals. For example, analysis of the LEAD program in Albany, New York, shows that less than 8 percent of LEAD-eligible cases were diverted by Albany police to public health and social services. Why? Approximately two-thirds of Albany police officers expressed less than favorable attitudes about the LEAD program because they viewed the work to divert someone to LEAD as requiring more of their time than traditional police work and because they doubted the efficacy of the program.[60] Officer buy-in, then, clearly is critical. Without proper identification and referral of participants, the program cannot function.[61]

In other jurisdictions, participants' lack of transportation has interfered with access to treatment, and high caseloads have made effective case management challenging.[62] Still another problem is the lack of community-based resources for addressing the needs of individuals who should be or are diverted. For example, Seattle has experienced significant shortages of services for LEAD participants:

> Our community's ability to adequately respond to behavioral health crisis events is itself in crisis, reads a letter from the providers addressed to Mayor Jenny Durkan and King County Executive Dow Constantine, as well as members of county and city councils and law enforcement agencies. Without urgent action, people living with behavioral health conditions, the staff and organizations who care for them and the community at large are at serious risk.[63]

Another prominent diversion effort is CAHOOTS, or Crisis Assistance Helping Out on the Streets. It is a version of a Mobile Crisis Team (MCT) approach that originated in Eugene and Springfield, Oregon, in the late 1980s. CAHOOTS began as a volunteer-run crisis unit that responded with the police on crisis calls. It evolved into a civilian mobile crisis unit that is dispatched to mental health and related situations through the 911 system. The 911 dispatchers in Eugene and Springfield have been trained to recognize situations that require a CAHOOTS response but that do not involve a clear threat of violence.

CAHOOTS mainly responds to calls involving mental health, homelessness, suicide, and welfare checks. In contrast to LEAD, CAHOOTS operates as an alternative to a police response. Analysis of 911 calls and responses in Eugene shows that CAHOOTS diverts between 5 and 8 percent of 911 calls.[64] Similar approaches successfully divert cases as well. For example, the Denver Support Team Assisted Response, or STAR, program is based on the CAHOOTS approach. A six-month evaluation revealed that STAR diverted 30,000 calls received by the Denver dispatch system.[65]

Responders typically consist of a crisis worker (trained in de-escalation techniques and counseling) and an emergency medical technician (EMT) or nurse. They are unarmed, but police are available if needed, which seems to be the rare exception. An analysis of the Eugene CAHOOTS program revealed that only 150 out of 23,000 calls required police backup. In some cases, police are the first responders and can then call in the CAHOOTS EMT and crisis worker.

Limited research on MCTs like CAHOOTS has been conducted. Extant evidence, though, provides insight into how well this approach to managing behavioral health crises works either with or without police involvement. The University of Cincinnati Center for Police Research and Policy has summarized the findings. MCTs typically provide crisis response, screening and triage assessments, de-escalation and crisis resolution, coordination with behavioral health and medical services as needed, and follow-up. One of the goals of MCTs is to increase connections to community-based services. The evidence shows that MCTs facilitate those connections to services and relieve pressure on the mental health system by reducing hospitalizations and emergency room visits. There is also some evidence that MCTs are cost-effective by reducing law enforcement involvement in these cases as well as avoiding hospitalization and ER costs.[66]

CIT, LEAD, and MCT diversion programs have served as models for dozens of alternative crisis response programs in the United States. These include programs in cities such as San Francisco, Orlando, Oakland, Portland, Oregon, Albuquerque, Olympia Washington, Rochester, Dallas, Toronto,

Los Angeles, Ann Arbor, and New York, among others. Some rely on hybrid models. For example, the Anne Arundel County, Maryland, Crisis Intervention model has both a Mobile Crisis Team and a Crisis Intervention Team. The county relies on the latter for cases deemed to be too dangerous for just mental health responders. Another example can be seen in the Dallas-developed Multi-Disciplinary Response Teams approach, which consists of a team of licensed mental health professionals, paramedics, and specially trained police officers.

Still another approach for responding to behavioral health situations is the Co-Responder Team model. Although they vary in design depending on the jurisdiction, the core logic centers on having the police respond to a crisis call with a clinician or other social services staff person. The co-responder may ride with the police to the call or arrive independently. The advantage of this approach is the presence of clinical expertise and security on-site. Research shows that the co-responder model leads to fewer arrests and increased de-escalation and diversion.[67]

The effectiveness of these approaches to pre-arrest or early diversion of individuals with behavioral health problems depends on having sufficient numbers of trained police and behavioral health responders, and appropriate and adequate treatment capacity available in the community. This includes emergency psychiatric services, detox, in-patient and out-patient treatment, housing, and case management and ongoing support.

These issues point to the critical distinction between crisis services and crisis systems. Individual services can and do play a fundamental role in enhancing behavioral health and reducing criminal justice involvement. However, when they work together in a coordinated crisis system with common goals, their effectiveness may be enhanced. Consider, for example, Balfour and colleagues' description of the Tucson system:

> In this model, health care and law enforcement stakeholders agree on a common goal of preventing avoidable jail, ED, or hospital use by providing care in the least restrictive setting that can safely meet the needs of an individual in crisis. . . . A Regional Behavioral Health Authority contracts with provider agencies to create an array of services organized along a continuum of intensity, restrictiveness, and cost. At all points along the continuum, easy access for law enforcement (e.g., 911 colocation, co-responder teams, and no-wrong-door policies) facilitates connection to treatment instead of arrest.[68]

Crime Prevention Strategies by Law Enforcement in Other Countries

Many other countries offer critical insights for informing how America can reinvent policing.[69] We start in New Zealand and then go to Scotland, Ireland,

and Europe. After doing so, we will step back and present a new prevention-focused model for American policing.

Since 2011, the Prevention First National Operating Model (Prevention First) has placed the prevention of crime as the top priority for policing in New Zealand. The key goals for the Prevention First model include (1) prevent crime and victimization; (2) target and catch those who commit crime; and (3) deliver a more responsive police service. The New Zealand Police describe Prevention First in the following way:

> Prevention First is a balanced approach that maintains a focus on resolving crime while emphasizing the immediate and longer-term benefits of integrating prevention into all aspects of how we police. . . . To make New Zealand the safest country, we must continue to embed Prevention First as our operating model. . . . We need to gain a better understanding of the underlying conditions that are driving offending and victimization and work together to reduce these over time. More than any other agency, our officers are in the homes of those most at risk collecting information and intelligence that, when shared, can improve decision-making by all agencies to prevent further harm and to ensure social services reach those who need them most. . . . We need to work together with other agencies, service providers and the community in finding solutions that address the underlying causes of social harm.[70]

The Prevention First model identifies six drivers of crime that their prevention efforts target: alcohol and drug abuse, youth, families, roads, organized crime, and mental health. These drivers may not necessarily involve criminal events, but they often require a police response, which can offer opportunities for preventing subsequent crime and harm.

Problem-solving policing and community policing stand as core strategies of the Prevention First model. Community policing facilitates the police working with communities and service providers to identify and resolve the underlying causes of criminality, resulting in greater crime prevention and declines in crime. Problem-solving is central to developing prevention strategies. Both approaches are viewed as central to improving relationships between the community, especially minority communities, and the police.

Although a policing initiative, the Prevention First model relies on the formation of partnerships in the community. The premise is that these partnerships are critical for identifying and mitigating the underlying causes of crime.

So, what do we know about the relative effectiveness of Prevention First in New Zealand? Den Heyer found that in a relatively short time since the implementation of Prevention First (2011 to 2014), reported crime declined by 20 percent, non-traffic prosecutions declined by over 41 percent, and crime prevention service delivery activities increased by nearly 6 percent.

A subsequent analysis of crime between 2014 and 2018 revealed increases in some crime. Since there are many reasons why crime can increase or decrease, we take these results as suggestive, especially since there was no control or comparison area. Even so, there were improvements in the perception of the police by the public and feelings of safety and security. Public satisfaction with the police improved, as did public trust in the police and feelings of safety at night.

Ayrshire, a county of 366,000 people in southwest Scotland, developed and conducted a pilot of the Prevention First model in 2014. The stated goals and approach are

> to prevent crime, reduce victimization, and reduce locations where offending takes place, through a partnership and early intervention approach which gets to the heart of issues and identifies the best way to solve problems and tackle community concerns. . . . The programme encapsulates a partnership approach to tackling violence, anti-social behaviour and community concerns regarding violent crime. The main ethos of the programme is that violence is preventable, not inevitable and that crime, violence, and anti-social behaviour are driven by underlying social conditions and span the household, community, and school environments, entailing a multi-agency approach to address them.[71]

The Prevention First model seeks to balance deterrence-based prevention with prevention efforts that address the underlying causes of crime. Rather than rely on a police-only approach, it involves the collaboration of a variety of organizations and agencies.

A descriptive statistical analysis of crime in Ayrshire shows declines in violent crime and anti-social behavior after implementation of Prevention First. It also shows reductions in carrying of offensive weapons, especially knives and bladed weapons, public alcohol consumption, disturbances, incidences of public nuisance, and other public order crimes. These results included comparisons of crimes prior to implementation of the Prevention First pilot. A review of internal Prevention First documents and interviews conducted with police officers, partner agencies, local government officials, and the public led the evaluators to conclude that Prevention First should be a best practice. They conclude:

> As experienced police scholars, we are convinced that "Prevention First" is a powerful and innovative tool in contemporary policing. The "Prevention First" process augments, supports, and amplifies existing community policing. . . . It builds effective and efficient policing practices. We genuinely believe that "Prevention First" has the potential to move beyond traditional community policing, towards a new era of genuine multi-agency policing. . . . The innovative combi-

nations of utilizing community policing, crime prevention, early intervention, and information sharing is a sophisticated advancement.[72]

Policing in Scotland more broadly has embraced crime prevention, largely an outcome of the Police and Fire Reform Act 2012, which among other things led to the creation of a single police force called Police Scotland. The 2012 act also prioritized crime prevention by focusing police resources on reducing harm. Reinforcement of prevention also came from the ten-year strategy agenda, Policing 2026, and emphasized the importance of addressing community-level problems like inequality, poverty, and vulnerable populations, and individual-level problems like mental illness, drug and alcohol abuse, and domestic abuse.

A 2021 assessment of Scotland's emphasis on crime prevention showed a strong commitment by the police to collaboratively working in partnership with community organizations. The research highlighted the need to broaden the range of organizations that the police work with in crime prevention and harm reduction efforts:

> The cases illustrate the police working with a broad range of other organizations which bring additional and different resources and professional skills to collectively tackle issues of shared concern. It is insufficient, and ineffective for the police to apply their unique competence in law enforcement to prevention in isolation.[73]

Another example of Scotland's crime prevention priority can be seen in the Scottish Violence Reduction Unit (SVRU), a component of Police Scotland. The Scottish government treats violence as a preventable disease and therefore a public health problem (in keeping with the World Health Organization's declaration in 2002).[74] The SVRU uses evidence-based interventions at the community level and the individual level to mitigate the conditions that allow violence to develop and spread, early intervention with the goal of harm reduction if prevention has not been possible, and responding to violence after the fact, treating its effects and assisting the areas and rehabilitating the individuals involved. The SVRU initiative entails a partnership between Police Scotland, Social Services Scotland, Education Scotland, and other agencies and organizations as well as community members. At the same time, tougher sentences for knife crimes have been implemented as well as control over alcohol consumption.

Early signs indicate that the SVRU has significantly contributed to declines in a variety of crime measures, especially gang activity involving the use of weapons. Importantly, SVRU activities have increased community satisfaction.[75]

In 2017, the Irish Garda issued a report, "Crime Prevention and Reduction Strategy: Putting Prevention First," that placed crime prevention as their top priority, in conjunction with traditional deterrence-based approaches to addressing crime. The outcomes that the strategy is anticipated to achieve are increased crime prevention capacity, reduction of crime and fear of crime, reduction in the risk of victimization, enhanced community safety and security, and a reduction in recidivism. The strategy consists of a variety of initiatives and approaches:

- Interventions should be based on scientific evidence regarding the causes of crime.
- Crime prevention requires a multi-agency approach.
- The Garda alone cannot prevent crime; it requires engagement by state agencies, institutions, community and nongovernmental organizations, and the business sector.
- A wide variety of interventions is required to maximize effectiveness.
- Crime prevention should be integrated into all relevant social and economic policies and programs including social services, health, education, and employment with a special emphasis on communities, families, children, and youth at risk.
- Rely on community policing and a problem-solving approach.
- Use situational crime prevention, crime prevention through environmental design, hot spots policing, and social crime prevention (i.e., address the underlying causes of crime).
- Ensure a culture of crime prevention is established through Garda training.

In 2011, the UK's Home Office published "A New Approach to Fighting Crime." The report cited high crime and recidivism and lack of trust and confidence in the police as the motivation for launching a new approach. Also mentioned was a failure of the police to understand the underlying causes of crime, such as drug and alcohol abuse, poverty, and unemployment. It called for a new approach centered on crime prevention. The mission of policing in the UK is to reduce crime, but as noted in the report, reducing crime requires much more than catching and convicting those who have committed a crime. It also requires prevention by tackling the risk factors that drive offending and the factors that increase crime rates.

Germany, Belgium, France, Sweden, Canada, Finland, Norway, the Netherlands, and Poland are additional examples of nations that have embraced crime prevention by attempting to mitigate the underlying causes of crime. This emphasis aligns with the United Nations' policy statement on crime prevention, Guidelines for the Prevention of Crime (ECOSOC Resolution 2002/13):

There is clear evidence that well-planned crime prevention strategies not only prevent crime and victimization, but also promote community safety and contribute to the sustainable development of countries. Effective, responsible crime prevention enhances the quality of life of all citizens. It has long-term benefits in terms of reducing the costs associated with the formal criminal justice system, as well as other social costs that result from crime. Crime prevention offers opportunities for a humane and more cost-effective approach to the problems of crime.[76]

Prioritization of crime prevention can be seen as well by the European Union's development of the European Crime Prevention Network, designed to compile and disseminate research-based methods of crime prevention. The knowledge base consists of international research findings on crime prevention as well as information about specific crime prevention programs in locations throughout the Union.

Two patterns stand out in this brief review of international policing policies. First, many nations are pursuing crime prevention that seeks to address the underlying factors responsible for many crimes. Second, the United States is not doing so. Exceptions exist in some American police departments, but even then, prevention generally does not serve as the priority and instead serves as a modest augmentation to traditional policing. Indeed, across America, prevention activities are (1) the exception rather than the rule across policing agencies; (2) constrained by inadequate community-based behavioral health resources and unavailability of properly trained police responders; (3) hampered by a lack of broad police buy-in; (4) primarily reactive, in response to a 911 call, rather than a result of proactive community outreach; (5) limited mainly to behavioral health situations, such as mental health crisis calls; (6) often impeded by a lack of collaboration between police and other community agencies; and (7) not often a priority over the traditional activities like responding to 911 calls, routine patrol, and traffic enforcement.

Before proceeding, we should emphasize that many others have called for a crime prevention approach to policing, and for the use of a public health model for doing so. We have discussed many of them already. A prominent example—one that occurred just as the United States embarked on its four-decade get-tough era—is the U.S. Surgeon General's characterization of violence as a health problem and of the police as potentially playing an important role in addressing it. The Centers for Disease Control followed suit and launched what became known as the Division of Violence Prevention. The National Institute of Justice recognized, too, that law enforcement and public health officials have increasingly recognized the common ground associated with poverty, violence, and a variety of other social problems.[77]

A good example of the public health collaboration in crime prevention is the focus on ACEs.[78] Evidence shows that poverty is highly comorbid with exposure to adverse experiences. In turn, ACEs are strongly linked with a variety of negative outcomes like abuse and neglect, exposure to violence, poor educational attainment, and parental incarceration. All of these, in turn, are criminogenic.[79]

Crime control approaches historically, and still today, have not typically conceptualized crime in these ways or, by extension, adopted public health responses. That needs to change if we are to make any lasting, appreciable improvements in public safety and the role of the police in making society safer.

A New Model for American Policing

A fundamental reinvention of policing is needed. And, fortunately, many examples exist from which to draw. Our proposal builds on them and calls for a new model of American policing. It includes a balance of crime prevention and some types of traditional policing (e.g., hot spots policing, community policing, and problem-solving policing), with priority given to proactive prevention measures.

Critical to this model and its success is a lead public safety agency whose sole charge is to promote, guide, and coordinate crime prevention efforts. Police effectiveness in contributing to crime prevention hinges heavily, if not entirely, on the integration of what they do within a broader, coherent plan for preventing crime among individuals, groups, and communities.

Given such an agency, the presumptive police role would be that of guardian, and community strengthener, rather than warrior. The police would operate with a multi-agency approach, which establishes highly functional, long-term collaborations with a variety of governmental and nongovernmental agencies and organizations that bring the variety of resources and expertise necessary to effectively prevent crime and recidivism and promote public safety. The goal is to develop a holistic, collaborative, and multidisciplinary approach to public safety.

We simply cannot continue relying on a criminal justice response that evidence has overwhelmingly proven to be ineffective. It is as simple as this medical analogy. You break your leg, then go to the ER. They X-ray it and identify that, yes, the leg is broken. Then they send you home with pain medication. They did nothing to fix the leg. They just treated the symptom. That would be considered medical malpractice. Our current approach is to arrest the symptom with doing little to fix the underlying condition. How is that not malpractice?

It is worse than that. We do the functional equivalent of waiting for people to break their legs, then we treat the symptom. When that happens to someone, the leg barely heals. Then the person is predisposed to fall and break the leg again. And we repeat the process. Meanwhile, we do nothing to prevent individuals from falling and breaking their legs, or to address why, for some reasons, rates of broken legs are higher in some areas than others.

Fine-tuning police departments will not work. What is needed is a wholesale change of policing and other participating organizations and agencies. There needs to be a coherent public safety approach that promotes clarity of mission, the sharing of resources, and collaborative and cooperative efforts to achieve the collective goal of crime prevention and justice.

In a time when police legitimacy appears to be at an all-time low, and when there have been calls to defund the police, there is an obvious question: Why should the police play a prominent role in crime prevention and public safety? The simple answer is that some institution—whatever one calls it—has to be embedded in communities and positioned to facilitate crime prevention as well as to respond to crime when it happens. It is critical that the individuals who would undertake such work, though, be uniquely positioned to learn about, understand, and help communities to address crime.

The police are uniquely situated to play a prominent role in a broader, systemic approach to crime prevention for a number of reasons. First, they are the front-line governmental agency charged with dealing with crime. Second, they already engage in traditional crime prevention on a routine basis. Third, they are routinely on the ground—in communities, in residences, patrolling, walking beats, interacting with the public, gathering information, watching and listening, some engaging in problem-solving policing and community policing. The problems that lead to crime exist in neighborhoods, and include poverty, racism, lack of collective efficacy, gangs, and under-resourced schools, as well as individual-level factors, such as drug and alcohol use, mental illness, neurodevelopmental and neurocognitive disorders and impairments, educational deficits, unemployment, homelessness, and a variety of other circumstances. The police observe these criminogenic circumstances first-hand or do or can learn about them from individuals, organizations, and businesses in the communities where they work. That provides them with a critical vantage point from which to learn about crime, to address it directly, and to work with communities and other organizations to prevent crime.

Of course, a police presence will not help much with crime prevention if officers adhere to a tough-on-crime, warrior culture. The reinvention of policing, therefore, requires changing that culture to one that emphasizes a guardian and collaborator role. That is one reason for a lead agency that oversees public safety and to whom the police—along with other agencies, institutions, and organizations who directly or indirectly play a role in addressing crime—must respond. The police would not, in this model, lead public safety. Instead, they would play a key role in crime prevention. An essential part of their effectiveness would be the ability to work closely with communities and other agencies to foster and implement crime prevention efforts. This idea dovetails directly with the view in Europe: "In most European countries policing isn't viewed primarily as a top-down, law enforcement perspective, but rather part of a bigger solution to social problems. It's not, There's a problem, send the police. It is, there's a problem, let's work together to find a solution."[80]

A fourth rationale for leaning heavily on the police to foster crime prevention is that the infrastructure for law enforcement already exists. Efforts like problem-solving policing and community policing align well with a prevention approach and can be found in many police departments. They are not, in and of themselves, sufficient, but they represent an important momentum-building start that can help to prioritize prevention.

A fifth rationale is that the police in the United States are, with exceptions of course, in the midst of a crisis of legitimacy and trust, especially in poor and minority neighborhoods, and shifting the focus of the police from a warrior or crime-fighter model to a crime prevention one could help to address that problem. In so doing, it could improve trust and the legitimacy of the police. Could we do away with the police? Perhaps. Yet, virtually any replacement institution would encounter significant barriers to establishing trust and legitimacy. Crucial to our model is the requirement that the police take direction from a lead agency that mandates crime prevention as a priority and a need to work with, not against, communities.

The idea of substantially expanding crime prevention makes sense. After all, if we ever hope to effectively reduce crime, victimization, recidivism, and cost and truly accomplish public safety, we must recognize that the criminogenic circumstances or root causes of crime must be addressed. That is, in our view, the largest missing piece in criminal justice policy. We now turn to discussion of some of the important components of our proposed new model of policing.

1. A Lead Agency Charged with Promoting Public Safety

The first and most important piece of the new model is the necessity of a lead agency charged with promoting public safety, with crime prevention as the priority. As Mears has argued, virtually any major public policy effort will fail if there is no lead agency or organization to prioritize it. That has been the problem in American criminal justice—it operates in an out-of-control manner, with no lead agency to prioritize crime prevention and to coordinate the efforts of the major institutions that we have, such as the police, courts, and corrections, for ostensibly addressing crime.[81] There is no coherent, systemic approach to preventing crime.

That point warrants emphasis because it sets the stage for why a lead agency is needed, and why policing must be reinvented. We have highlighted throughout this book that what is lacking in the criminal justice system—and in local, state, and federal government, and in public policy more generally—is any institutional responsibility for crime prevention and public safety. Stand-alone and piecemeal efforts can be identified, but no coordinated, funded, collaborative, scalable, and sustainable infrastructure for crime prevention and public safety exists. Consider this in the context of many, many federal agencies that are designed to prevent workplace accidents (OSHA), prevent aviation accidents (FAA), protect the environment (EPA), protect food and drugs (FDA), regulate transportation (DOT), prevent transportation accidents (NTSB), regulate business practices (SEC) and commerce (FTC), prevent disease (CDC and HHS), protect the homeland (DHS), and protect parks and wildlife (DOI). There are also state and local equivalents of many of the agencies mentioned above, not to mention the hundreds of thousands of local, state, and federal regulations designed to regulate and control behavior.

We are not alone. The UK Police Foundation states in their *Redesigning Policing and Public Safety for the 21st Century* that their policing is primarily reactive rather than preventative. Like the United States, they lack a centralized authority charged with promoting public safety through prevention:

> No one is responsible for crime and harm prevention. . . . No one owns the task of prevention. What is required if we are to move prevention to the heart of our public safety efforts is a much more systemic approach. We have a justice system, but we lack an explicit and institutionally anchored public safety system, whose focus is on promoting safety and preventing crime.[82]

Without a strong organizational lead, we are left with a disorganized, haphazard patchwork of participants and agencies that lack a clear, unified mission or coherent, concerted strategy of crime prevention. What we propose is a new, independent, officially designated government entity that is a locally accountable, organizational structure consisting of a variety of governmental and nongovernmental agencies, nonprofits, community organizations, civilian groups, and criminal justice agencies that bring different skills and resources to the table, that communicate and share information freely, and that collaborate and cooperate to achieve the common goal of crime prevention and public safety.[83] Depending on particular circumstances, these would include public health agencies, social service providers, first responders, alternative responders, affordable housing and shelter facilities, schools, community development organizations, citizen patrols, violence interrupters, prosecutors, researchers and academics, business and property owners, community groups, and neighborhood associations.

In the UK, the Police Foundation calls for the creation of a Crime Prevention Agency, a flagship organization that has ownership of crime prevention and public safety. The UK has the strategic advantage of being able to develop a Crime Prevention Agency at the national level, just as they have much greater control over police training with the College of Policing. But the logic for a flagship organization applies equally well at state and local levels.

The Center for American Progress recommends the creation of what they call Offices of Neighborhood Safety. As civilian organizations, these would serve as a "permanent pathway for community members to participate in the jurisdiction's public safety agenda and priorities . . . [and] the infrastructure and resources necessary for successful community-based public safety efforts."[84] Community involvement is a critical part of crime prevention, as we will discuss. But the Neighborhood Safety approach excludes the police and the rest of the criminal justice system, as well as other government agencies. That misses an opportunity to create a more effective system of crime prevention, and does not directly address the need for collaboration.

Is it feasible for state and local government to create an entirely new public safety institution that prioritizes crime prevention? Absolutely. Consider that after 9/11, the United States created an entire, brand-new cabinet-level agency, the Department of Homeland Security. One of the motivations was the chaotic and disjointed approach to the country's security. Consider, too, that states frequently can and do take dramatic steps quickly. After the Marjory Stoneman Douglas High School mass shooting in Parkland, Florida, the state legislature set aside $400 million for a medley of responses, and did so within months of the incident.[85] And, of course, almost all states took dramatic steps to start, escalate, and sustain mass incarceration. From that vantage point, creating a new institution charged with developing and overseeing a coherent strategy for public safety constitutes a more than viable undertaking.

This agency needs to have the production of public safety as its primary mandate. Priority should be placed on crime prevention at all three levels—primary (universal), secondary (selective), and tertiary (indicated). And all efforts of any constituent agency, institution, legislative or city council policy, or the like would be overseen and coordinated by this agency. Importantly, this agency would oversee not just the police but also efforts by the courts and corrections and other governmental efforts to prevent and address crime.

The agency's charge? Create, then implement, a coherent plan for crime prevention and coordinate the efforts of the different agencies as well as any government-funded programs or policies for addressing crime. The agency should prioritize collaboration and communication, including clarifying how different agencies or groups can help and are helping to prevent crime. This step reinforces all parties that the focus is on prevention, and it helps to identify potential conflicts or redundancies as well as changes that might be needed. It also should prioritize accountability, measuring and evaluating processes and outcomes and ensuring that community input and participation are integrated into crime prevention efforts, not as nice "add-ons" but as essential parts of coproducing public safety.

In some cases, crime prevention will be primarily a police responsibility, such as employing deterrence-based hot spots policing and responding to 911 calls and making arrests, especially for serious crimes. There is a place for traditional policing tactics, but more limited than is the case today. In other instances, crime prevention will involve collaborations between the police and other organizations and agencies through efforts like community policing. And in still others, the police role in crime prevention will be more limited. For example, they may serve to offer insights to citizens, community leaders, and businesses about steps that they could take to prevent crime, including identifying groups or resources that might be available to help.

One illustration of this type of collaborative, community-centered role for the police can be seen in the Local Initiatives Support Corporation (LISC),[86] which was created in 1994 with the goal of improving public safety and revitalizing decaying neighborhoods through partnerships with police and community residents, business owners, and community developers, among others. According to the Department of Housing and Urban Development (HUD), approximately fifty cities participate in the LISC initiatives. Strategies include buying abandoned, blighted property and developing affordable housing on those sites, cleaning up vacant lots, and applying principles of situational crime prevention as well as crime prevention through environmental design, all with critical input from police. The logic of this model is that the police are on these streets, in these neighborhoods, and they know what kinds of crimes occur where and have insight about what makes some places more and less attractive opportunities for crime. That knowledge and insight plays a fundamental role in community development decisions about planning and developing spaces, as HUD highlights:

> The success stories of cities such as Los Angeles, Philadelphia, and other target communities in LISC Community Safety Initiative have demonstrated that innovative community-police partnerships and holistic community development efforts can significantly reduce crime, enhance community safety, and replace troubled areas with quality affordable housing, businesses, and parks that positively transform neighborhoods.[87]

As promising as such initiatives may be, their effectiveness will be muted if they occur without an overarching, well-coordinated focus on public safety. That problem arises with many promising initiatives or "evidence-based" practices, programs, or policies. "Evidence-based" simply means that under certain conditions, we might observe some benefit. But these benefits depend heavily on those conditions being met. And they can come at a cost—for example, investing in an evidence-based program in one area might divert resources from where they might be more needed. A lead agency arrangement can avoid this problem by ensuring that all policing efforts—along with those of related government entities—focus on crime prevention, and do so based on a coherent, comprehensive plan that heeds real-time changes and conditions in communities and in participating agencies or organizations.

One can argue about whether this arrangement is feasible and the many challenges that would arise. Here, though, we simply would highlight that no government agencies' lifespan is set in stone. Government exists to serve the public, not to serve bureaucracy. As we discussed in Chapter 4, any coherent plan for systemic, comprehensive crime prevention requires straightforward steps: measure crime, identify and measure its causes, target the causes that cost the least to address and simultaneously may yield the largest returns, and so on. As currently configured, our criminal justice and correctional systems take none of these steps. An agency whose sole charge was to promote public safety through crime prevention and responses to crime when it occurs would take them. It could guide the police, advocate for the importance of policing that prioritizes crime prevention, identify ways to coordinate police agency efforts with communities and other institutions, and evaluate the police based on their contributions to crime prevention and to ensuring justice for all citizens.

2. Research Guidance on Crime and Its Causes

Despite decades of policymakers calling for government accountability and evidence-based policies, we operate our criminal justice systems with no infrastructure for ensuring that these goals are achieved.[88] How would we know if there was accountability? How would we know if there was use of evidence-based policy? More than that, how would we know if, for example, the police implemented policies and protocols appropriately? Or that crime prevention funds targeted known causes of crime? Or that the public trusts the police or courts? Or is willing to work with them? Or, in every instance, what factors contribute to these views?

Presently, our public safety institutions, the police included, operate with no credible answers to these types of questions. They might have information on one practice at a particular time, based on a one-time study. But they do not have such information on a regular basis, much less for the panoply of practices and policies that they undertake.

That has to change. More to the point, it has to change if public safety efforts are to be effective. Otherwise, we are left randomly allocating resources here or there.

Policymakers sometimes say that government should be run like a business. Any successful business, though, must do research. They must monitor all aspects of their business and what makes it more efficient or responsive. They must continually identify ways to improve performance and new ways to operate more effectively. That all makes sense, and it all requires research that provides credible information.

Further below, we discuss the importance of research for evaluating the implementation of police practices and policies—and how to improve implementation—as well as their impacts and cost-efficiency. A prior step, though, entails proceeding from accurate information about the problem that we wish to address. Our focus here is primarily on crime, but the same logic holds for any effort to address disparities in, say, court sentencing.

Briefly, and following the arguments presented in Chapter 4, public safety and police efforts must be guided by research on the prevalence and distribution of crime, as well as its causes. The bulk of traditional policing ignores this basic step. It entails reactive responses. Even practices like community policing and hot spots policing, which can be effective when implemented well, tend to be driven by a focus on areas where crime is highest. We, thus, miss an opportunity to prevent increases in crime.

The simple solution at the individual level is to systematically identify at-risk individuals (i.e., those who have higher levels of or exposure to factors known to increase the probability of offending) and intervene early. This approach requires investment in the capacity of schools and social service agencies to carefully assess when individuals might benefit from services or supports. It warrants emphasis that this capacity is typically minimal. Schools, for example, face numerous mandates and so typically reserve their resources for the most glaring behavioral problems. Children or youth who display indicators of potential problems go unnoticed and unassisted. (We recognize that at-risk individuals might be targeted for control-oriented or get-tough intervention. That obviously would be counterproductive and so needs to be prevented.) The police constitute an obvious front-line contact with many such youth, and can play a role in promoting diversion. This approach only works well, though, if the diversion programs draw on accurate information about the risks and needs of youth, and if the programs address these risks and needs.[89] The same argument applies to adults with whom the police come in contact. There must be the institutional capacity at social service agencies and within police departments to make credible assessments of risk and need, and a willingness and commitment to prioritize using this information to help at-risk individuals obtain services and support.

At the community level, public safety agencies and the police can conduct surveys of citizens and knowledgeable stakeholder groups—the police, social service providers, businesses, and so on—to identify criminogenic conditions. They can rely as well on merging different sources of secondary data. The U.S. Census Bureau supplies an abundance of information that can be used. But these data can be augmented with local sources of data as well, along with the citizen surveys. Armed with such information, researchers can identify areas where crime is on the rise and, just as importantly, the potential factors that may be contributing to crime. The police then can work with other agencies and community members to take stock of these causes and identify others that may be relevant. Importantly, they can help identify as well different strategies for effectively intervening, and which ones may be most feasible to implement.

In short, investment in research must happen if we are to avoid investing in needless or ill-advised policies and practices. It must happen to document problems, including disparities and injustices. It must happen to identify causes of these problems. It must happen, too, if we are to demonstrate effectiveness and identify ways to improve it. Not least, it must happen if we are to create solutions that fit local conditions. What may be possible to implement in one community may not be possible to implement in another.

As part of a reinvention of policing, research should not be a "would-be-nice" if resources permit undertaking. It *must* happen. In addition, the police should be required to guide and evaluate their efforts based on research. One function of a lead agency is, in fact, to use research-based metrics for evaluating police performance.

3. Multi-Agency Policing

Effective policing means that the police cannot go it alone. They must collaborate with other agencies and, as we discuss further below, communities. There are many examples of a "multi-agency policing" approach. For example, the 2007 Los Angeles Multi-Agency Task Force consisted of the LAPD, the LA School District Police, the FBI, the Burbank Police Department, the California Department of Corrections, the Bureau of Alcohol, Tobacco and Firearms, and the LA County Probation Department. They focused on gangs and tagging crews who were involved in criminal activity. Called Operation Heat Wave, it entailed a hot spot, deterrence-based approach.

That specific approach is not, in fact, what we recommend. We mention it both to highlight that multiple agencies can work together and to emphasize that a multi-agency approach that relies on what traditional policing emphasizes (e.g., deterrence) is not sufficient. We need a much broader approach that utilizes the resources of a wide variety of organizations, agencies, and communities that serve to mitigate the many criminogenic factors that underlie offending and reoffending in the collaborative production of crime prevention and public safety.

The World Health Organization (WHO) in 2002 argued for a broader, multi-agency approach to crime prevention in a paper defining violence as a public health issue, and concluded that addressing violence requires a collective, collaborative inter-agency approach. For example, consistent with what we outlined in Chapter 4, the public health model of violence prevention identifies the underlying causes and correlates of violence at various levels (societal, community, family, individual), identifies prevention strategies, and, finally, identifies local agencies that likely need to be involved in efforts to prevent violence (e.g., health care providers, police, educators, schools, social service providers, and government agencies). The logic for collaboration with multiple agencies and individuals is compelling. As the World Health Organization states,

> In many efforts to date, in both industrialized and developing countries, priority is often given to dealing with the immediate consequences of violence, providing support to victims and punishing the offenders. . . . Because violence is a multifaceted problem with biological, psychological, social and environmental roots, it needs to be confronted on several different fronts at once. . . . The overlap between the set of risk factors for different types of violence suggests strong potential for partnerships between groups with a major interest in both primary and secondary (traditional) prevention: local government and community officials, social housing planners, the police, social workers, women's and human rights groups, the medical profession and researchers working in each specific field.[90]

Many public health approaches have been successful at reducing violence and other crime and minimizing collateral harms.[91] These approaches identify the structural determinants of violence in communities and then target prevention strategies at them. This idea can be illustrated by hospital-based violence prevention, which relies on trained community members to be on-site in a trauma unit and to serve as violence interrupters, often in situations involving gang members. Research identifies significant reductions in gang retaliations and violent crime through such strategies.[92] A different illustration comes from a national effort—access to health care through the

Affordable Care Act's provision for expansion of Medicaid—that also is associated with reductions in violent and property crime.[93]

Many other such illustrations exist. For example, programs such as Cure Violence and Advance Peace help reduce neighborhood violence by strengthening anti-violence norms and peer relationships. Engaging with and supporting youth has been shown to reduce involvement in violence.[94] Enhancing street lighting substantially reduced serious crimes committed at night in public housing developments in New York City.[95] Research shows that participation in summer youth employment programs reduces arrests and convictions for at-risk youth, both while in the program and subsequent to participation.[96] And housing assistance is shown to decrease homelessness as well as crime, increase employment, and improve health.[97]

These and other examples are not restricted to focusing on at-risk individuals—they focus on communities. In so doing, they have the potential to have a greater impact on public safety. The examples also highlight the importance of a comprehensive focus that tailors solutions to local conditions. A considerable amount of research has focused on the effects of restoring blighted land, increasing greening of vacant lots, and cleaning up neighborhoods.[98] Intervening in place-based, high-risk areas has been shown to reduce crime by nearly one-third with no evidence of displacement. Using a randomized control trial of over 500 vacant lots in Philadelphia, the researchers implemented a strategy that included cleaning up the selected lots, planting grass and trees, building low wooden fencing around the perimeters, and providing regular maintenance. The controls received no intervention:

> Participants living near treated vacant lots reported significantly reduced perceptions of crime, vandalism, and safety concerns when going outside their homes, as well as significantly increased use of outside spaces for relaxing and socializing. Significant reductions in crime overall, gun violence, burglary, and nuisances were also found after the treatment of vacant lots in neighborhoods below the poverty line. Blighted and vacant urban land affects people's perceptions of safety, and their actual, physical safety. Restoration of this land can be an effective and scalable infrastructure intervention for gun violence, crime, and fear in urban neighborhoods.[99]

Whether the approach is cleaning and greening vacant lots, enhancing street lighting, violence interventions in hospital ERs, taking a public health approach to crime, or addressing homelessness and unemployment, the guiding focus centers on crime prevention and a wide variety of participants and strategies. In some instances, it may rely directly and exclusively on police intervention through more traditional tactics, such as responding to violent crime or relying on hot spots policing, or a concerted community policing and problem-solving effort in collaboration with community organizations and other agencies. Regardless, the goal remains the same—prevent crime rather than wait for it to happen.

Reinventing policing is, in our view, about reinventing our broader approach to public safety: The police can play a critical role in this approach, but, under the proposed model, they are coproducers of public safety. Communities and other government and nongovernmental organizations are essential producers as well. They can help to prevent crime on their own, but they also can help the police to do so, and the police can be agents of change for communities.

4. Addressing Crime through Police Specialization and Improved Training

Police specialization and improved training are sorely needed. Tracey Meares, a law school professor and policing expert, highlights the point: "Just look at what police are doing right now and ask, 'In which of these situations do I need an armed first responder?' If we don't need an armed first responder, why are police doing it in the first place?"[100] The obvious answer is that we are sending armed responders to situations where they are not needed because few other alternatives exist.

American policing has been and continues to be largely a one-size-fits-all enterprise. And, due to mission creep, the police have become the dumping ground for all manner of responsibilities that do not logically fit with them. That creates bureaucratic pressure to simplify training. Case processing pressures force organizations to adopt this approach. But the content of the training is not generic. Instead, tough-on-crime policies have resulted in uniform training on, and socialization in, the tactics of crime control. Policing culture has followed suit and supports that way of thinking, so much so that many officers resist adopting any other approach.

As we continue below to elaborate on a new model for reinventing American policing, it will become evident that we envision a much more specialized police force than currently exists. We are not alone in this vision. Barry Friedman, law professor and director of the New York University Policing Project, has articulated a similar proposal. Rather than a one-size-fits-all approach to training, Friedman proposes a focus on specialization of skills that more appropriately meet the needs of different situations. His proposal calls for recruiting and training officers for different specialties and for hiring civilians onto the police force who have the necessary expertise for certain types of incidents. He also suggests that many of these specialists could be non-sworn members of the police department.

There is nothing unusual about a differentiated workforce, and we believe that as the job requirements become more specialized, so should the training. One specialization is the more traditional police role of responding to 911 calls, especially calls involving serious, violent crime. Special weapons and tactics (SWAT) requires specialized training, as does working in such areas as explosives, cybercrime, aviation, K-9, marine patrol, and investigations. Other specializations include community policing, problem-oriented policing, and community building. Skills and knowledge specific to these activities consist of understanding the individual-level and community-level factors and circumstances that contribute to crime and recidivism, protective factors that reduce crime risk, situational crime prevention, crime prevention through environmental design, creating and maintaining community partnerships, collective efficacy, de-escalation, critical thinking, mediation, leadership, and conflict resolution.

Another potential specialization is mental health training, like that received by members of Crisis Intervention Teams. However, to ensure clarity of mission, the police should not be the go-to agency for incidents involving mental health crises. All police should be trained to understand signs of mental illness and ways that it may affect interactions, but in cases involving a priori evidence of mental health crises, the more effective and appropriate strategy is to call on mental health professionals. Police can be available if the need arises on a given call.

Chuck Wexler, the executive director of the Police Executive Research Forum, clearly and directly expresses how academy training needs to change:

> In many ways, we still train our officers to think of their job as just rigidly following a convoluted set of rules and regulations, which keep getting more complex by the latest "reforms" dictated by state legislatures and city councils.... To achieve real and lasting reform, we need to start by blowing up the traditional police academy approach and begin training cops in a fundamentally different manner. We need to teach officers how to identify and solve problems, not by adhering to a checklist of "do's and don'ts," but by thinking critically and acting ethically.[101]

Assessments of U.S. police training reveal that departments require relatively little training compared to other Western nations. Moreover, they typically adopt a militaristic approach, with most of the time spent on crime control training. To reinvent police training will require changing from the military, boot camp method, and it also will require expanding the duration and content of training. Curricula require a dramatic overhaul.

The President's Task Force on 21st Century Policing makes the point that with the increasing complexity of the situations and issues police face, substantial changes to recruitment, socialization, and in-service training need to occur: "The skills and knowledge required to effectively deal with these issues requires a higher level of education as well as extensive and ongoing training in specific disciplines."[102] Although the task force did not focus specifically on prevention, they introduced recommendations that align well with what we propose.

With over 650 police training academies across the country, there is a need for consistent standards and high-quality curricula. The President's Task Force recommends that the federal government take the lead in creating training innovation hubs for developing evidence-based, state-of-the-art training methods and curricula. Academic institutions can partner in this process. Training should balance tactical skills with social interaction skills, such as critical thinking, implicit bias, fairness and impartiality, and trust building. The task force also makes a point of requiring mental health crisis intervention training for all officers. Another important recommendation involves the U.S. Department of Justice partnering with colleges and universities to create a national post-graduate program for senior executives that focuses on enhancing leadership skills. Moreover, there should be incentives for higher education for officers.

Requiring a core general curriculum for all recruits and then specialized training for subsets of them constitutes a simple and effective way to improve training. The general curriculum would focus on traditional topics, such as criminal law and criminal procedure, self-defense and weapons training, driving skills, traditional crime prevention tactics, etc. It also would include a variety of interaction skills, such as those recommended by the President's Task Force.

Specialized training then would occur and focus on such topics as community policing, problem-solving policing, criminology, different approaches to crime prevention (and recognizing differences between primary, secondary, and tertiary prevention), and the variety of skills mentioned above, such as community building, collective efficacy, critical thinking, and leadership. Individual officers could self-select into these specializations, or they could be directed there based on aptitude, personality testing, or other skills assessments.

This approach is far from radical. It logically flows from thinking about the challenges, conditions, people, and incidents that officers can and do face. And it flows from thinking about what can be covered in only a few months of training. Yet, the approach is radical when contrasted with the minimal and generic training that all officers typically receive. There is no free lunch—if we want the police to effectively implement, say, problem-solving policing, they must have sufficient training in it. Specialized training should be a priority, not an afterthought.

Greater specialization and improved training have an additional benefit— they can improve the culture in police agencies. Specialization can help to avoid the tension that many police feel when they face seemingly conflicting mandates. Training can help by ensuring that officers have the skills that they need to perform their work well. In the end, though, a strong and positive police culture requires leadership that sends a clear message about priorities and commitments. That is why a critical foundation for the model we propose begins and ends with a lead agency for public safety and an institutionalized, widespread commitment to crime prevention.

5. Crime Prevention through Collective Efficacy and Informal Social Control

Crime is fundamentally related to poverty and disadvantage. One of the pivotal explanations for this involves a neighborhood's ability to exercise informal social control to prevent crime. The term "social disorganization" was coined by the Chicago school to refer to a set of social, economic, and demographic processes that inhibit a community's ability to effectively muster informal social control to mitigate crime. As we discussed above, Sampson and colleagues clarified and extended the theory of social disorganization by emphasizing key mechanisms of common values, mutual trust, cohesive relationships, and the willingness to intervene for the common good of the neighborhood. Neighborhoods high in collective efficacy are characterized by neighbors who are motivated to take collective action to reduce crime. Research shows that collective efficacy mediates the relationship between poverty or concentrated disadvantage and crime.

Most of the research on collective efficacy has been on the extent to which it reduces crime. Little attention has been given to undertaking studies on how to increase collective efficacy and, in so doing, expand a neighborhood's ability to effectively exercise informal social control to prevent crime. One important exception is research on the role that the police can play in facilitating the creation of collective efficacy, informal social control, and crime prevention. Yesberg and Bradford recently conducted an assessment of the research and evidence on policing as an antecedent to collective efficacy. They focused on several mechanisms. The two most important are trust and confidence in the police and particular types of policing strategies, such as community policing. When residents believe that the police are a reliable, effective, capable resource and are fair and just, they may be more likely to engage in informal social control and intervene when problems arise. Place-based policing strategies that focus on enhancing community engagement may facilitate the development of collective efficacy by providing opportunities for residents to become more involved in community matters as well as establishing relationships with police and access to police resources:

As a result of community policing—and the specific strategies it entails, such as neighborhood watch meetings and other community events—residents are expected to build new social ties and expand their neighborhood networks, develop mutual trust with other residents and become emboldened to work collectively with neighbors to solve local issues.[103]

Another aspect of community policing thought to facilitate collective efficacy and informal social control is police presence. Police visibility may provide a sense of safety and reassurance, allowing residents to engage in informal social control with less fear of crime.

The review of existing research by Yesberg and Bradford found a fairly consistent relationship between trust in police and collective efficacy. Specifically, trust in the effectiveness or capability of the police, as well as whether residents believe the police act in a fair and just manner, is related to higher levels of collective efficacy and informal social control.

The research on community policing has tended to focus on police presence as well as how police engage with the community. Findings here point to a similar pattern. When done well, community policing contributes to greater satisfaction with police visibility and engagement; this, in turn, contributes to greater social cohesion and informal social control.[104] Yesberg and Bradford also highlight two field experiments that found beneficial effects of community policing on collective efficacy and informal social control. One tested collaborative problem-solving and police presence. The researchers found positive short-term effects on informal social control and positive longer-term effects on social cohesion. The second field experiment found that community policing increased informal social control.

Kochel and Weisburd surveyed the research on the relation between policing and collective efficacy and informal social control. They find consistent evidence for two mechanisms through which police influence collective efficacy. First, police presence can reduce fear of crime and increase perceived police accessibility, in turn increasing informal social control. Community policing was found to be the most effective form of police presence for reducing fear of crime. The second mechanism—confidence and trust in the police, as well as satisfaction and perceived legitimacy of the police—has been found to promote collective efficacy, willingness of residents to become engaged in neighborhood issues, and increases in informal social control.[105]

Weisburd and colleagues have focused attention on policing, collective efficacy, and informal social control on micro-geographies, especially crime hot spots.[106] They have convincingly established the relevance of collective efficacy and informal social control at the micro-area level, in particular crime hot spots, down to the street-segment level. The theoretical basis for the finding is that hot spots and street segments can be viewed as micro-communities that have collective efficacy and informal social control, just as is the case with larger geographic areas such as blocks or neighborhoods. What, though, does research show?

One study assessed the impact of the Assets Coming Together to Take Action (ACT) program in Brooklyn Park, Minnesota.[107] A police-led effort designed to build collective efficacy and problem-solving at crime hot spots, the ACT program components include establishing relationships with and among residents, enhancing trust between police and residents, and developing shared expectations. These activities clearly align with community policing and problem-solving policing, and serve to increase collective action and collective efficacy in the targeted areas. Findings from the study indicate that ACT can increase collective action and collaboration among residents and with the police, as well as prevent crime.

Another study tested the cooperation hypothesis in crime hot spots.[108] This hypothesis holds that when residents perceive the police to be a viable, capable, supportive, and reliable resource, they will engage in more informal social control. The research assessed three police interventions in seventy-one crime hot spots—a collaborative problem-solving approach, a police presence approach, and a directed patrol approach. Their summary assessment follows:

> We can conclude from these findings that hot spots policing strategies can impact collective efficacy in a micro area, especially on residents' willingness to engage in informal social control behaviors. The results provide support for the cooperation hypothesis in that when police implemented hot spots policing strategies, that reduce crime in the area, residents were more inclined to take action to address problems. . . . Faith in the capabilities and competence of police and the effectiveness of police at reducing crime can improve informal social control.[109]

The strongest effects emerged for police presence (directed patrol), but beneficial effects of problem-solving surfaced as well over the long term. The authors suggest that the lack of short-term effects from problem-solving policing likely stems from the police not fully engaging with area residents. The beneficial effect in the long term, then, likely derives from community problem-solving, which provides opportunities for resident interaction.

Using panel survey data from seventy-one crime hot spots, Kochel and Gau compare the impacts of the amount of police presence reported by residents versus residents' awareness of police-community engagement strategies used to enhance safety, confidence in police, social cohesion, and informal social control. Their results indicate that showing up does not suffice. What matters is how often officers are seen in the area and satisfaction with the tactics police use to effectively engage with residents. High satisfaction, in turn, predicts greater confidence in the police, safety, social cohesion, and perceptions of informal social control.

Kochel and Gau observe that what matters is residents' sense of a meaningful connection with police, and that they can trust and rely on officers to promote safety and the interests of the neighborhood. That cannot be achieved simply by being visible. Rather, police need to be trained and incentivized to build relationships with community members and to facilitate residents' willingness and ability to engage in informal social control. This requires that police leadership fosters a culture in which officers play a critical role in community building and in developing the social fabric of neighborhoods. That requires meaningful continuous interaction and engagement that has collaborative problem-solving as a priority. As Kochel and Gau state,

> Meaningful community engagement may go beyond knock and talks, neighborhood block parties, basketball games with youth and other social activities and instead focus directly on collaboratively addressing problems and improving safety through systematic problem solving and enduring partnerships.[110]

We have touched indirectly on community policing and problem-solving policing above and now turn directly to them. Both approaches can be, we argue, important tools for coproducing collective efficacy, social cohesion, informal social control, and crime prevention.

In reviewing research on community policing, Braga and colleagues conclude: "Community policing should be the foundation of any police-led violence reduction strategy."[111] The President's Task Force on 21st Century Policing identifies community policing and problem-solving as one of the six main pillars or sets of recommendations for policing going forward. The task force concludes: "The 'co-production' of public safety by police and citizens through collaborative problem-solving is the core tenet of community-oriented policing."[112]

As Skogan describes it, community policing does not consist of a set of activities, programs, or initiatives—it constitutes a way of thinking that involves changes in decision-making and culture. He also describes it as "an organizational strategy that leaves setting priorities and the activities that are needed to achieve them largely to residents and the police who serve in their neighborhoods."[113] Its three primary components are citizen involvement, decentralization, and problem-solving.

Community policing is not what is often pejoratively described by police as "social work," but can be a highly effective tool for crime prevention and public safety. However, fundamental changes to the implementation and practice of community policing are required. Stephen Mastrofski calls for "profound experimentation with the innovative elements of community policing."[114] He poses a set of questions that highlight dimensions that quite likely greatly influence the implementation and effectiveness of community policing, and highlight the work necessary to ensure that it can prevent and reduce crime:

- What happens if community members are given a greater say in who patrols their neighborhood?
- What happens if officers engaged in community policing are assigned to work an area for several years, rather than rotated annually or more frequently?
- What if officer performance evaluations include how well the officer knows the people and customs of his/her assigned turf?
- What if the availability of career advancement were to depend heavily on how well officers perform on things that are essential to community policing, rather than the usual arrests, clearances, and calls answered statistics?
- What happens if community stakeholders have a significant role in training officers about serving their constituents?
- What if the principles and tactics of community policing become the guiding force for all units of the police department?
- What if officers and community members are given extensive training and ongoing support to engage in community outreach and problem solving?
- What if policing structures, procedures, and practices are actually transformed to promote community policing, rather than merely tolerate it?[115]

Many of these "what ifs" have been addressed, at least in part, in the neighborhood policing efforts in the UK, which can provide guidance to U.S. efforts.[116] They also highlight a central tension. With too much variation in what counts as community policing, it arguably becomes difficult to use the term in a consistent and meaningful manner. By the same token, like many policies, it may be unreasonable to think that one can "manualize" every aspect of community policing. The underlying logic and spirit of this approach clearly centers on collaboration between the police and citizens. As long as that remains in focus, it may not matter a great deal whether one community policing effort differs along one or more of the "what if" scenarios above. That is not to say these dimensions don't matter. They likely do. But attention to them and losing sight of the central guiding logic of collaboration would not be terribly effective. The details matter, but so too does the commitment to the overarching spirit of community policing.

Alongside of community policing is problem-solving policing. Leading policing experts identify it as an effective approach to addressing crime. As Rachel Santos observes, "If policing is to have a prevention role, crime reduction strategies must be focused and approached in a systematic way through the problem-solving approach."[117]

The problem-oriented policing paradigm as defined by Goldstein includes police identifying problems, gaining a deep understanding of each problem, and addressing problems by thinking creatively about specific solutions to the problems.[118] In the process of problem-solving, police should prioritize prevention. They should seek solutions that do not exclusively depend on the criminal justice system. And they should engage community members and public and private sector entities. Problem-solving policing, thus, provides a platform for thinking differently about the roles and responsibilities of police and aligns well with the model that we propose, which includes increasing investment in problem-solving policing.

Greater investment will be critical to community policing and problem-solving policing. For example, in writing about the latter, Braga and Weisburd identify a disconnect between what problem-solving should be and how problem-solving is implemented in many jurisdictions.[119] They also ask whether it is reasonable to expect policing agencies to implement problem-oriented policing at the level necessary to significantly affect collaborative problem-solving efforts and, in turn, reduce crime. They conclude that it may be "unrealistic to expect every police officer to continuously engage in full-fledged problem-oriented policing."[120] They point, for example, to police organizational structure and culture as factors that inhibit adopting innovative approaches.

The challenges are real. A recent Pew Research Center survey found that only 39 percent of patrol officers indicated that they had patrolled on foot for 30 minutes or more in the past month.[121] It is, though, unrealistic to expect all officers to have expertise in community or problem-solving policing, hence the need to invest in specialization. For example, recruit and train select officers to serve full-time as long-term community policing and problem-solving officers. In his book *Uneasy Peace,* Patrick Sharkey recommends precisely this approach. As part of New York City's effort to reduce crime in public housing, the police developed what they called neighborhood coordination officers, whose job was to serve as a new kind of community or neighborhood guardian:

> If police officers are to become a different kind of urban guardian, they will need assistance. Funding is necessary to implement new training and to allow departments to hire new officers whose role is not to enforce the law but rather to build relationships with community residents. Community policing is an old idea that has come to mean many different things to different people—but the

neighborhood coordination officers in New York City, whose explicit job description is to build stronger relationships between officers and residents, provide a model for what the next stage of neighborhood policing should look like.[122]

Building trust, strengthening communities, and working with residents—many of whom have a long-standing mistrust of the police—to identify crime problems in their community and to develop collective efficacy and informal social control is hard work. It requires expertise. Accordingly, you get what you pay for. Invest little in training and organizational commitment to community policing and problem-solving policing and there should be little return. A reinvention of policing requires a shift in priorities that recognizes the value, importance, and challenges of these types of policing.

6. Crime Prevention through Alternatives to the Police

There are many examples, both in the United States and abroad, of civilian, governmental, and quasi-governmental groups that serve as alternatives to police. We have discussed at length the role of mental health services in responding to many 911 calls. Another prominent example is that in thinking about public safety, it should be apparent that the police should not be engaged in traffic control. That function can be fulfilled by unarmed traffic control personnel who are not sworn police offices. These individuals would be responsible for accident investigation, speed enforcement, road safety, and other day-to-day traffic matters. They would not be responsible for criminal law enforcement.[123] They could and should be trained in mediation, de-escalation, violence prevention, and self-defense, given the potential risks that can arise in traffic stops. However, they would not have the authority to escalate situations into investigations of criminal activity, thus reducing the risk of violence. In cases where danger exists, the traffic personnel could call the police for assistance. It warrants emphasizing here that a diverse range of alternatives for improving compliance with traffic laws exist, and they do not need to require personnel or officer involvement. They include more widespread reliance on video camera surveillance, environmental design (e.g., speed bumps, build-outs), and signage.[124]

Shifting responsibilities in this way would clarify the primary mission of the police—to prevent and address crime. It also would free up a substantial amount of police time and resources. And it would reduce one of the primary complaints against police, which is the traffic stop as a pretext to search a vehicle. Such tactics have been implicated in complaints about racial profiling, harassment, and a variety of Fourth Amendment concerns such as drug searches. Not least, it would reduce fear associated with being approached by a police officer for a minor infraction.

There are many other examples of civilian or quasi-government alternatives to police in fulfilling public safety, guardian, and informal social control functions.[125] For example, in the United States, there are many types of informal and formal community patrols and community outreach groups that perform various public safety and guardian functions as well as provide support for vulnerable populations like the homeless. Increasingly popular are violence interrupters or violence mediators. These are community members, often former gang members, who intervene to de-escalate conflicts. They attempt to leverage information and relationships with active gang members to mediate ongoing disputes before they result in shooting events. The Vera Institute concluded that the evidence base warrants recommending the establishment of civilian-staffed community violence intervention agencies.[126]

In England and Wales, such individuals are called Neighbourhood Wardens and Community Support Officers. They provide visible patrols and serve to reduce low-level disorder. In France, they are called Social Mediation Agents. They serve on public transport and conduct night patrols to enhance public order and engage with community members to strengthen social ties. Belgium has Prevention and Security Agents who serve as a presence on public transportation and at apartment complexes, shopping areas, high-risk neighborhoods, and recreation areas to promote safety and security. In Western Australia, the Nyoongar provide foot and vehicle patrol and use non-coercive methods to prevent or de-escalate harmful and antisocial behavior.

Most of these types of initiatives are relatively new, thus the evidence base is incomplete. However, it seems fair to conclude that the evidence that does exist on the effectiveness of these types of alternatives to police is best characterized as promising. There is, too, the question of the point of comparison. What is the effectiveness of the police in undertaking these activities? For example, how well does sporadic, non-random enforcement of speed limits—not in theory or in isolated experiments, but rather as practiced nationally—reduce crime? We have little systematic evidence to answer that question. As a logical matter, then, we can view the situation from a blank-slate perspective: On what theoretical or other grounds should we anticipate that the police are best suited to effectively help individuals who are having mental health crises or to effectively reduce speeding, as compared to the diverse array of alternative approaches to achieving these goals? A good debater might come up with several reasons, but they would not stand up to close scrutiny. In the end, there is no credible reason to stick to a status quo arrangement that has the police involved in activities that do not clearly and directly relate to crime and, in particular, serious crime.

7. Crime Prevention through a Systematic Approach

It can make sense to focus on a discrete event, like a robbery, and declare that we should target resources at the individual who committed it. From a crime prevention standpoint, though, that approach makes no sense, unless we are simultaneously investing substantially in a diverse range of prevention strategies. Presently, that does not happen. We invest little in prevention, and focus the bulk of our resources on responding to avoidable crime.

The U.S. criminal justice system, as we know it, should not be the go-to solution—but is—for many of the problems that communities face. Clearly, arrest, prosecution, conviction, and punishment are appropriate for many individuals who commit crimes. However, we should not lose sight of the reality that the vast majority of them will not have successful outcomes. One need only look to recidivism rates as evidence for that conclusion.[127]

Catching someone who commits a crime is a benefit. Of greater benefit is preventing the individual from committing the crime in the first place. Not only does that avoid the financial costs of the criminal justice system, it also avoids the social costs of the crime, the harm caused to the victim, and the erosion of public safety.

The model we propose—based on the ideas and research of experts in policing— attempts to decrease reliance on the justice system by preventing more crimes and seeking alternative solutions to crime-related problems. Policing will always involve responding to crimes, and in many of those instances, especially serious violent crime, arrests can be viewed as a success. But the bigger successes consist of what does not happen—crime.

There is nothing simple about what we propose, and it certainly is ambitious. It calls for a lead public safety agency, and it asks the police to collaborate with a broad mix of other agencies, organizations, governmental entities, and community members to shift much of the focus of policing and public safety to prevention. Many tools, backed by research, already exist. Community policing, problem-solving policing, and hot spots policing have been in existence for decades and are practiced, for better or sometimes worse, in many jurisdictions around the country. When implemented well, police partnerships with citizens, community organizations, and businesses can reduce crime. Hot spots policing is demonstrably effective in reducing crime in micro-areas and also can be effective for building collective efficacy. Situational crime prevention, crime prevention though environmental design, addressing physical disorder like vacant lots and abandoned buildings, greening open spaces in urban areas—these are all evidence-based strategies.[128] Under certain conditions and with high-quality implementation, they can be effective. Many of these interventions and practices not only prevent crime in more traditional ways, such as through deterrence or limiting opportunities for crimes to occur, but also prevent crime by increasing collective efficacy and informal social controls in communities.

Diversion serves as a critical tool for crime prevention. This can occur prior to any police involvement, or it can occur pre-arrest, post-arrest, or pre-booking. In our view, the public health community must work with the police and prosecutors in determining who needs diversion, what type of diversion, and how soon. These determinations must be balanced with considerations of risk. This underscores the importance of a collaborative approach that brings police, public health practitioners (e.g., psychiatrists, psychologists, clinical social workers, addiction medicine experts), and prosecutors together in the decision-making process.[129] That is especially important given that the police and courts frequently encounter situations that involve behavioral health problems where diversion would be appropriate.[130]

Comprehensive crime prevention requires focusing on individuals, households, micro-geographies like hot spots, schools, neighborhoods, and communities. And it entails identifying and mitigating the criminogenic circumstances, discussed above, confronting individuals and communities. Not least, it entails doing so in a careful, systematic, planned manner.

There is no cookie-cutter solution here. Local communities, towns, and cities need to be able to identify individuals at risk of any or increased offending and areas where crime may occur or increase. They need to be able to identify the causes. They need to take stock of their capacity to address these causes. And then they need to develop a coherent plan for systematically and comprehensively addressing it. Only then can specific crime prevention efforts that the police or others might pursue make sense. A simple analogy follows: A hospital decides to buy a new and expensive magnetic resonance imaging (MRI) machine, and does so because a few physicians said it would be helpful. In so doing, though, the hospital risks diverting resources from where they might most be needed or best be utilized. Perhaps the MRI purchase should happen. But whether it is needed more than additional staff or other technology can only be determined from the vantage point of a hospital's broader goals, capacities, and needs, including the types and volume of particular types of medical problems.

So, too, with policing. One can justify adoption of almost any intervention, including those that are "evidence-based." But the only effective and cost-efficient way to proceed is to rely on careful, research-based planning that empirically maps out the types and volume of problems, their causes, existing solutions, and ways to improve them, and theoretically and empirically grounded alternatives or additional approaches.[131] Then one must evaluate their implementation, improve them, assess their impacts, and make any needed adjustments. Such an approach perforce must be undertaken in a systematic manner. The risk otherwise is piecemeal change that achieves little and may, as with the MRI analogy, interfere with our broader goals.

8. Crime Prevention through Improvement of 911 Call Systems

Juxtaposed against these broad changes is a quite specific one—improve 911 call systems. We discussed 911 reform in Chapter 5 and highlighted that nearly a majority of 911 calls required actions that did not need a traditional police response. In these cases, an alternative response to a sworn police officer would have been appropriate. When those options are not available, cities, towns, and counties default to a one-size-fits-all response. That is not good for the police, it is not good for the caller, and it is not good for the community.

If jurisdictions follow the recommendation to create multi-agency policing and specialization of police roles, determining who to send in response to 911 calls will become more complex. In part, that is because the response options will increase. For example, the responses could involve the police and, if the police, a particular type of officer, or a public health responder, homeless advocate, clinical social worker, and so on. In part, it is because the information necessary to make correct decisions will need to be accurate and specific. Recent research shows that current 911 systems misinterpret or misclassify mental health situations by a substantial amount, resulting in dispatching inappropriate responders (i.e., armed police).[132] A jurisdiction can have the best qualified and trained mental health responders, but if they are not dispatched when and where needed, they are of no help.

This is an illustration: The City of Austin recently changed their 911 system. When someone calls 911, they are given the traditional options of police, fire, or EMS and, now, a fourth option of selecting mental health emergency. After this change, thousands of calls were diverted from the police to mental health professionals. The vast majority of these were "true diversions," meaning that once the mental health response is selected, police are not subsequently involved.[133] This is just one example of how 911 innovation can have significant impacts on initial responses to problems. What we lack are outcome data regarding how the mental health emergency is resolved. It is, however, reasonable to anticipate that their resolution would be better when handled by mental health professionals than by the police.

Necessary changes to 911 will require a significant revision of the computer-assisted dispatch (CAD) scripts currently used as well as enhanced interviewer training for dispatchers. The call-takers need to be trained in a much broader set of circumstances (generalists, as Barry Friedman calls them[134]) who are better able to match the information provided to the appropriate responder and, at the same time, to correctly prioritize the response.

This change is significant, especially since 911 reform, as we discussed in Chapter 5, entails many challenges. But given that 911 is the primary conduit for reporting a wide variety of problems and issues to government, it is essential that we get that right. Absent a highly functioning 911 system that is tailored to the multi-agency approach and police specialization of roles and responsibilities, this model we propose will not be as effective as it could be. For that matter, the effectiveness of the current model—traditional policing—is compromised as well.

It bears emphasizing that 911 improvements are not simply a way to help triage cases (and the individuals that the cases represent) to those entities best equipped to address them. They also provide a way to help gauge crime distribution and prevalence. That information, in turn, can assist with efforts to identify where crime prevention resources would best be placed.

9. Leverage Public Support for Reinventing and Evaluating Policing

We turn next to a much more diffuse, but no less critical, part of our proposed new model—namely, the reinvention of policing should take advantage of the fact that the public *wants* changes to happen. This public support provides an opportunity to enact reforms that can have a large and lasting effect on improved crime prevention.

What does the public want? Many surveys provide insights about the public's views on the use of force, abuse by police, racism, lack of accountability, and lack of trust in the police, and what should be done. For example, a majority believe that police use force when they do not need to, and that police killings constitute a systemic problem.[135] There is also strong support for the use of body cameras, requiring officers to report misconduct by fellow officers, establishing clear standards for use of force, prosecuting officers for use of excessive force, and penalizing officers for racially biased policing.[136]

But public views go well beyond concerns about police conduct. A recent (2020) Gallup poll found that most Americans believe that policing needs "major changes." The public supports requiring police officers to have good relations with citizens and neighborhoods through stronger community policing initiatives, and rethinking policing by promoting community-based interventions that target individuals who are at a high risk for violent crime. One-half of Americans support eliminating police enforcement of low-level, nonviolent crimes, a reaction to concerns about broken windows policing and stop-and-frisk policies.[137]

Crime prevention is a top priority for the public. Nothing new there—twenty years ago, a survey commissioned by the Open Society Institute found that respondents believe that it is the most important goal for the criminal justice system.[138] In addition, by a two-to-one margin, the public believes crime prevention entails addressing the root causes of crime and not relying solely on deterrence and punishment. Research shows that citizens put their money where their mouth is, and are willing to support tax increases for balanced approaches that include rehabilitation.[139]

Overall, 82 percent of Americans support greater community involvement of family services and other social programs in addressing underlying risk factors. In another survey, when asked, "What is the greatest barrier to public safety in your community?" the most common answer was "Not enough prevention programs to keep young people from turning to crime."[140] In the same survey, the vast majority of respondents supported moving funds from incarceration to community-based public safety programs like treatment, rehabilitation, job training, and other crime prevention services.

A 2020 survey underscores the public's strong preferences for prioritizing crime prevention, including community-based violence prevention, mental health and crisis response treatment, and changes to 911 systems, so behavioral health crises receive the appropriate response by trained mental health professionals.[141] The survey respondents overwhelmingly support federal funding for a variety of crime prevention measures, such as community-based and hospital-based violence prevention to help reduce the risk of youth getting involved in crime, expanding the number of mental health crisis responders, providing care to youth exposed to violence and other trauma, and broadening support for victims of violent crime.[142] Other surveys have found similar support for federal assistance for crime prevention and dealing with individuals having behavioral health crises.[143]

Public support for a balanced and nuanced approach to public safety can be seen in other views that the public holds. For example, a survey of likely voters provided very strong support (78 percent) for targeting police resources on serious violent crimes like shootings, robbery, aggravated assault, and homicide. At the same time, nearly three-quarters of respondents stated that the best way to facilitate the police priority on serious crimes is by having alternative responders for behavioral health and homelessness situations.[144] A large majority support creating new agencies of responders other than armed police for dealing with mental health and substance use crises, as well as non-emergency situations like welfare checks and people experiencing homelessness.[145] This support cuts across partisan divides as well as race. Moreover, there is little support for reducing the funding for law enforcement despite the initial momentum shown by the defund movement.[146]

In short, the public wants the police to do a better job and to adopt a crime prevention orientation. What they want aligns with research and logic—if we want less crime, we must address the causes of it, and the responses must take into account individual and community conditions. That includes taking into account historical practices that create concerns that marginalized communities have about reforms that include more of the same type of policing.[147]

A corollary to leveraging public support to create change is that how we evaluate policing should change as well. Crime is, in general, the central outcome that should be used to judge how well government achieves public safety. But there are other dimensions, as Lum and Nagin and other scholars highlight, that are either important in their own right or provide insight into mechanisms that can contribute to crime or to preventing it.[148] For example, citizens should not just be safe, they should *feel* safe. They should have trust in the police and the criminal justice system; they should view both as legitimate. That is not just important on its own—greater trust and legitimacy translate into a greater willingness to call the police for help and to cooperate with them.[149] For the same reasons, the public should have confidence in the police. Effective policing should engender confidence that, when called on, they will act ethically and effectively. Using these and other dimensions (e.g., perceptions about how well the police listen to concerns or the extent to which they treat all groups fairly) to evaluate policing is not an extra—it should be central to assessing their effectiveness.

10. Research Evaluation of Implementation, Effectiveness, and Cost-Efficiency

The final part of the model we present emphasizes research that evaluates the implementation of policy, its effectiveness, and, not least, its cost-efficiency. Consider community policing—it can be implemented well or poorly. Its effectiveness will depend greatly on implementation. How, though, do we know if it is implemented well? We have to conduct research. There simply is no shortcut if we want to be able to evaluate not only the level and quality of implementation but also what affects it. The latter enables us to take corrective action.

We need this information for all police practices, and it should be monitored on a regular basis. We need information, too, on the impacts of these practices. What is their effectiveness? How large are the impacts? What harms might they have? How does their effectiveness vary in comparison to other approaches? And, not least, we need information on cost-efficiency. Are the impacts sufficiently large, relative to the costs, to warrant continuing the practice? These are basic questions. With answers to them, the police can make evidence-based decisions—that is, ones grounded in credible empirical information rather than gut instinct or personal belief. Importantly, there must be credible information about community views and different agencies' views of the police, as well as their ideas for what changes should happen.

Researchers have, fortunately, provided plenty of tools for collecting and quickly collating information, and presenting it an accessible manner. The real challenges to reliance on research are twofold. First, policymakers and practitioners tend not to understand or value research. That means that they will make incorrect inferences, or simply ignore research altogether. Second, the police—and, by extension, local and state governments—simply do not invest much in research. There is, unfortunately, no free lunch. One-time studies by researchers can be helpful, primarily in a piecemeal manner, but they cannot substitute for ongoing monitoring and evaluation of police officer and agency performance, or that of a public safety system more broadly. Currently, much of what happens in policing goes unmonitored and unevaluated. That needs to change. It must change if we are to improve policing and public safety.

A final point is that a system of public safety that rests on continuous monitoring and evaluation, and that draws on insights from the police, citizens, communities, and more, will be one that avoids becoming trapped in ineffective or harmful practices. It can, therefore, help to prevent dramatic swings in practice and policy. Put differently, it will always be reforming itself, making adjustments when needed, and always staying focused on public safety.

What Has to Happen for the Reinvention of Policing to Be Successful?

The answer to what has to happen for the reinvention of policing to be successful depends on what one means by criminal justice reform. A first step is to acknowledge that punishment-focused crime control—especially when it occurs with no appreciable crime prevention emphasis—does not work.[150] The evidence could not be clearer. The incarceration binge, the War on Drugs, and other myriad efforts to threaten and punish bad behavior out of people has been a phenomenal failure. Even allowing for incapacitation and some possible general deterrent effects, we are left with a failure to invest in evidence-based policies in a systematic or comprehensive manner. And we are left, too, with the many harms that can and do result from a near-exclusive emphasis on tough-on-crime policies.

Second, the evidence is also quite clear that the path to meaningful, effective, cost-efficient criminal justice reform is one that addresses the reasons people commit crime or why some communities experience high crime rates. Many individuals, for example, enter the system with complex comorbidities—substance use disorders, poverty, trauma, mental illness, neurodevelopmental impairments, educational deficits, ACEs, and many more. Punishment does nothing to change any of these conditions and disorders. It, like warrior-centered policing, also does nothing to improve the conditions in communities that contribute to crime. To be clear, we do need prisons and jails as a way to separate from society those individuals who commit serious or violent crimes. And we need police responses to these crimes. But they represent a fraction of the crimes—and the individuals who commit them—that the justice system sees on a daily basis.

What we propose for policing aligns directly with an evidence-based, systems approach to preventing crime and recidivism. In fact, the policing piece of criminal justice reform is in many respects the most important. Evidence shows that criminal justice and juvenile justice involvement can be criminogenic. To the extent that the front line of the criminal justice system can help prevent crime and therefore keep individuals from coming in the front door, it can help to avoid that problem. It is a win-win situation.

Address Barriers to Reinventing Policing

Even so, changes to policing will encounter barriers. We recognize that and discuss several critical barriers because they must be addressed if we are to successfully improve policing. We also recognize that the model we present constitutes an ideal state, not necessarily one that is politically viable. But without a vision for where we should go, it is difficult to get there. As we have emphasized throughout, the current risk is that we continue down the road of piecemeal changes that accumulate into appreciable or longstanding reduction in crime. They provide sources of light, but in many ways distract from the root problem of a broken, poorly designed system of policing and public safety.

Funding

Public safety (police, fire, and EMS) consumes large portions of city budgets. Counties also pay considerably for sheriffs, jails, courts, and probation. Even so, additional funding will be required for fundamental changes to policing and public safety. Our recommendations for relying on alternatives to police (e.g., traffic enforcement, community patrols, and mental health responders) will help reduce demand on police time and resources. More, though, will be needed.

The truth is that we have no way to accurately estimate what will be required in terms of resource investments in police reorganization, recruiting and training police, changes in roles and responsibilities, alternatives to police, modifying the culture of policing, or supporting research, analysis, and evaluation. What we know is that it will be substantial, and it will fall primarily on city and county governments to underwrite. At the same time, state and federal governments have a tremendous stake in public safety; thus, we would certainly expect them to provide funding, necessary statutory changes, and technical assistance to local jurisdictions.

Ultimately, an improved policing and public safety approach means that we will have less crime and more justice. We will need to rely less on probation and prison. Reducing prison and jail populations alone would provide cost savings to offset investing in crime prevention. One of the most obvious ways to proceed is to incentivize prevention. For example, communities that spend more on prevention and send fewer individuals to prison could receive payments from state coffers. That, too, is a win-win situation—more prevention and less crime, and a reduced burden on states given that corrections expenditures consume a large part of their budgets.[151]

Organizational Inertia

Most organizations resist change. Organizational inertia is the term used among business experts to describe an internal momentum to stay the course or conduct business as usual. In important respects, organizations operate on autopilot, doing things a certain way because that is how they have been done in the past. In the business world, external threats or pressures may force an organization to change to survive in a competitive environment. Effective leaders seek evidence-based guidance on launching and navigating organizational change.

That same inertia exists in the public sector. Yet, governmental agencies operate in environments and ways that make change more difficult. Police departments are subject to a changing political environment that can cause turnover in leadership. Policy changes can be dictated from local politicians, who also control budgets. The complex of stakeholders, often with conflicting demands, make developing new policy especially difficult.

The changes we recommend require the dedicated participation of police leadership and line officers. But they also require the support of local government leaders as well as government agencies, NGOs, and local interest groups and stakeholders. We believe that a political middle ground exists, that the public wants improvements that accord with what we have presented, and that many police officers support change. Substantial reform and reinvention can happen. Yet, organizational, structural, and political challenges will need to be addressed. We see no silver bullet solution to doing so. One option, though, is to rely on consulting organizations (e.g., McKinsey & Company, Accenture, and Deloitte) that have expertise in public sector transformation and change management.

Police Culture

Transitioning a police department to one that has a reasonable balance between law enforcement and responding to crime on the one hand and crime prevention on the other requires a significant shift in ways of thinking about crime and human behavior. It requires a conversion from a warrior cop to a guardian orientation, as well as expansion of evidence-based strategies like community policing and problem-oriented policing. It requires accepting the "social work" and community builder role as a significant part of policing.

Police culture stands as one of the greatest obstacles to fundamental change. Cynicism is a common trait used to describe police.[152] The reality of the job rarely places police in a situation where things go well. They regularly and frequently encounter situations where the world has gone sideways—it may be minor problems, such as noise complaints, or it may be major problems, such as assaults or murder. The work can create a siege mentality. A survey conducted by Arthur Rizer, a former officer and currently a researcher at the R Street think tank, asked officers if they would want their child to become an officer. The majority said no, because they do not feel supported in their work, and they felt that they were at war with the public—the "us versus them" way of thinking.[153] A recent large-scale police survey conducted by Pew found that the vast majority (84 percent) worry about their safety at least some of the time and four in ten worry about it all of the time or often. That creates what Michael Sierra-Arévalo calls the "danger imperative," or a preoccupation with the fear of harm and violent death.[154]

The vast majority of officers (86 percent) also believe that the public does not understand the risks that they confront.[155] Few ever fire their service weapon while on duty (27 percent), but about one-third report having a physical confrontation with someone in the past month. Although nearly 80 percent stated that they were thanked by a community member in the past month, two-thirds were verbally abused.

It should not be difficult to appreciate that such experiences, and this world view would lead to resisting changes to roles and responsibilities, much less to ones that depart substantially from primarily responding to 911 calls and to enforcing the law. Much of the literature on police culture focuses on how culture contributes to police misconduct, brutality, use of force, the "bad apple" versus the "rotten barrel," and officer shootings. Unfortunately, not as much addresses transforming police culture in a way that allows it to do business in a substantially different way.

The Police Executive Research Forum clearly sees the need for changing the police culture. It starts with training: "Changing how we train officers is critical, but it isn't enough. Changes in training must be viewed as part of a bigger push to fundamentally change the culture of policing."[156] Improved academy training and field training will go some way, but changing policing requires changing the organizational culture as a whole.

Police leadership is not trained in organizational and culture change. We believe that to truly create a new culture that can mitigate the issues of police misconduct, as well as provide the environment necessary for transitioning policing to what we have proposed, will require external experts. As noted above, there are many companies that provide expertise in change management, and they serve as one potential source on which to draw. There is, at the same time, the need for political support for change. That, again, is one reason for a lead public safety agency. It could serve as the catalyst for promoting change in police culture and working with policymakers and the public to help that to happen.

Police Unions and Police Associations

Police unions and associations play a large role in police organizations, police policies, and the job of the police officer. Bureau of Labor Statistics data show that nationwide, about 55 percent of officers are union members and 58 percent are covered by a collective bargaining agreement.

Unions typically function as collective bargaining agents who protect members' job security and enhance salaries and benefits. Some police unions go further by promoting provisions to make it more difficult to discipline and fire officers accused of improper conduct. That can be beneficial when procedures do not suffice to protect officers from being scapegoated for poor management, but it can be harmful when it covers for misconduct or ineffectiveness. Another complicating factor is that police unions enter into the political arena by endorsing and funding sympathetic candidates. That may benefit the police, but it also politicizes policing.

Given the importance of police unions and associations, it is unfortunate that relatively little scholarship has assessed their impact on police effectiveness.[157] What does exist tends to focus on the relation between unions and matters dealing with use of force, lethal force, racism, choke holds, no-knock warrants, and other types of problematic or illegal behavior.

What we do not know much about is the effect of union and association presence on the types of reforms we propose. It seems reasonable to anticipate that some changes, such as improved training, might be embraced, while others, such as eliminating certain police functions, might be resisted. Yet, none of the changes entail putting the police out of a job. They focus on improving their effectiveness and both their own safety and that of the public. Keeping that in mind may help to facilitate not only police officer and union acceptance of change but also a willingness to collaborate in making it more effective.

Resistance to Criminal Justice Reform

Perhaps one of the more significant motivators for reform is homicide. Increases in homicide in the 1980s contributed, without doubt, to part of the rise of the punitive era in criminal justice.[158] In recent years, murder has risen again, and has led to new discussions about criminal justice reform. (Actually, criminal justice reform seems to surface as a prominent policy focus every few years. But murder seems to be an acute motivator for reform.) Murders increased by roughly 30 percent between 2019 and 2020, the largest one-year spike since 1905. That increase brought the homicide rate to the highest level since 1996, but still below the rates between the 1970s and the early 1990s. A sample of homicide in twenty-two cities in 2022 shows a continuing increase in murder in 2021, although at a slower rate (5 percent).[159] This increase has had significant consequences. A Pew Research Center survey found that 61 percent of Americans identify violent crime as "a very big problem" in July of 2021. That is a 20 percentage point increase from June 2020.[160] At any given time, increases in crime, especially murder, may mute the public's eagerness for fundamental change. That may be all the more the case when economic conditions decline and leave citizens and policymakers looking to reduce costs.

Resistance to fundamental change comes from other corners as well, as can be seen in the pushback that reform-oriented prosecutors have faced. For example, Chesa Boudin, the DA of San Francisco who was elected in 2019, faced a recall election over what his critics said was a soaring crime rate and a failure to prosecute as many cases as he should; a vote led to his recall. Radley Balko of the *Washington Post* investigated and found that the two arguments for Boudin's recall were incorrect.[161] George Gascón, a progressive prosecutor elected in Los Angeles in 2020, faced a recall as well. Other progressive prosecutors have encountered significant challenges to their efforts at creating "big" change. Among those who have been targeted include Kim Foxx (Cook County, Chicago), Marilyn Mosby (Baltimore City), José Garza (Austin), John Creuzot (Dallas), Aramis Ayala (Ninth Judicial District, Florida), Rachael Rollins (Suffolk County, Boston), Alvin Bragg (New York City), and Wesley Bell (St. Louis), among many others. Police unions and police associations have been some of the most vocal critics of reform-oriented prosecutors, as have been more traditional, tough-on-crime prosecutors.

Policing and politics go hand in hand, and that creates a critical hurdle for systematic, comprehensive change. The solution, in our view, requires embracing that reality. And it requires putting accurate, credible information out in the public arena so that it is simultaneously easier to see the types of changes needed and more difficult to make false claims. Policing and public safety are complicated undertakings. But what is not complicated is that failing to address the causes of crime will leave society trapped in a vicious cycle from which it cannot escape.

Create Incentives for Reinventing Policing

Overcoming the above and other barriers will be necessary to achieve large-scale meaningful change. Another strategy for achieving this goal is to incentivize police departments and states and local jurisdictions to embrace it. Here, we offer a few suggestions.

Public Safety and Government Accountability

We made the case that efforts to reduce crime and recidivism have largely failed. Research confirms that criminal justice policy is responsible for a fraction of the declines in crime over recent decades, and recidivism rates speak to the effectiveness of our tough-on-crime, punishment-focused approach. We have emphasized the point already but believe it cannot be overstated—no governmental entity has responsibility for crime prevention and public safety. That situation is all the more shocking when we consider the size and expense of the American criminal justice system and, need it be said, the tragic consequences of serious crime.

The roadmap we have laid out identifies crime prevention and public safety as largely the responsibility of government, with a clear role for communities in the coproduction of prevention and public safety. We believe that the existing scientific evidence supports our model, and therefore, when implemented (in whole or part), should significantly prevent crime and increase public safety.

This is the easy argument to make. Public safety is a critically important public good. It is time that government fulfills its responsibility, both by taking the lead in addressing one of the greatest challenges we face and by working with a variety of community organizations, agencies, and groups in collaboratively accomplishing public safety.

Accountability requires that government take action. Highlighting this fact may go some way in motivating government to enact much-needed large-scale reforms, including the reinvention of policing and, more broadly, creating public safety agencies.

There are different ways to incentivize accountability. One is to require it. We believe that many of the changes that we call for should, in fact, be required. Police agencies, for example, should be evaluated based on their ability to meet performance metrics, including not only crime but also responsiveness to the public.

A second is to tie financial incentives to these metrics, an approach that has success in different arenas of criminal justice and corrections.[162] Local public safety and police agencies could be rewarded for adopting certain changes and meeting benchmarks. Federal and state governments could play a role in funding these incentives.

A related one is to advertise publicly the performance of these agencies. In the "big data" era, it is especially easy to collect, analyze, and present data in an easy-to-interpret format. That includes monitoring trends in public perceptions of the fairness and legitimacy of the police. Such monitoring can motivate police agencies to demonstrate their effectiveness, and it also provides them protection from overgeneralizations about their performance based on what may be isolated negative incidents.

Financial Considerations

Although what we propose will be expensive, it is important to emphasize that public safety is a highly valued public good. In a democratic society, it is a deeply rooted expectation that citizens should be protected from crime and victimization and that they should both feel and be safe. Yet, added to the intrinsic value of public safety are the profound financial gains from effective crime prevention. We spend hundreds of billions of dollars annually on direct criminal justice costs. The War on Drugs has cost an estimated $1 trillion over the past fifty years.

Crimes prevented translate into reductions in direct criminal justice costs from police to prisons and everything in between. Reducing recidivism has benefits that policymakers and elected officials often seem to overlook. Not only will preventing a crime from occurring in the first place or reducing recidivism have financial benefits in the moment, but every time someone does not reoffend, all of those criminal justice costs are avoided. Interrupting cycles of reoffending results in longer-term financial benefits that are considerable.

Moreover, there are substantial tangible and intangible costs associated with crime, including costs to crime victims, pain and suffering, lost economic productivity, reduced property values, and many more. Estimated

Murder	$7,809,000
Rape	$400,800
Robbery	$43,700
Assault	$38,800
Motor Vehicle Theft	$10,800
Household Burglary	$5,370
Theft	$4,780

costs of crime put the financial issues in stark relief. For example, Miller and colleagues estimate the total tangible and intangible costs by selected crimes, per crime, in 2017 dollars as follows[163]:

They then develop direct costs of crime (e.g., police, court, incarceration, victim services, medical and behavioral health care, the value of property loss) and intangible costs such as loss of quality of life and pain and suffering.[164] The results are stunning. The 121 million crimes committed in the United States in 2017 had estimated direct costs of $620 billion. The intangible costs were $1.95 trillion, for a total cost of $2.6 trillion per year. That amounts to approximately $8,000 per person per year in the United States. It also exceeds the annual gross domestic product (GDP) of all countries in the world, with the exception of the United States, China, Japan, and Germany.

The clear challenge is that there is not one entity that incurs the costs and reaps the benefits. These are spread over fifty states, 3,143 counties and county equivalents, and 19,500 cities and towns in the United States. Nevertheless, from a strictly economic perspective, it is not difficult to make a strong argument for the financial benefits of crime prevention and public safety.

Reducing the Burden

Another defining feature of the American criminal justice system is that it is overwhelmed by the number of people with which it deals. Prisons and jails are crowded, probation and parole caseloads are unrealistic and unmanageable, court dockets and prosecution caseloads require that 95 percent or more of felonies and misdemeanors are plea negotiated, and the police routinely spend large portions of their time responding to calls—everything from serious crime to welfare checks, traffic accidents, and many, many calls that have little or nothing to do with crime. Anyone with any familiarity with the criminal justice system—including those who work within it—knows that it operates much more like a large-scale manufacturing facility. It produces, as David Heilbroner, a former assistant district attorney, aptly put it, "rough justice."[165]

In short, one incentive for the changes that we propose is that they should reduce the burden of case processing and allow for "people processing," the kind that allows for individualized justice and treatment. It would allow the police to conduct their work in a more reasonable manner, at a pace that permits developing relationships with people in the community. It would allow police departments to make necessary changes well before a crisis forces piecemeal reform.

Political Benefits

"Smart on crime" has been the tagline for criminal justice reform for more than a decade. Public opinion clearly supports limited use of incarceration, less punishment, and more diversion and treatment, all of which can be viewed as smart-on-crime approaches. In addition, evidence-based strategies, like community policing and problem-solving policing, are relatively straightforward approaches to sell. So, too, are reforms to 911 call centers and, indeed, the bulk of what we have proposed. Science and public opinion support large-scale reform and the reinvention of policing, and the prioritization of crime prevention. Given that, there would seem to be benefits to members of either of the two major political parties in the United States in enacting such change. Indeed, improvements in public safety enable policymakers to fulfill an obligation to the public, and approaching public safety through ways that the public supports does so as well.

Moral and Ethical Benefits

As we noted earlier, the Kerner Commission concluded fifty years ago that we do little to get at the underlying root causes of crime. Not much has changed since then. That is not only inefficient, but it constitutes an indictment of government, not only for allowing needless suffering to occur but also for allowing an ineffective criminal justice system to contribute to inequality. Poverty and racial and ethnic discrimination are intertwined in criminal justice. The inequalities begin with community-level disadvantages and extend to the challenges of navigating a system that does not focus on helping but instead on intensive punishment and that, in many places in the country, directly or indirectly enables discrimination to occur.

A simple example follows: A good lawyer is a necessity for navigating the courts, but those who cannot afford one (which characterizes the vast majority of criminal defendants) must rely on the public defense system. Many good lawyers work in that system, but they are underpaid and overworked. By contrast, wealthier defendants can afford to purchase stronger representation from attorneys with greater expertise and more resources at their disposal.

Many who work within the criminal justice system, and this includes the police, operate with integrity. To say that discriminatory practices, intended or otherwise, occur in no way impugns their character. To ignore this situation, though, is to ignore reality. And to continue down the same path that has been followed for the last several decades—a path that is, again, flawed in design—simply does not make sense, especially when it contributes to inequality and when an alternative exists that is sensible, grounded in theory and research, and accords with public opinion. We submit that business as usual is immoral and unethical. We can and should do better.

By targeting the causes of crime, we may be able to begin to change the extent and consequences of poverty and racism. Similarly, to the degree that a new approach to policing and public safety generates greater trust and confidence in the police across all communities and all racial and ethnic groups, we have a foundation for promoting both safety and justice.

We see that as a moral and ethical good, and one that could be used as a metric for evaluating the police and a broader system of public safety. Individuals and organizations tend to take action in line with how they are evaluated. One way to incentivize adherence to a new model of policing is to ensure that measures of performance and effectiveness are used to evaluate police and public safety agencies, and to tie financial incentives to them. Those measures should include outcomes that gauge such dimensions as officer and departmental compliance with the law (a foundational requirement of legitimate law enforcement and any governmental undertaking[166]), equity in how all citizens are treated, cultural sensitivity to different groups, and a sincere willingness and ability to work with communities.

Reality: Pragmatic Considerations and Reinvention of American Policing

It is obvious that what we propose here is, to put it mildly, a massive enterprise. Added to the barriers just discussed is the fact that there are 18,000 police departments in the United States, some large departments in large cities and some very small departments in rural jurisdictions. Some are in more liberal areas, some in conservative areas. The fact that criminal justice policy has become a lightning-rod wedge issue makes the likelihood of implementing any of what we propose a matter of which side of the wedge one falls.

It is certainly not our expectation that there will be wholesale policing and public safety reform nationwide. Rather, our goal is to present a blueprint for reinvention that will hopefully stimulate thought, discussion, and policy change to the extent possible. As we have emphasized, large-scale change is unlikely to occur without a clear vision for what should happen. It is our hope that the blueprint that we present can help to guide efforts to put American policing and public safety on a better footing.

Our concern, which motivated this undertaking, remains—pursuing piecemeal change creates the pernicious and unintended consequence of enabling government to avoid making the larger changes required to improve safety and justice. In our view, it will be a significant advance if we can move past piecemeal change and begin the path toward the large-scale structural changes necessary to make appreciable gains in public safety and justice.

Conclusion

In this chapter, we have argued for a fundamental change to—a reinvention of—policing. We stand by the guidance from Chapter 5: Simply eliminating what does not work or is not appropriate for the police will go a long way to improving policing. So, too, will continuing or expanding traditional policing strategies, such as hot spots policing, that can be effective. Investing in higher-quality implementation of these strategies will help as well. Such an approach accords with the "clean-slate" design that we discussed in Chapter 4. Relying on evidence-based strategies is a cornerstone of effective policy and practice.

The problem with this approach is that it leaves a flawed design in place. We are still left with a situation in which there is no widespread commitment to crime prevention, and with no agency whose sole goal is to promote public safety. We are left, then, with the proverbial problem of shuffling the chairs on the deck of the *Titanic* while it is sinking. There may be the appearance of progress but, meanwhile, peril awaits. The difference is that the changes discussed in Chapter 5 can make a positive difference. They simply do not go far enough.

Accordingly, Chapter 6 outlined what the reinvention of policing can look like and, again, took heed of the "clean-slate" ideas outlined in Chapter 4. The reinvention begins, first and foremost, with a commitment to crime prevention that targets at-risk individuals and, simultaneously, at-risk communities. That aligns with what we identified in Chapter 4 as a basic building block of effective crime prevention. Gleaning insights from the efforts that have slowly emerged throughout the country and in other countries will be essential. These efforts provide a template for how to proceed, but more is needed.

As part of the commitment to prevention, there are essential steps to take that collectively constitute what we present as a new model of policing. They include (1) charging a lead agency with guiding and overseeing public safety, and coordinating the efforts of the police and other agencies whose mission directly or indirectly bears on crime and justice; (2) undertaking research on the distribution and causes of crime in order to guide prevention activities; (3) using multi-agency policing; (4) specializing police work, with training that supports the diverse mandates that confront the police; (5) investing in efforts to promote collective efficacy and informal social control in communities; (6) relying on alternatives to the police where possible and appropriate, with reliance on police for traffic control representing the poster child for an activity that should be the purview of a different agency; (7) developing a comprehensive and systematic approach to crime prevention; (8) improving 911 call systems; (9) responding to public support for change and for effective and just policing; and (10) investing in research to evaluate implementation, effectiveness, and cost-efficiency.

No doubt, adopting these changes is a tall task, and there will be many barriers that impede their adoption. We discuss some of the most obvious barriers, such as funding and organizational inertia, and we identify ways to incentivize change. The bottom line is that, with political courage and a calibrated set of incentives, they can be overcome. At the least, this model helps to cast in stark relief the problems with contemporary policing and where we need to go.

7

Better Policing and Public Safety Mean More Justice

OUR MAIN FOCUS IN THIS BOOK has been on how policing can be improved in ways that promote greater public safety. We would be remiss, though, if we did not highlight its importance for justice. Indeed, justice goes hand in hand with policing and public safety. In a society where individuals feel that justice exists, they are more likely to support and participate in efforts to prevent and reduce crime. That includes collaborating with the police and other public safety institutions. The reformation and reinvention of policing that we present sets down a foundation that we believe would increase not only public safety but also justice. Accordingly, below, we briefly sketch the reasoning and do so primarily to underscore that any efforts to address public safety should take into account justice. Indirectly, we seek to highlight that this focus has been missing in criminal justice policy for many decades. The near-exclusive focus on get-tough responses has relegated justice to the back burner. That needs to change.

What Is Justice?

No universal definition of justice exists. Scholars have expended substantial energy highlighting diverse ways to define and think about it. We will cling here to a simple notion—justice occurs when laws are implemented in a fair and consistent manner, when citizens feel respected, and when government gives appropriate attention to an individual's or group's unique circumstances and conditions that might affect the experience and effects of punishments.

This definition has roots in many different accounts of justice. Over two thousand years ago, Aristotle, in his Nicomachean Ethics, presented complex arguments about the nature of justice.[1] For example, he argued that equality of punishment is not just when two individuals occupy different ranks, or occupy different statuses, in society. Accordingly, just punishments would need to include a "corrective" component to create equality across individuals of different ranks or statuses.[2] Justice entails equal treatment, but what "equal" means can vary. Aristotle highlights the centrality of the law to justice—to abide by the law, for example, is to be just. Notably, though, laws themselves may vary in how effectively they guide individuals to ideal behaviors and away from those that harm. The law is an imperfect instrument. Regardless, the notion remains—for Aristotle, laws should be well-designed and help to create a just citizenry.

Justice, thus, can be seen as involving well-designed laws, effective governance, and citizens complying with laws. It also can be seen as a tool of society. Why? It is society that determines the values, rights, beliefs, and so on that matter. And it is society whose social conditions structure opportunities for individuals and groups. To say that is not to absolve individuals of responsibility. It is to acknowledge a simple fact—social conditions influence what we can do, how we view and respond to others, and more. These conditions are not randomly occurring, but rather structured in ways that can advantage some groups and disadvantage others.

That situation has direct bearing on any discussion of justice. For example, conditions that may give rise to crime may be unequally distributed across some groups.[3] That makes them more likely to engage in crime and, logically, to encounter governmental policies or practices designed to respond to offending. The unequal exposure to conditions that foster crime itself can be viewed as unjust. Of course, society should respond when crime happens. It is, though, a strange form of justice that lets some individuals or groups be exposed to more criminogenic conditions and waits for crime to happen. That is both inefficient and, arguably, unjust.

Layered onto this issue is the fact that punishments themselves, as Aristotle emphasized, do not exist in a vacuum. They have no absolute force; rather, their effects vary depending on the individual and their social context. Missing several days of work, for example, might not greatly harm some individuals, but for others could result in losing their job.

The goals of punishment also play a critical role in defining and identifying just responses to crime. Notably, we can even see evidence of this idea from watching children. They obviously hold views that society shapes. Regardless, if children hold strong and particular views about justice, that would reflect the importance society places on it. Consider one of the most famous works in psychology, *The Moral Judgment of the Child*. In it, Jean Piaget highlighted the fascinating and complex moral worlds of children.[4] He and his colleagues identified, for example, that young children might "emphasize the vindictive aspect of punishment" and, at the same time, a "theory of preventive punishment." In the latter instance, for example, one child, commenting on another, noted, "a given punishment is not sufficient because 'it wouldn't make her [become] good enough.'"[5] Piaget found, too, that young children placed a premium on reciprocal punishments, or expiatory (retributive) justice, so that the "[transgressor] should realize the results of his actions."[6] That can be viewed, alternatively, as an educative or moralizing function of punishment. As children grow older, however, they place more weight on restitution, and notions of equality, rather than retribution.

In short, society expects a lot from punishment, as can be seen in the diverse goals associated with it. For example, we want it to deter individuals who have been punished (specific deterrence) and those who might commit crime (general deterrence); we want it to rehabilitate, possibly as a morally preferable approach; we want it to generate an appropriate level of retribution; and we want it to educate individuals and the citizenry at large about the law and societal values.[7] All of these goals play a role in defining justice.

To illustrate, severely punishing a minor transgression might be unfair to the individual, but perhaps would generate a substantial general deterrent effect. Unfair to the individual, yes, but perhaps justified if it advances a societal interest? There is, too, the question of whether a minor punishment should be issued in instances of low-severity crime. Perhaps the individual is unlikely ever to commit a crime again. We cannot know what will happen. Regardless, why punish them for something that they might do? Diversion programs in juvenile justice engage in this type of calculus—they seek to err in the direction of reducing a low-probability event even though the intervention might actually cause more harm than good.[8] One standard response is retribution. Some type of response must occur. There must be accountability.

There are, then, these numerous complexities that swirl around a discussion of justice. We have justice as an idea that stems from societal values and goals; something that requires adherence to laws; something that can inhere to or be violated by how laws are designed; and an outcome of society using governmental institutions, such as the police and courts, to achieve a myriad of goals through punishment. Even more complexities can be identified.

To illustrate, one view is that justice stems from and is embodied by fair processes. When government relies on unfair processes, the outcomes are, or can be viewed as, unjust. The credibility of legal systems rests on this idea. To tolerate improper processes, for example, is to enable punishments that never should have been applied in the first place. They allow innocent people to be punished, but they also lead to disparities that, even if guilty people get punished, undermine the real or perceived legitimacy of criminal justice, government, and, ultimately, society. One view of justice, then, is that it operates in a procedurally just manner.

Another view is that justice requires the production of substantively just outcomes. Thus, we can distinguish between procedural justice and substantive justice. This distinction is widely recognized in scholarly accounts. Tom Tyler, for example, differentiates procedural justice, which involves consistent and appropriate adherence to rules, protocols, or the like when enforcing the law, and distributive justice, which involves an appraisal of the fairness of outcomes in general or to specific individuals or groups.[9] This idea—that just processes may differ from just outcomes—is one that sociologists have long confronted. Early founders in sociology, such as Max Weber and Émile Durkheim, recognized that societies wrestle with creating legitimate authority, and that they rely on diverse structures, or approaches, to achieving it.[10] But these structures or approaches themselves cannot magically create legitimacy.

Justice thus can involve not only reference to evaluation of procedures but also evaluation of outcomes. Consider what the sociologist Robert Merton termed "deviant ritualism," a situation where one conforms strictly to rules or procedures even when doing so will produce a harmful or antithetical outcome.[11] For example, police can issue speeding tickets if a driver exceeds the speed limit by only one mile per hour. Doing so for every passing car, though, would not only consume a substantial amount of an officer's time, but likely engender hostility toward law enforcement and undermine their perceived legitimacy. That can lead to an unwillingness to cooperate with the police. It seems like a trivial example, yet it illustrates the fact that the police, like the courts, face situations where protocols cannot ensure substantively just outcomes—that is, decisions that most citizens would view as appropriate and fair given the circumstances. Justice somehow requires both fair process and fair outcomes.

What, though, is a substantively just outcome? No cookie-cutter formula exists. Too many competing considerations come into play. In addition to those that we have discussed, there is the matter of inequality. As Robin Engel has noted, a central theme in accounts of justice is the argument that "injustice is often the result of the tensions between individual rights and equity."[12] Unequal distributions of wealth, for example, may create differential probabilities of offending as well as capacity to navigate the court system. Laws, therefore, may have a disproportionate impact on some groups, such as individuals who live in poverty. Equitable processing and punishment, thus, would take such possibilities into account, and ideally would be addressed in the formulation of law, not just its implementation and enforcement.[13]

There are still more complexities—such as consistency in enforcing laws—that bear on a discussion of justice. What we know is that both within and between different local jurisdictions or within and between states, there can be tremendous variation in how the police, courts, and correctional systems operate and the decisions that they make. How can such variation be defended? In what way is the variation just? Government typically offers little clear answer. It is, in fact, difficult to defend, though one might point to arguments about the value of local government in making decisions that best fit local culture and conditions. That general rationale undergirds arguments since the founding of the United States for local government. And it makes sense as a general matter, not just historically but as a logical matter. Yet, it alone does not provide any coherent rationale for a particular view of, or approach to, justice. In so doing, it opens the door to inconsistent and varying approaches to justice across places and time, from one election, police chief, or set of prosecutors or judges to the next.

An illustration of this idea can be seen in the rise of restorative justice, an approach to justice that has found a home in some parts of the world and in the United States.[14] This approach emphasizes, among other things, providing individuals who have committed a crime a setting where they can meet the person who they victimized, explain why they did what they did, listen to the other person, and apologize. The approach emphasizes much more. For example, it calls for a process that respects all individuals. In some cases, members of the community play a role in the process. The process itself is held to reduce offending by helping individuals to be empathetic and to take responsibility for their behavior, but it allows them to retain their dignity. At the same time, a restorative approach provides a specific vision of justice. It views justice as emanating from a compassionate, empathetic process that requires accountability, including acknowledging harms to others. It views justice as emanating as well from a process that empowers victims.

Here is the point: Whether one encounters this vision of and approach to justice will depend on where you live. The same observation holds for other philosophies, such as strongly retributive or rehabilitative orientations or ones that promote diversion. For example, whether one will receive probation or a prison term can depend greatly on the specific court and community. This observation is not new, but the fact that it so readily is accepted obscures the fact that such variation can constitute or contribute to injustice.

What Do Police Reforms and the Reinvention of Policing Mean for Justice?

Against such complexities, what should be done? We have argued that society must fundamentally shift its approach to how it addresses crime. That entails prioritizing crime prevention and creating a coherent systematic approach to doing so. A simple starting point is to have a lead agency charged solely with

promoting crime prevention and the effective integration of diverse governmental efforts to prevent and, secondarily, respond to crime. The police play
a critical role within this broader focus but cannot go it alone. Nor can they
compensate for failures to create societal conditions that prevent crime. Recognition of that fact is essential for appreciating what reforms or changes to
the police can or cannot achieve.

Within a broader set of systemic changes to public safety and justice, the
police can contribute a great deal to preventing crime and to more effective
responses when crime occurs. We have detailed how they can do so through
improvements to traditional policing (see Chapter 5) and through reinventing policing (see Chapter 6). At the heart of what we propose is an emphasis
on crime prevention; better specialized and general training of police officers; using research to identify the causes of crime in particular areas and
to monitor and evaluate strategies to prevent and respond to crime; police
collaboration with diverse agencies; police working with and strengthening
communities; and the need for all police activities to relate back and be evaluated by a lead agency to ensure a constant focus on effective crime prevention
and to avoid slipping into a reaction-driven approach that has led to the crisis
in contemporary policing.

Long ago, Jerome Skolnick's classic work, *Justice without Trial,* highlighted
the pressures that confront the police, including motivations to process cases
in ways that take into account how prosecutors will process cases or that demonstrate fidelity to political pressures to prioritize order.[15] David Heilbroner's
Rough Justice, which illuminated the inner workings of the Manhattan DA's
office, identified similar concerns.[16] Prosecutors and the police, he highlights,
face case processing pressures and confused or competing priorities, and make
decisions that many times reflect little to no consideration of community
conditions, experiences, or views. Contemporary scholarship underscores that
such problems persist. That is why a fundamental shift must occur that includes
reforms but also a reinvention of policing.

The changes would, we submit, produce important benefits. Most important is the enhanced legitimacy of the criminal justice system in general and
the police in particular. As we and others have argued, legitimacy lies at the
foundation of any governmental efforts. When members of society view the
police, for example, as legitimate authorities and as acting in a legitimate
manner, they will be more likely to cooperate with and support their efforts.
This legitimacy comes from how government efforts are designed and implemented. Process is critical, which is why the changes that we propose put
process at center stage.

The coproduction of public safety requires meaningful participation by a
variety of government institutions and, most importantly, the community.
By involving these groups—especially marginalized communities who have

experienced structural racism or discrimination and have reason to mistrust "business-as-usual" policing[17]—and using research to guide, evaluate, and adjust policing efforts, legitimacy can be maintained or increased. One key reason is that those affected by the police have a significant voice in guiding and evaluating what the police do. As Anthony Bottoms and Justice Tankebe highlight,

> Those in power (or seeking power) in a given context make a claim to be the legitimate ruler(s); then members of the audience respond to this claim; the power-holder might adjust the nature of the claim in light of the audience's response; and this process repeats itself. It follows that legitimacy should not be viewed as a single transaction; it is more like a perpetual discussion, in which the content of power-holders' later claims will be affected by the nature of the audience response.[18]

Shifting the onus of public safety to being a collaborative endeavor avoids the problems that attend to a go-it-alone, or silo-like, approach to policing. That approach can lead to prioritizing bureaucratic goals, such as high clearance rates, or succumbing to political pressures, such as demonstrating a tough-on-crime stance.[19] And it can lead to de-prioritizing public safety. Community members are far less likely to lose sight of public safety as a primary goal. They also are more likely to highlight inequalities and discriminatory practices that affect them.

Legitimacy can be viewed as important in its own right. Citizens want authority to be exercised appropriately and with care. But legitimacy also can be viewed as essential to effective police efforts to prevent and respond to crime.[20] Colin Bolger and Glenn Walters, for example, conducted a meta-analysis of studies that examined procedural justice, legitimacy, and the willingness of citizens to cooperate with the police.[21] They found that citizen views of police fairness served as an important performance metric in its own right but also enhanced the ability of the police to effectively address crime: "Citizen perceptions of police procedural justice would appear to have both a direct impact and indirect effect on citizen cooperation, the latter by way of police legitimacy beliefs."[22] This outcome can stem from many factors, including a willingness to work with the police or simply to call them. As Bolger and Walters note, "when victimization experiences are not reported to the police, criminals become emboldened and their inclination to believe they are above the law grows even stronger."[23]

An approach to policing that creates and enhances legitimacy should necessarily give rise to increased justice.[24] It should enhance the willingness of citizens to work with and collaborate in preventing and responding to crime. And it should create a greater ability to effectively balance procedural and substantive justice. This greater ability stems from the involvement of diverse stakeholders, including other public safety–related institutions and communities, and reliance on research monitoring and evaluation. Monitoring and evaluation are essential—not just for ensuring effective and efficient policing but also for police officer and police department compliance with the law.[25] No perfect balance exists, but the combination of a collaborative and research-based approach can help to avoid swings too far in one direction or the other. It also creates transparency so that corrective steps can be taken.

Is such an approach realistic? Yes, as we have discussed in previous chapters, a variety of strategies exist that align with it. Recent experimental evidence suggests that its potential effectiveness is not just hypothetical. Consider, for example, a three-city randomized controlled trial that tested the effectiveness of hot spots policing guided by an emphasis on procedural justice versus the traditional hot spots policing approach. Impetus for the study stemmed from concerns that hot spots policing can engender mistrust among community members. The intervention generated a range of improvements: "Trained officers were more likely to give citizens a voice, demonstrate neutrality, and treat people with dignity and respect. They were also significantly less likely to be disrespectful."[26] In addition, "community members who had contact with procedural justice officers perceived the interaction as significantly fairer and were more likely to report that officers were neutral decision makers and showed more care and concern."[27] And, not least, "procedural justice hot spots had about 14% fewer incidents during the study relative to standard condition hot spots" despite officers initiating fewer arrests during the period of observation.[28] This is but one example, but it illustrates that, as the authors emphasized, "police fairness and effectiveness are not competing goals."[29] And it illustrates the centrality of citizens, legitimacy, and justice to efforts to promote public safety.

Conclusion

The supreme irony of long-standing problems with policing is that traditional policing practices can worsen crime. How? They may do so directly, by engendering hostility toward law enforcement, the courts, and the criminal justice system writ large. That can result in an unwillingness to cooperate with or help the police. In turn, the police cannot effectively prevent or respond to crime. Studies of community policing highlight the tension—in communities with high crime rates, there can be higher rates of mistrust of the police. Thus, in the very places where community policing might be needed, it can be especially difficult to implement, all the more so with insufficient staffing, policing training, or incentives to prioritize community collaborations. Poor implementation then can lead to greater mistrust and unwillingness to cooperate in police efforts to address crime.

Contemporary policing approaches also may contribute to crime indirectly—they divert attention away from preventing crime. It is the classic mistake that attends to almost any reaction-centered policy: Let problems emerge, then try to treat them. Pretty soon the problems become so endemic that reaction becomes the sole priority. The strategy amounts to investing more and more in emergency units at hospitals while failing to invest in health care prevention. It is a loser's bet. Spend more and more while watching a problem worsen.

This situation amounts to a form of injustice. Allowing crime to occur—allowing *preventable* crime to occur—simply is unjust. It amounts to a fundamental failing of government. No one wins in this situation. Not the police, most of whom, in fact, want to play a positive role in addressing crime. Not citizens in general, who expect accountable and effective governance and who want their taxes used to good effect. Not those who are victimized. And not the family members or friends of these individuals or the communities in which they reside.

Allowing preventable crime to occur results in a related type of injustice—since the causes of crime are not equally distributed in society, a less than robust approach to crime prevention means that some groups and places will disproportionately shoulder the burden of crime. A compound form of injustice results. Unequal social and economic conditions exist, they cause more crime, and then members of these communities encounter a criminal justice system that may increase rather than decrease recidivism and can operate in a discriminatory manner. A focus on crime prevention, then, is not simply about public safety, but also it is about promoting greater justice for all groups and places, especially those most at risk of experiencing crime.

8

Conclusion

Public Safety First

THERE ARE A FEW BASIC THINGS that any well-functioning society should be able to do, such as ensuring that citizens can obtain gainful employment, affordable housing, and food. And it should keep citizens safe. By that measure, the United States—like many "developed" countries—falls well short. At national, state, and local levels, it relies on a fragmented, poorly designed, and inadequately funded system that does little to prevent crime and mainly focuses on reactive measures, like punishment. Citizen safety and justice get left behind as a result. Who benefits? The purveyors of fragmented and reactive policies, and public and private contractors who implement a flawed system of justice. Consider prisons—they are so institutionalized into American crime policy that they amount to a monopoly on public safety investments. Only crumbs are left over to invest in crime prevention.

The solution is clear—a well-designed system for promoting public safety is needed, it needs to be adequately funded and implemented well, and it needs to be continuously evaluated and improved. Public safety as a priority must be institutionalized into policy rather than stand as a sound bite while society continues to invest in piecemeal, reactive policies, laws, and programs that lead us ever further away from the possibility of cost-efficient crime prevention.

One obvious starting point is to reform society's approach to policing. That makes sense because of the widespread and continuing concerns about problematic and failed policing practices. But it makes sense as well because in any well-designed approach to public safety, there need to be organizations and institutions that play a prominent role in reducing and responding to crime. Yet, as we have argued, focusing on the police alone will fail. No amount of changes to policing can correct problems with our laws, courts, and correctional system; minimal investment in crime prevention; and the lack of any integration or oversight of these diverse institutions and approaches to public safety.

What to do? Improve policing—it is an obvious starting point. But simultaneously we need to improve our entire approach to public safety. A focus on policing alone will not work because policing occurs within a broader community and systems context. So, we need a systemic and comprehensive approach that focuses on reducing crime in our communities and offending among those who come into contact with our criminal justice system. What does this approach require? It will require improved lawmaking, court processing, and correctional system practices. It will require investing in crime prevention and prioritizing justice. It will mean listening to communities and the diverse groups affected by crime. And it will require continuous research feedback, without which we are lost and left with, well, the current epic failures in American crime and justice.

Here, then, we conclude by identifying the contours of this new approach to policing and public safety. We highlight the proverbial "forest" and "trees." The broad-based focus on the "forest" is essential. If we as a society—and the government officials and agencies who serve us—get too buried in specifics, we risk becoming entrapped by the all-too-narrow policies and practices that diverted us from making public safety a priority. As we argue, one way to avoid that problem is to create a public safety agency, one charged with maintaining a crystal-clear focus on preventing and reducing crime, and coordinating all efforts for achieving this goal. That said, the "trees" obviously are important. Fortunately, research has identified an abundance of strategies that can improve policing and public safety.

A brief recapitulation of the book is first in order. Recall that Chapter 2 provided guidance about what led us to the current state of problematic policing and approaches to public safety. It is relevant for helping to diagnose what has gone wrong and what needs to be done differently going forward. Chapter 3 pointed to the litany of problems in American policing and served as an indictment of policing in the United States, while providing a roadmap of some of the dimensions along which policing and approaches to public safety can be improved. Chapter 4 illuminated that an effective approach to crime prevention and public safety would look much different than current approaches, and set the stage for appreciating the arguments presented in Chapter 5, which identified ways to reform traditional policing, and Chapter 6, which identified ways to reinvent policing and the approach that the United States takes to public safety. Chapter 7 then detailed ways in which reinventing policing and our approach to public safety can contribute to improved justice.

In what follows, we discuss key implications and recommendations that flow from each chapter. We then step back to identify "big" takeaway points that we argue flow from the different chapters and that will be essential for putting public safety first.

A Litany of Problems (Key Points from Chapter 2)

Many critiques of policing and criminal justice amount to ad hoc points about this or that critical problem. We do not mean to diminish any one problem. To the contrary, any one problem—such as disparities in the treatment of minority citizens—can and should be front and center as a public policy and moral concern. One limitation of this approach, however, is that we fail to see the broader, systemic problems that demand attention in their own right and may contribute to other problems, such as disparities in police approaches with some groups.

Chapter 2 highlighted this issue. There are indeed a litany of problems in policing. These include flaws in the very design of policing. Most important is the lack of any central crime prevention agency that oversees, supervises, and coordinates the efforts of police to help reduce crime. The police instead operate as what amounts to an independent fiefdom. All manner of problems flow from this central design flaw. We lose sight of the goals of policing. Mission creep occurs, whereby we dump onto the police ever increasing sets of responsibilities, with little thought or attention to whether they constitute the best group for taking on these responsibilities or to providing proper funding and training.

The police by and large do not do much of anything that resembles crime prevention. Instead, they primarily react to calls. They also do little to address the root causes of crime. Again, they react after crime happens. Increasingly, the police have become militarized, cementing a more reactive and control-oriented culture that leads away from systemic crime prevention. And their efforts occur independently of the courts, corrections, and lawmaking. One could hardly design a worse or more ineffective strategy for policing.

The problems go well beyond design flaws. As we highlighted, much policing not only is ineffective, it creates harms. That can be seen most clearly in the all-too-frequent occurrence of excessive use of force and racial and ethnic bias. A public safety institution that does not reduce crime effectively or efficiently and that simultaneously creates harms quite rightly and understandably has led to widespread condemnation and calls for a better approach.

There are, too, rampant operational problems. We demand much of the police, yet provide too few resources, too little training, and too little support for what research highlights constitutes one of the most stressful and de-manding jobs that exists. These types of problems remain endemic. Ignoring them has not magically led them to disappear.

Inattention to the nature of policing and the stress it places on officers is a related problem. Officers face numerous dangers, stressful encounters with citizens, and frequent criticism of their work and themselves. This all takes a toll on their mental and physical health as well as their families. That in turn means they cannot execute their responsibilities to their best. The end result? Less public safety and more public disenchantment with the police.

On a parallel front, there are the experiences and perceptions of the public. Widespread problems prevail here as well. Citizens frequently report dis-satisfaction with the police, with some groups reporting more dissatisfaction than others. They too-frequently experience unjust treatment, and, whether the perception is justified or not, they often view the police as unjust. That translates into a lack of cooperation or outright hostility, neither of which are good ingredients for effective crime prevention efforts.

Just as important is the lack of research, monitoring, and oversight. With-out continuous and high-quality research on all aspects of policing, there can be no systemic corrective efforts. Instead, problems go unnoticed until they reach such profound levels that a crisis occurs. Effective corrections do not typically occur at these moments because of the levels of mistrust and the politicization of the problem. At most, piecemeal responses occur. Then policing continues to occur in the equivalent of a "black box."

All of these problems stand as indictments of contemporary policing, but they also point the way to the contours of an effective solution. Most impor-tantly, they highlight the largest consideration—policing must be system-atically reinvented, integrated with a larger set of institutions and activities designed to promote public safety, and evaluated.

Why Policing Is Broken and Needs to Be Reinvented (Key Points from Chapter 3)

Chapter 3 detailed how we got to this place. It is a long and complicated story, but some key features stand out. One is that policing was flawed in its design at the outset, and then evolved largely as an independent institution. That never should have happened. At the end of the day, the issue is simple—the police, or an institution like them, are supposed to take actions that promote public safety. That would mean coordinating police activities with those taken by other institutions. This never happened. Instead, the police increasingly developed into a larger and more independent institution. Policing in turn became increasingly reactive. When you are trying to prevent crime but your efforts exist in a vacuum, you quickly realize that you cannot do much to address the causes of offending or high crime rates in communities. You have no ability to assist at-risk individuals or groups or to improve communities, for example. So, what do you do? You react to crime and do so with ever more force.

This problem then was amplified by the political unrest of the 1960s, and the broader politicization of crime-fighting. The get-tough era of the 1980s paved the way for a "warrior cop" culture to emerge. It did not help that for a brief period of time in the mid-1980s to the early 1990s, violent crime dramatically spiked. This confluence of factors ushered in a new era of policing that became increasingly militarized. The police actually received more funding. That seemingly could be a productive development, but it simply led to more of the same. Well, not the same. It led to even more demands on the police, with continued inattention to the design and operational flaws that have plagued policing from the outset. Most recently, dissatisfaction with the police has led to calls to defund policing.

What lessons can be gleaned from these developments? Policing is, quite simply, broken. If we are to improve public safety, we need an approach to policing that can actually have a fighting chance to prevent and reduce crime and—just as importantly—to work with and for citizens, and be seen that way, rather than against them.

A Clean-Slate View of How to Improve Public Safety
(Key Points from Chapter 4)

A critical barrier to improving public safety is a lack of appreciation for the profound flaws and problems in policing and society's broader approach to crime prevention. Chapters 2 and 3 served to highlight this issue and, ideally, to foster awareness of these flaws and problems.

What, though, is a better way? We felt that one way to appreciate what needs to be done is to begin with a blank slate. Accordingly, with Chapter 4, we began with the idea you and we were charged with preventing and reducing crime. What would we do?

Answering the question leads to what we believe are straightforward insights. We want, for example, crime prevention and public safety to be our paramount goals. We want information about the actual occurrence of recidivism and crime in communities. We want information about their causes. And then we want to work on two tracks, one that employs evidence-based strategies to reduce offending among at-risk individuals and a second that employs evidence-based strategies to prevent or reduce crime rates in communities. In each instance, we want to address the causes of crime. We also want to work at multiple levels. That includes primary (universal) prevention, in which we implement interventions to prevent crime from happening. It includes secondary (selective) prevention, in which we target interventions at individuals or groups at above-average risk of offending or communities where crime and above-average risk of increased crime exists. And it includes tertiary (indicated) prevention, in which we target our interventions at the individuals who already have committed crime and are at high risk of committing more, and at communities with the highest crime rates.

Not least, we want our diverse efforts well-coordinated. Tracking crime, its causes, and intervening in these different ways will require substantial information and attention. No one institution can do it all. But one institution likely needs to exist to coordinate the different efforts of the institutions that would be needed. And, of utmost importance, this central institution will need continuous research and assessment to guide its efforts. The assessments would entail monitoring and evaluation of policy implementation, impacts, and cost-efficiency. And they would include insights from citizens to ensure that their voices inform and guide the interventions that, if well-designed and implemented, should keep them safe.

All of these ideas amount to common sense. But that has been lacking in nationwide and state and local approaches to public safety. A piecemeal approach instead has prevailed. The attendant problems have gone on too long. It is, we submit, time to reinvent policing and our public safety efforts so that the police can be effective and so that our public safety institutions work together to effectively and cost-efficiently prevent and reduce crime.

Reforming Policing (Key Points from Chapter 5)

Chapter 5 began with the premise that much of what the police do is flawed in design—it simply cannot or is unlikely to effectively prevent crime or promote public safety. At the same time, it recognized that many activities that the police undertake either are or can be effective. Not least, society needs an institution that undertakes many of the critical tasks that the police do. The implication is clear: Eliminate unnecessary and ineffective practices, and retain and improve those that are, or can be, effective.

What should be eliminated? It is not complicated. We should stop investing in police practices that are flawed in design and that have the potential to create harm. These include random foot patrols, which require allocating resources to areas low in crime, even though we know that crime tends to be concentrated in a small number of communities. In these places, targeted efforts, not a random presence of officers here or there, are needed. Eliminate traffic enforcement—it is dangerous for officers, cannot be scaled up to a meaningful level, contributes to mistrust of the police and to actual or perceived racial and ethnic disparities in criminal justice responses, and, not least, is largely irrelevant to the task of preventing or reducing crime. Many other options exist to prevent traffic violations: Video camera enforcement of speed limits, speed bumps, improved signage, and more can be scaled up to amount to the equivalent of primary (universal) prevention—that is, a prevention strategy that targets everyone, not just select areas or groups. Eliminate mental health calls. The police are not trained as mental health counselors. It simply does not fall under their area of expertise. Might their help be needed in some cases? Sure. But they should not be the presumptive go-to responders.

What else should go? Eliminate police in schools. There simply is too much confusion that comes from this practice. The police in such settings have been likened to traditional law enforcement officers, mentors, and counselors. That simply is untenable. In addition, it creates the risk of criminalizing age-typical low-level misconduct. And without scaled-up staffing, there is little likelihood that they can effectively prevent much crime, including, unfortunately, school shootings. Predictive policing also should be eliminated. Inaccuracy inherent to this approach is a critical problem, and it does little to nothing to guide intervention. This list is not complete, but it highlights substantial room for removing distracting and ineffective practices so that the police can focus on crime prevention.

What do the police do well, or do that could be improved in ways that promote public safety? A great deal, in fact. One of the main problem areas centers around 911 calls. Dispatchers are the gatekeepers to the criminal justice system. Unfortunately, 911 systems frequently suffer from poor implementation. That should be corrected, and must be if responses to crime—including the potential to prevent it—are to be effective.

Similarly, hot spots policing can be and frequently is effective. But it, too, must be implemented in ways that maximize its effectiveness and minimize the risk of displacing crime to other areas. Both problem-oriented policing and community policing can be effective as well. They depend heavily, however, on quality implementation. That includes recruiting and training officers in the spirit or philosophy of these approaches, how to interact in culturally sensitive and appropriate ways with local citizens, strategies for de-escalating situations and for developing collaborative relationships with neighborhood residents and stakeholder groups, and more. Proactive policing, too, warrants retaining and improving. As with hot spots, problem-oriented, and community policing, the design, or theory, is sound, and research indicates that it can be effective. As with these approaches, however, the disjuncture between theory and practice is substantial. To be effective, all of these approaches must be funded sufficiently and thoughtfully implemented, with evaluation monitoring to ensure consistent and responsive implementation.

That is not all. There is a continued need, too, for police recruitment and training that draws on effective strategies. It is inescapable—without high-quality and well-trained police, there can be no effective prevention of or responses to crime. With it, we have a chance. At the same time, the vision for policing must change. The traditional "warrior" philosophy must go. A military approach has repeatedly proven to be ineffective—it engenders mistrust and hostility, which undermine crime prevention. And it amounts to a diversion of the police from activities that could prevent crime. Shifting toward a guardian philosophy orients police to acting in ways that create trust and relationships with local citizens, and in turn supports problem-oriented, community, and proactive policing. Changing culture is, of course, difficult. Without such change, though, we will be tied to a foundation that sinks any chances of appreciable crime prevention or substantial gains in public safety or justice.

Reinventing Policing (Key Points from Chapter 6)

A central argument of the book is that even with the reforms discussed above and in Chapter 5, contemporary policing cannot appreciably improve public safety unless an overhaul in the structure and design of policing occurs, and unless such change occurs within a broader context of changing our approaches to crime and justice. Reform without fundamental changes to policing and to how we approach public safety more broadly is a dead end.

For this reason, Chapter 6 argued for a reinvention of policing. A foundation for this reinvention comes from reforms that we described in Chapter 5, including removing some functions that the police currently handle but should not because they have little connection to public safety. Chapter 6 built on this foundation and argued that many current reform efforts, though well-meaning, simply are too narrowly focused and do not address the central overarching problem—no well-structured and well-coordinated focus on preventing crime.

To be sure, many of the proposals make sense. For example, the President's Task Force on 21st Century Policing identified six pillars of reform, with a series of recommendations under each. We believe that many of the recommendations rest on sound science and should be implemented. By and large, though, many current and proposed reforms amount to tinkering around the edges, and fail to create a framework and foundation for crime prevention. In so doing, they consign us to a continuing and endless cycle of ineffective policing, avoidable tragedies that lead to more calls for reform, implementation of more of the same (with new names), and yet still no appreciable fundamental change to how society goes about achieving public safety.

Our premise, which guides Chapter 6 and derived from the "clean-slate" arguments presented in Chapter 4, is that the reinvention of American policing must begin and end with a systematic focus on crime prevention. All efforts should be guided by primary (also called "universal"), secondary (or "selective"), and tertiary (or "indicated") prevention. The first two should be prioritized. The last is important, but it amounts to waiting until individuals commit crime or communities experience high levels of, or dramatic increases in, crime. To effectively prevent crime, efforts are needed that promote primary and secondary prevention as well. Primary (universal) prevention entails creating strong communities everywhere, while secondary (selective) prevention entails targeting resources toward at-risk individuals and communities. The police are uniquely positioned to participate in secondary (selective) prevention, to work with higher-risk individuals and communities to help avoid crime and, at the same time, to develop supports and institutions that strengthen them.

In making the case for crime prevention as a central guiding mission, we recognize that the police cannot lead the effort or do so alone. Indeed, perhaps the most significant failure of public safety efforts since the founding of the United States is the lack of a centralized, comprehensive, systematic approach to public safety that prioritizes prevention. Chapter 6 therefore highlights ways to reinvent policing, and part of that reinvention entails creation and implementation of just such a centralized approach, with a lead agency whose primary mandate is public safety.[1] Without one, criminal justice and corrections are and will remain chaotic, ill-coordinated endeavors, each of which engages in activities centered around control and reaction rather than prevention. Will such a transition be difficult? Yes. But, as a logical matter, no other alternative stands a chance of appreciably and effectively promoting crime prevention and public safety on a large scale. Presently, virtually no criminal justice or correctional system agency has as its primary mission the prevention of crime. The agencies and systems operate almost universally in a reactive manner, thus consigning criminal justice to, at most, tertiary (indicated) crime prevention efforts.

With a well-coordinated system of crime prevention, what role can the police play? An absolutely essential one. They are positioned to understand the causes of crime and to work with communities, local leaders, social service systems, and more to aid this understanding, develop appropriate and effective responses, and undertake or assist with implementation of them. They can work with a lead public safety agency to secure resources and identify how best to coordinate and concentrate efforts to prevent crime. They alone cannot identify all individual-level or neighborhood-level criminogenic conditions, but they can work with others to do so, and then to develop or implement policies and practices to address these conditions. One of their most important roles can be to increase collective efficacy among communities. Doing so can strengthen the communities and provide a broad-based foundation for prevention.

What, then, are the ways to reinvent policing? First, prioritize crime prevention. It is at once that simple and, given the history of policing and crime control in the United States, complex.

Second, expand the crime prevention efforts that have slowly emerged throughout law enforcement agencies across the country. These include the CIT approach for helping police to manage individuals with a mental health condition and divert them to treatment; the LEAD approach for diverting low-level crimes, especially among individuals with behavioral health problems, to programs and services to address criminogenic circumstances in their lives; and CAHOOTS, an MCT approach to identifying situations where a social service crisis intervention approach would be the more appropriate and effective alternative to a police response.

Third, learn from and adopt crime prevention policing approaches used in other countries. Guidance from the international community abounds. There is, for example, New Zealand's Prevention First model, which draws on problem-solving policing and community policing and entails coordinated efforts with other agencies. The police do not "go it alone." There is Scotland's conceptualization of violence as a preventable health problem that calls for efforts to address criminogenic forces at individual and community levels. Ireland, too, has adopted a similar overarching platform, one that more explicitly identifies the importance of diverse groups, communities, community organizations, and local and state agencies to participate in crime prevention. This theme is echoed in efforts in the UK and Europe. There is, in addition, the call from the United Nations to ground crime prevention efforts in research. In all cases, the countries recognize the critical importance of deterrence and punishment. They differ from the United States, however, in more deliberately thinking about and placing resources into prevention.

Fourth, adopt a comprehensive and systematic approach to crime prevention. The new model that we present, which draws on the ideas presented in Chapter 4 and from our review of the literature, includes many of the critical pieces of what this approach could entail. It is not an exhaustive listing, but illustrates how we can approach crime prevention in a way that gives the United States a chance to appreciably improve public safety and do so in a sustained manner.

1. The model emphasizes the importance of a lead agency, one that over-sees and coordinates all crime prevention efforts. The police cannot be effective, or as effective, in their work if what they do is not guided by and integrated with other local and state as well as court and cor-rectional system efforts to prevent crime.

2. A second necessary starting point is accurate information about the distribution and causes of individual-level and community-level crime. Relying solely on calls to the police is a recipe for failure. These do not provide sufficiently accurate information about the prevalence or distribution of crime, and they, of course, say nothing about the causes of it. Any public safety agency, along with the police, needs the latter to guide their efforts.

3. The model emphasizes the importance of multi-agency policing that is, by its very design and nature, collaborative. The concept of multi-agency policing underscores that the police do not solely make society safe. Rather, they coproduce public safety through collaboration with other agencies and, more broadly, with communities.

4. In addition, the model calls for addressing crime more effectively by relying on police specialization and improving training. Differentia-tion is called for when certain tasks require unique sets of skills. Those required to de-escalate a domestic violence incident vary, for example, from those required to investigate a homicide or to promote collective efficacy through collaborations with citizens.

5. It calls as well for crime prevention through efforts that promote col-lective efficacy and informal social control. We know that perhaps the biggest "bang for the buck" in reducing crime comes from strengthen-ing communities. Yet, historically, our public safety efforts have not prioritized this approach. The police can play a pivotal role in helping communities to help themselves. Doing so requires a different kind of policing, one that can help to not only address crime but also improve the actual and perceived legitimacy of the police. It can entail problem-solving policing and community policing, but only when these are well-implemented. It can entail far more as well, but whatever the ap-proach, ongoing collaboration and communication, and the develop-ment of trust, are essential.

6. Our model calls for relying on alternatives to the police wherever possible and appropriate. Traffic control, for example, should be di-verted almost entirely to a different agency. Speed limit enforcement is illustrative—there simply is no compelling theoretical or empirical basis for having the police monitor speed limits and issue tickets. Shedding unnecessary work—that is, activities that do not directly and

appreciably contribute to crime prevention or addressing crime—can help to crystallize more clearly what should be the guiding mission of the police, crime prevention and justice, and free them to concentrate more fully on that mission.

7. The model points to the central importance of a systematic and comprehensive approach to crime prevention. Although the contours of what that can include may be broadly similar across communities, the specific dimensions invariably will depend on local conditions. At its most basic level, a systematic and comprehensive approach requires targeting efforts at the causes of crime at the individual and community levels. Without this approach, the police will revert to reacting to crime rather than helping to prevent it in the first place. And the police, and society at large, will be left with a patchwork of efforts that do not merge into a coherent overall plan.

8. The new model emphasizes the need to radically improve 911 call systems, and to do so in ways that contribute to crime prevention. These systems are plagued by inefficiencies and errors that can have life-threatening impacts. They can place officers at risk as well. Given that 911 calls typically are a central gateway to activating the police, we need to ensure that calls are properly routed. Under the new model, responding to 911 calls will be even more challenging, but it also constitutes a critical point from which to ensure more effective responses.

9. A fundamental piece of the new model centers on the public—they are the ultimate constituency. Reforming and reinventing the police is supported by the public. Government accountability requires adopting policies that, except in limiting instances (e.g., support of discrimination), respond to the public will. At the same time, the broad-based support for changes to policing provides a critical platform for introducing a much-needed rethinking of the structure and nature of policing and, more broadly, our approach to public safety. In addition, a focus on the public is essential for evaluating effectiveness. Successful policing should create greater public safety, but it also should lead the public to feel safer, to view the police and criminal justice system as just and legitimate, and to be willing to call on and cooperate with them to address crime. Scholars study these dimensions, yet criminal justice systems operate with little institutionalized need to consider anything other than arrests and clearance rates, or avoiding the fallout from scandals. That should change if the police are to be effective and if they—and the institutions that are supposed to keep society safe—are to be held accountable.

10. The new model requires substantial investment in, and use of, research. Continuous research and assessment must occur. Policymakers

thus must invest substantially in the research infrastructure for generating relevant information to guide implementation and evaluation of effectiveness and cost-efficiency, as well as to guide corrective actions for improving policing activities. This includes collecting information directly from citizens and those with boots-on-the-ground insights about the individuals caught up in our system of public safety and the communities it serves.

In presenting this model, we recognize that many barriers to its implementation exist. We discuss them—including challenges in securing sufficient funding, organizational inertia and police culture that fight against any meaningful change, police unions and associations that oppose change, and resistance to reform in general—and ways that they can be overcome. We discuss, too, incentives for change. The most obvious is that crime prevention and public safety are something that the public wants, but that also can be incentivized through different strategies, including financial rewards for performance. We highlight that financial considerations weigh heavily in favor of change, especially if we consider the monetary benefits of avoided crime. We highlight a related benefit—by reducing crime, there is less pressure on the criminal justice system, and an ability to allow it to contract. There are, as well, political benefits and, not least, a moral and ethical argument for adopting a model of policing that not only can appreciably prevent and reduce crime but can also prevent and reduce racial and ethnic, social class, and other disparities in public safety and justice.

Not least, we discuss the pragmatic reality that implementing this model—or advances of any appreciable amount in reforming or reinventing policing and public safety—will be a challenge. But without a clear vision for where we should go, society will be left tinkering at the edges, enacting more of the same reforms that will, once again, barely make a dent in crime and injustice. We can and should do better.

Improved Public Safety Means More Justice
(Key Points from Chapter 7)

We set out to focus on policing, quickly realized that improved policing could not happen without an improved system of public safety, and then realized in turn that justice is part and parcel of any discussion of crime prevention. A hallmark of democracies is an approach to justice that recognizes the importance of due process. Crime prevention that does not place justice at center stage will not be terribly effective and it would create problems. That includes the problems that undermine contemporary criminal justice, such as actual and perceived disparities in how the poor, racial and ethnic minorities, immigrants, juveniles, women, and disadvantaged communities are treated by the police, courts, and correctional system.

Chapter 7 set out to emphasize these points and highlight how an improved approach to policing and to public safety can benefit from a focus on justice and, simultaneously, can improve justice. How? The first and most important is that it should prevent and reduce crime. This should necessarily have a greater benefit for those groups and communities who are most affected by crime.

A second and related way it can improve justice is by not contributing to crime. A society that causes more crime is, by definition, acting in an unjust manner. Traditional approaches to public safety and policing typically have failed to address the causes of crime. Put less charitably, they have let these causes persist and grow, enabling crime to happen, and then have applied incapacitation- and deterrence-based punishments. That is, quite simply, unjust.

A third way the proposed model can improve justice is by coproducing public safety. Doing so can increase the real and perceived legitimacy of the police and other public safety agencies and institutions. Preventing crime and promoting justice can be more effective by including the voices of those who are affected by crime and who experience inequalities that can contribute to injustice. Here, recall that the United States has a criminal justice—not a victim justice—system. Yes, victims increasingly have a role in and are served by the police, but not in any systematic way and not to scale. This situation not only does a disservice to victims, it disproportionately affects those groups and communities that experience the most crime and injustice.

Any effective approach to public safety requires insights about the causes of offending and crime. Who better to ask than individuals and community citizens who are most affected by their occurrence? Theory and research play a critical role, but so, too, do the insights of populations and areas where crime occurs. We argue that effective public safety must institutionalize feedback, insights, and guidance from these groups. They should not be "given" a voice. Rather, their voices should be a given. Doing so provides a critical form of justice—the ability to be heard and to take action. And it helps to ensure that public safety efforts are responsive to and heed the insights of those most affected by crime.

We argue that the model that we present—which emphasizes crime prevention and the coproduction of public safety through multi-agency and community collaborations—provides a platform for empowering communities. And it provides a vehicle through which diverse groups' and communities' voices can be heard.

Conclusion

It is, perhaps, all too human to proceed from a place of good intentions when developing a course of action. And to proceed with our first instincts and plans. And then, when confronted with repeated evidence of flaws in this approach, to persist nonetheless in a stubborn belief that somehow or someday, the approach will work. But the end result can be—and, in the case of crime and justice in the United States, is—tragedy.

The founders of our contemporary criminal justice system and approach to policing took a stab at how best to improve public safety. Some of the strategies made sense. But not all of them. Rather than step back and alter the design, though, the United States has committed to and reinforced it. This approach results in more crime and injustice.

We wish that we could claim credit for that insight, but the reality is that scholars, policymakers, and the public have highlighted the numerous problems with how our society addresses crime. That includes ignoring prevention and enabling injustice.

An unchecked tragedy is becoming an even greater one. It will increasingly be difficult to revamp not only policing but also our entire criminal justice system. Time, then, truly is of the essence.

The solution is, in many respects, simple—we need to prioritize crime prevention and create institutions, or agencies, that commit to this goal. That is the foundation of the new model that we present. All the rest is details. Important, yes, but the far more important change is to commit to crime prevention. Without this commitment, we will endure further piecemeal change. And the groups most affected by crime and injustice will have to endure much more.

It simply does not have to be that way. American society is wonderfully adept, when it wants to be. In difficult times, it has created unprecedented responses. The problem with crime may be that, even in times where it increases, our attention simply cannot stay on it for very long. A war, perhaps. But not a problem that ebbs and flows, and has become so politicized. Whatever the reason, we want to emphasize, it simply does not have to be that way. We can do better.

We can and should reinvent policing. That is not just our view. In writing this book, we encountered numerous instances of scholars, policymakers, and the public calling for large-scale change. The international community understands the issue as well, and in many instances have made greater strides than the United States has in correcting their own flawed designs for public safety.

Once we commit to this reinvention, the path to follow becomes clear. We need to prevent crime. Punish, yes, but persist in prioritizing prevention.

To do so requires that public safety agencies operate with accurate informa-tion about the distribution and causes of crime in their communities. They then need to devise strategies to prevent or reduce crime, with a focus on at-risk individuals and, separately, at-risk communities. They need to work with, not against, citizens. For that, the agencies must have institutionalized approaches to communicating, cooperating, and collaborating with com-munities. They should work to strengthen communities to create lasting protection against crime and an ability to support just responses. Not least, the agencies need consistent and credible research on implementation and effectiveness, and on how the public experiences and views the ways that government responds to crime and pursues justice.

So, we set out to reinvent policing. But along the way, it has become clear that our entire system of criminal justice—our approach to public safety and justice—must change. The police cannot go it alone. The most effective police agency in the world cannot compensate for a society that does not invest in crime prevention, that gives the courts few options other than punishment, and that gives correctional systems even fewer options.

If, as a country, we are serious about creating more effective and just polic-ing, we need to create a system that supports this approach. We need more than piecemeal change to the police. But we also need more than piecemeal change to the institutions on which we have come to rely—especially the courts and correctional system—for taking care of crime and justice.

What we stand to gain from reform and reinvention of policing is much bigger than crime prevention and public safety. There are dividends in terms of the amount and quality of justice, the reduction of the psychic and financial costs to crime victims as well as the broader social costs of crime, improve-ments to public health, enhanced economic productivity, lower criminal justice costs, improved quality of life and life-course outcomes, reduced de-pendence on public assistance, and others. These all constitute ripple effects that flow from investing in crime prevention. It is time to take a better path toward policing and public safety.

Notes

Preface

1. Quoted in Lentz and Chaires (2007:77).

Chapter 1

1. Madeo (2018).
2. Hayes (2020).
3. McLaughlin et al. (2016).
4. Chalfin (2015).
5. Morgan and Truman (2020).
6. Kelly (2021).
7. Lyon (2019).
8. Kelly (2016).
9. Kelly et al. (2017).
10. Kelly et al. (2017).
11. Centers for Disease Control (2018); Merrick et al. (2018).
12. Kelly et al. (2017).
13. Raine and Yang (2006:205-6).
14. Raine (2018:2).
15. Kelly et al. (2017).
16. Mears (2004).
17. Kelly et al. (2017).
18. Allen (2008).
19. Gramlich (2020b).

20. Bayley (1996:25-26).
21. Kelly (2016).
22. Open Society Foundations (2002).
23. Alliance for Safety and Justice (2020:4).
24. Lake Research Partners (2017).
25. American Civil Liberties Union (2017).
26. Samuels (2016).
27. NORC (2020).
28. *Washington Post* (2022).
29. *Washington Post* (2022).
30. Cipriano (2021b).
31. Sullivan (2021).
32. Eder et al. (2021).
33. National Registry of Exonerations (2022).
34. Davis (2020).
35. The systems-focused accounts include Mears (2010, 2017, 2019, 2022), Mears and Cochran (2015), Kelly (2015, 2016, 2021), and Kelly et al. (2017).

Chapter 2

1. Rossi et al. (2004); Mears (2010).
2. Antenangeli and Durose (2021:1).
3. Kelly et al. (2017); Mears (2017).
4. Mears (2017).
5. National Research Council (2004:4).
6. Nix et al. (2017); Bandes et al. (2019); Brunson and Wade (2019); Alang et al. (2021).
7. Lum and Koper (2017:8).
8. Sherman (1983:149).
9. Neusteter, Mapolski, et al. (2019).
10. Welsh and Farrington (2012).
11. MacKenzie (2006); Lipsey and Cullen (2007); Latessa et al. (2014); Kelly (2015); Mears and Cochran (2015).
12. Sampson et al. (1997); Pratt and Cullen (2005); Rosenfeld (2006); Messner and Rosenfeld (2009); Sampson (2012).
13. Alonso et al. (2019).
14. Reisig (2010).
15. Rossi et al. (2004); Mears (2010).
16. Vitale (2020).
17. Skogan (1995:60); see, generally, Mears and Cochran (2015).
18. Clinton (1996).
19. American Civil Liberties Union (2014).
20. Akpan (2018).
21. Kraska (2007).

22. Akpan (2018).
23. Kelly et al. (2017).
24. Kelly (2021).
25. Scheiber et al. (2000).
26. Trotta (2020).
27. Glock and Kurtz (2020:3).
28. McCorkel (2020).
29. Mears (2010).
30. Tonry (2014).
31. Mears (2010, 2017); Mears and Cochran (2015).
32. Roeder et al. (2015).
33. Bump (2020).
34. Roeder et al. (2015).
35. Weisburd, Braga, et al. (2017); Weisburd and Majmundar (2018); Braga, Brunson, and Drakulich (2019).
36. St. Martin (2019); Snider and Szilak (2021).
37. Antenangeli and Durose (2021).
38. Mears and Cochran (2015).
39. Kindy et al. (2021); Thompson (2021).
40. Graham (2021).
41. Sinyangwe (2021).
42. Lopez (2020).
43. Jackman (2021).
44. Office of Civil Rights Evaluation (2018:2).
45. See, generally, Muhammad (2019) and Russell-Brown (2021).
46. Tonry (2011, 2012); Baumer (2013); Avery and Cooper (2020).
47. Heilbroner (1990).
48. Morin et al. (2017).
49. Mears, Craig, et al. (2017).
50. Harrell and Davis (2020).
51. Harris (2020).
52. Harris (2020:4-5).
53. Andrews (2016); Pierson et al. (2020).
54. Mears, Craig, et al. (2017).
55. Lenehan (2017); Stolper and Jones (2018); American Civil Liberties Union (2020); *Boston Globe* Editorial Board (2020); Levchak (2021); Vito et al. (2021).
56. Levchak (2021).
57. Choudhury (2018).
58. *Boston Globe* Editorial Board (2020).
59. American Civil Liberties Union (2015).
60. Lenehan (2017); Levchak (2021).
61. Coviello and Persico (2015); Levchak (2017, 2021); Kramer and Remster (2018).
62. Lenehan (2017).
63. American Civil Liberties Union (2022).

64. American Civil Liberties Union (2022).
65. American Civil Liberties Union (2022).
66. Harrell and Davis (2020).
67. Edwards et al. (2018).
68. Joseph (2022:181).
69. See, for example, Brunson and Miller (2006) and Brunson and Wade (2019); see, generally, Mears, Cochran, and Lindsey (2016) and Mears, Craig, et al. (2017).
70. Ofer (2016).
71. Thusi and Carter (2016).
72. Kindy et al. (2021).
73. Morin et al. (2017).
74. Langer (2021).
75. Pew Research Center (2020).
76. Ekins (2020).
77. Barned-Smith and Dexheimer (2020:1).
78. Armstrong (2020).
79. Adachi (2017).
80. Khazan (2021).
81. Horton (2021).
82. Tchekmedyian (2022).
83. Buehler (2021).
84. Weichselbaum (2020); Buehler (2021).
85. Weichselbaum (2020).
86. Lantigua-Williams (2016).
87. Morin et al. (2017).
88. Burke (2017).
89. Skolnick (1966); Heilbroner (1990); Moskos (2008).
90. Howard (1994).
91. Mears and Bacon (2009).
92. U.S. Department of Justice (2011:xv).
93. U.S. Department of Justice (2017).
94. Engel (2003).
95. Engel (2003).
96. National Emergency Number Association (2021).
97. Dewan and Oppel (2015).
98. Karma (2020b).
99. Mears and Bacon (2009).
100. Neusteter, Mapolski, et al. (2019): Neusteter, O'Toole, et al. (2020).
101. Karma (2020b).
102. Karma (2020b).
103. Lum, Koper, and Wu (2022).
104. Rubin and Poston (2020).
105. Asher and Horowitz (2021).
106. Lum, Koper, and Wu (2022).
107. Lum, Koper, and Wu (2022:269).

108. Mears and Cochran (2015).
109. Oudekerk and Kaeble (2021).
110. Kelly (2016); Mears, Cochran, and Cullen (2015); Mears, Cochran, et al. (2016); Loeffler and Nagin (2022).
111. Mears and Cochran (2015).
112. Morin et al. (2017).
113. Li and Mahajan (2021).
114. Brenan (2020).
115. Brenan (2020).
116. Schulte (2021).
117. Page and Lee (2021).
118. Associated Press (2020).
119. Cipriano (2020).
120. Elkins (2016).
121. Riley (2020).
122. Mazumder (2020).
123. Noppe et al. (2017); Jones (2020).
124. Worden and McLean (2018).
125. Mears (2017).
126. Lum and Nagin (2017).
127. Rosenfeld (2006).
128. Mears (2010, 2017); Santos (2014).
129. Montes et al. (2021).
130. Weitzer (2015:478).

Chapter 3

1. USAFacts (2020).
2. Uchida (1989).
3. Uchida (1989).
4. Lepore (2020).
5. Lepore (2020).
6. Uchida (1989).
7. Balko (2014).
8. Uchida (1989).
9. Uchida (1989).
10. Uchida (1989).
11. Lepore (2020).
12. Balko (2014:32).
13. Balko (2014).
14. Waxman (2017).
15. Waxman (2017).
16. Walker (1977).
17. Rawlings (1994).

18. Bump (2020).
19. Vera Institute (2022).
20. USAFacts (2020).
21. Statista (2011); Banks et al. (2016); Task Force on Policing (2022).
22. Lattimore (2022).
23. Lattimore (2022).
24. Bump (2020).
25. Mears (2010).
26. Flamm (2019:11).
27. Snyder and Kelly (1977).
28. Hinton (2015:103).
29. Hinton (2021).
30. See, for example, Piven and Cloward (1993).
31. Hinton (2015:107).
32. Kelly (2015, 2016); Mears and Cochran (2015); Kelly et al. (2017).
33. Eisen and Chettiar (2016).
34. Purnell (2020).
35. Fellner (2009).
36. Gramlich (2020a).
37. Pearl (2018); Drug Policy Facts (2020).
38. Stellin (2019).
39. Levine et al. (2013).
40. Lee (2021).
41. Forer (1994).
42. Vitale (2020).
43. U.S. Census Bureau (2020).
44. Karma (2020c).
45. Karma (2020c).
46. Treatment Advocacy Center (2016).
47. *Washington Post* Editorial Board (2021).
48. Neusteter, O'Toole, et al. (2020:12).
49. Speri (2019).
50. Harcourt and Ludwig (2006); Braga, Welsh, and Schnell (2015); Office of the Inspector General for the NYPD (2015); O'Brien et al. (2019).
51. See, for example, Tyler and Meares (2020).
52. O'Brien et al. (2019).
53. Balko (2014).
54. Balko (2014).
55. Barrett (2020); Mack (2021).
56. Balko (2014:96).
57. Barrett (2020); Mack (2021).
58. Balko (2014:154).
59. Balko (2014:210).
60. Balko (2014:254); Adachi (2017).
61. Adachi (2017).

62. McNamara (2006).
63. Montes et al. (2021).

Chapter 4

1. Rossi et al. (2004); Mears (2010, 2018); Bardach and Ptashnik (2020).
2. Junger-Tas and Marshall (1999); Gomes et al. (2018, 2019).
3. Vannette and Krosnick (2018).
4. Latessa et al. (2014).
5. Lipsey and Cullen (2007); Latessa et al. (2014); Mears and Cochran (2015).
6. Mears and Cochran (2015); Kelly (2015, 2016); Kelly et al. (2017).
7. Office of Juvenile Justice and Delinquency Prevention (2015).
8. Office of Juvenile Justice and Delinquency Prevention (2015).
9. Office of Juvenile Justice and Delinquency Prevention (2015).
10. Mrazek and Haggerty (1994:20-21).
11. Sampson et al. (1997).
12. Sampson (2012).
13. Lipsey and Cullen (2007); Latessa et al. (2014); Mears and Cochran (2015); Mears (2017).
14. Manning (2005).
15. Banks et al. (2016:1).
16. Mears (2010, 2017).
17. Rossi et al. (2004); Mears (2010).
18. Davis et al. (2018:1).
19. Mears and Lindsey (2016).

Chapter 5

1. Sherman et al. (1989); Weisburd, Bushway, et al. (2004).
2. Center for Evidence-Based Crime Policy (2010).
3. Asher and Horowitz (2021).
4. Karma (2020a).
5. Dexheimer and Barned-Smith (2021).
6. Texas Department of Public Safety (2020).
7. Pierson et al. (2020).
8. Baumgartner et al. (2018).
9. Stanford Open Policing Project (2022).
10. Mears and Lindsey (2016:68).
11. Simpson (2021).
12. Weill-Greenburg (2021).
13. Bacon (2021).
14. Weichselbaum et al. (2021).

15. Karma (2020a).
16. Woods (2021).
17. Harrison (2021).
18. Office of Juvenile Justice and Delinquency Prevention (2020).
19. Mears (2010).
20. National Research Council (2004:229); see also Taylor (2001).
21. See, for example, Harcourt (2001) and RAND (2022).
22. Braga, Welsh, and Schnell (2015).
23. See, for example, Heaton et al. (2017) and Kelly (2021).
24. Armenta and Alvarez (2017).
25. Mears (2001).
26. Agan et al. (2021).
27. Neusteter, Mapolski, et al. (2019).
28. *Washington Post* Editorial Board (2020).
29. *Washington Post* (2022).
30. Fialk (2020).
31. Butler and Sheriff (2020).
32. Flack and Fischer (2020).
33. Cipriano (2021a).
34. Wang et al. (2020).
35. Whitaker et al. (2019).
36. Snow et al. (2021).
37. Masterson (2017).
38. Brown et al. (2020).
39. Montes et al. (2021).
40. Mears, Montes, et al. (2019).
41. Mbekeani-Wiley (2017:4).
42. Gottfredson et al. (2020).
43. Sentencing Project (2013).
44. Sentencing Project (2013); Connery (2020); Gottfredson et al. (2020).
45. Gottfredson et al. (2020:929-30).
46. Kupchik (2010).
47. Chiu et al. (2018).
48. Mears, Moon, and Thielo (2017).
49. Santos (2019:375).
50. Perry et al. (2013); Hvistendahl (2016); Weisburd and Majmundar (2018); Meijer and Wessels (2019); Santos (2019); Lau (2020); Linder (2020); Browning and Arrigo (2021).
51. Browning and Arrigo (2021:303-4).
52. Richardson et al. (2019); Bhuiyan (2021); Browning and Arrigo (2021).
53. Browning and Arrigo (2021).
54. Neusteter, O'Toole, et al. (2020).
55. Neusteter, O'Toole, et al. (2020).
56. Parsons and Wunschel (2020).

57. Neusteter, O'Toole, et al. (2020).
58. Neusteter (2021:2-3).
59. Durkan (2021); Felitto (2021).
60. Mears and Bacon (2009); Kelly and Pitman (2018); Kelly (2021).
61. Gillooly (2020:791).
62. Gillooly (2020).
63. Karma (2020b).
64. Pew Charitable Trusts (2021).
65. Parsons and Wunschel (2020); Herscowitz (2021); Neusteter (2021).
66. Neusteter, O'Toole, et al. (2020).
67. Neusteter, O'Toole, et al. (2020).
68. Gillooly (2020); Neusteter, O'Toole, et al. (2020); Wunschel and Bodah (2020).
69. Neusteter, O'Toole, et al. (2020:305).
70. Telep et al (2016).
71. Braga, Turchan, et al. (2019:305).
72. Lum and Koper (2017).
73. Weisburd and Braga (2019).
74. Rosenbaum (2019).
75. Hatten and Piza (2022).
76. Rosenbaum (2019); Hatten and Piza (2022).
77. National Research Council (2004); Lum and Koper (2017); Telep et al. (2018); Weisburd and Majmundar (2018).
78. Rosenbaum (2019:317).
79. Rosenbaum (2019:319).
80. Lum and Koper (2017).
81. Caplan et al. (2015).
82. Marchment and Gill (2021:9).
83. Lum and Nagin (2017:350-51).
84. Lum and Koper (2017).
85. Hinkle et al. (2020).
86. Braga and Weisburd (2019:199).
87. Cordner (2014:5).
88. Cordner (2014).
89. Gill et al. (2014).
90. Peyton et al. (2019).
91. Crowl (2017).
92. Gill et al. (2014).
93. Crowl (2019).
94. Gill et al. (2014:419-20).
95. Lum and Koper (2017).
96. Skogan (2019:30).
97. Weisburd and Majmundar (2018:30).
98. Lum, Koper, Wu, et al. (2020).
99. Lum, Koper, Wu, et al. (2020).

100. Lum, Koper, Wu, et al. (2020).
101. Lum, Koper, Wu, et al. (2020).
102. Blumberg et al. (2019).
103. Armstrong (2020).
104. Armstrong (2020).
105. Lum and Koper (2017:160).
106. Blumberg et al. (2019).
107. Goh (2022).
108. Rahr and Rice (2015:3-4).
109. Morin et al. (2017:18).
110. Morin et al. (2017:19).
111. Morin et al. (2017:57).
112. Skolnick (2002); Ivković et al. (2018); Schuck and Rabe-Hemp (2022).
113. Rahr and Rice (2015:3-4).

Chapter 6

1. Mears (2017).
2. Kelly (2021).
3. Wexler (2021).
4. Police Executive Research Forum (2020).
5. Bell (2017); Cobbina-Dungy and Jones-Brown (2023).
6. Eder et al. (2021); Associated Press (2020); Jenkins (2021).
7. Mears, Craig, et al. (2017).
8. Wexler (2021:2).
9. Saletan (2021).
10. Romero (2020).
11. Ray and Neily (2021).
12. Petersen (2018:1).
13. Gest (2020).
14. Human Rights Watch (2020).
15. Neusteter, Subramanian, et al. (2019).
16. Advancement Project (2017).
17. Stoughton et al. (2020).
18. Police Executive Research Forum (2021).
19. President's Task Force on 21st Century Policing (2015); Lum, Koper, Gill, et al. (2016).
20. Lum and Nagin (2017:351).
21. Lum and Nagin (2017).
22. Mears (2017).
23. *Washington Post* Editorial Board (2021).
24. Mears and Cochran (2015); Kelly (2015, 2016, 2021).
25. See, generally, Mears (2010, 2017), Mears and Cochran (2015), Kelly (2015, 2019, 2021), Kelly et al. (2017), Kelly and Pitman (2018).

26. Targeting risk factors among individuals constitutes prevention, and may be especially helpful during childhood and adolescence—that is, during development from childhood into adulthood (see, generally, Welsh and Farrington 2012).

27. Welsh and Farrington (2012:130).

28. Welsh and Farrington (2012:130).

29. Bucerius et al. (2021).

30. Farrington, Loeber, and Ttofi (2012).

31. Kelly et al. (2017).

32. Drake et al. (2009); Lee et al. (2012); Washington State Institute for Public Policy (2020).

33. Piquero and Jennings (2012).

34. Lösel and Bender (2012).

35. Farrington, Gaffney, et al. (2017:91-92).

36. Griffin et al. (2015); Willison et al. (2018).

37. Sampson et al. (1997).

38. Sampson et al. (1997:923).

39. U.S. Department of Housing and Urban Development (2016).

40. Sharkey and Sampson (2015:329).

41. Pratt and Cullen (2005).

42. Sharkey et al. (2017:1233).

43. Ohmer (2016:700).

44. Ohmer (2010).

45. Collins et al. (2014).

46. Telep and Hibdon (2018).

47. Skogan (2012:184).

48. Sampson and Raudenbush (2001); Keizer et al. (2008).

49. Branas, Kondo, et al. (2016); Branas, South, et al. (2018); Moyer et al. (2019).

50. Moyer et al. (2019).

51. Heinze et al. (2018).

52. Branas, South, et al. (2018).

53. Branas, Kondo, et al. (2016).

54. Tallon et al. (2018).

55. Tallon et al. (2018).

56. Dempsey et al. (2020); Balfour et al. (2022).

57. Law Enforcement Assisted Diversion (2022c).

58. Law Enforcement Assisted Diversion (2022b).

59. Pearl (2018).

60. Vera Institute (2018).

61. Worden and McLean (2018); Law Enforcement Assisted Diversion (2022a).

62. University of Cincinnati Center for Police Research and Policy (2021a).

63. Kroman (2021).

64. Eugene Police Department Crime Analysis Unit (2020).

65. Beckett et al. (2021).

66. University of Cincinnati Center for Police Research and Policy (2021b).

67. Balfour et al. (2022).

68. Balfour et al. (2022:661).
69. Piza and Welsh (2022).
70. New Zealand Police (2017:3-5).
71. Smith et al. (2018).
72. Smith et al. (2018:109).
73. Bland et al. (2021:1888).
74. Krug et al. (2002).
75. Firman (2019).
76. United Nations (2002:3).
77. Schweig (2014).
78. Kelly et al. (2017).
79. Hughes and Tucker (2018).
80. Adam and Noack (2020).
81. Mears (2017); see also Rubin and Feeley (2022).
82. Police Foundation (2022:61).
83. See Mears (2017) for a fuller account of this idea; see also Rubin and Feeley (2022).
84. Pearl (2020:5).
85. Sanchez and Yen (2018).
86. Ryan (2011).
87. Policy Development Research (PD&R) Edge (2014).
88. Mears (2017).
89. Mears (2012); Mears, Kuch, et al. (2016).
90. Krug et al. (2002:15, 16, 244).
91. Branas, South, et al. (2018); Doleac (2018); Branas, Buggs, et al. (2020); Pearl (2020); Alexander and Sered (2021); South (2021).
92. Rodriguez (2021).
93. Doleac (2018).
94. Branas, Buggs, et al. (2020).
95. Chalfin et al. (2019).
96. Kessler et al. (2021).
97. Cohen (2020).
98. Branas, South, et al. (2018); Branas, Buggs, et al. (2020); South (2021).
99. Branas, South, et al. (2018:2946).
100. Cheatham and Maizland (2020).
101. Wexler (2021:3).
102. President's Task Force on 21st Century Policing (2015:51).
103. Yesberg and Bradford (2021:420).
104. Yesberg and Bradford (2021).
105. Kochel and Weisburd (2019).
106. Weisburd, Davis, and Gill (2015); Kochel and Weisburd (2019); Weisburd, White, and Wooditch (2020); Weisburd, Gill, et al. (2021).
107. Weisburd, White, and Wooditch (2020).
108. Kochel and Weisburd (2019).
109. Kochel and Weisburd (2019:919).

110. Kochel and Gau (2019:315-16).
111. Braga, Brunson, and Drakulich (2019:547).
112. Lum, Koper, Gill, et al. (2016:28); see also President's Task Force on 21st Century Policing (2015).
113. Skogan (2019:28).
114. Mastrofski (2019:63).
115. Mastrofski (2019:63-64).
116. Colover and Quinton (2018).
117. Santos (2013:44).
118. Goldstein (2018).
119. Braga and Weisburd (2019).
120. Braga and Weisburd (2019:197).
121. Morin et al. (2017).
122 Sharkey (2018:158).
123. Vera Institute (2021b).
124. Mears and Lindsey (2016).
125. Gray (2007).
126. Vera Institute (2021a).
127. Mears and Cochran (2015).
128. Braga and Bond (2008).
129. Kelly et al. (2017); Kelly (2021).
130. Heilbroner (1990).
131. Mears (2010, 2017).
132. Graham (2022).
133. Thompson (2022).
134. Friedman (2020).
135. Crabtree (2020).
136. Associated Press (2020).
137. Crabtree (2020).
138. Open Society Foundations (2002).
139. Cullen et al. (2000); Nagin et al. (2006).
140. Lake Research Partners (2017).
141. Alliance for Safety and Justice (2020).
142. Alliance for Safety and Justice (2020).
143. Data for Progress (2020).
144. Ferner (2021).
145. Winter et al. (2020); Buckwalter-Poza and McElwee (2021).
146. Associated Press (2020).
147. Cobbina-Dungy and Jones-Brown (2023).
148. Lum and Nagin (2017); Mears, Craig, et al. (2017).
149. Bolger and Walters (2019); Braga, Brunson, and Drakulich (2019).
150. Mears (2010); Mears and Cochran (2015); Mears (2017); Kelly (2015, 2016, 2018, 2021); Kelly et al. (2017); Kelly and Pitman (2018).
151. Cullen et al. (2017); Mears (2017).
152. Witkin (2021).

153. Beauchamp (2020).
154. Sierra-Arévalo (2020).
155. Morin et al. (2017).
156. Wexler (2021).
157. DiSalvo (2020).
158. Mears and Cochran (2015); Mears (2017).
159. Task Force on Policing (2022).
160. Gramlich (2021).
161. Balko (2021).
162. Cullen et al. (2017).
163. Miller et al. (2021).
164. Miller et al. (2021).
165. Heilbroner (1990).
166. Meares (2021).

Chapter 7

1. Aristotle (2012[350 BCE]).
2. Chroust and Osborn (1942).
3. Mears, Cochran, and Lindsey (2016).
4. Piaget (1932).
5. Piaget (1932:212).
6. Piaget (1932:215).
7. Gibbs (1975); von Hirsch (1976); Ashworth et al. (2009).
8. Mears, Kuch, et al. (2016).
9. Engel (2005); Tyler (2006).
10. Weber (1978); Gould (1993).
11. Merton (1957).
12. Engel (2005:448).
13. Rawls (1999).
14. Braithwaite (2002).
15. Skolnick (1966).
16. Heilbroner (1990).
17. Bell (2017); Muhammad (2019); Russell-Brown (2021); Cobbina-Dungy and Jones-Brown (2023).
18. Bottoms and Tankebe (2012:129).
19. Skolnick (1966).
20. Braga, Brunson, and Drakulich (2019).
21. Bolger and Walters (2019).
22. Bolger and Walters (2019:98); see also Tyler and Meares (2020).
23. Bolger and Walters (2019:93).
24. Braga, Brunson, and Drakulich (2019).

25. Meares (2021).
26. Weisburd, Telep, et al. (2022:6).
27. Weisburd, Telep, et al. (2022:6-7).
28. Weisburd, Telep, et al. (2022:7).
29. Weisburd, Telep, et al. (2022:7).

Chapter 8

1. Mears (2017).

Bibliography

Adachi, Jeff. 2017. "Police Militarization and the War on Citizens." *American Bar Association Human Rights Magazine* 42(1). Available at https://www.americanbar. org/groups/crsj/publications/human_rights_magazine_home/2016-17-vol-42/vol-42-no-1/police-militarization-and-the-war-on-citizens.

Adam, Karla, and Rick Noack. 2020. "Defund the Police? Other Countries Have Narrowed Their Role and Boosted Other Services." *Washington Post*, June 14. Available at https://www.washingtonpost.com/world/europe/police-protests-countries-reforms/2020/06/13/596eab16-abf2-11ea-a43b-be9f6494a87d_story.html.

Advancement Project. 2017. "The Change We Need: 5 Issues that Should Be Part of Efforts to Reform Policing in Local Communities." Los Angeles: Advancement Project. Available at https://advancementproject.org/the-change-we-need-5-issues-that-should-be-part-of-efforts-to-reform-policing-in-local-communities.

Agan, Amanda Y., Jennifer L. Doleac, and Anna Harvey. 2021. *Misdemeanor Prosecution*. Cambridge, MA: National Bureau of Economic Research.

Akpan, Nsikan. 2018. "Police Militarization Fails to Protect Officers and Targets Black Communities, Study Finds." *PBS News Hour*, August 21. Available at https://www.pbs.org/newshour/science/police-militarization-fails-to-protect-officers-and-targets-black-communities-study-finds.

Alang, Sirry, Donna McAlpine, Malcolm McClain, and Rachel Hardeman. 2021. "Police Brutality, Medical Mistrust and Unmet Need for Medical Care." *Preventive Medicine Reports* 22:101361.

Alexander, Amanda, and Danielle Sered. 2021. "Making Communities Safe, Without the Police." *Boston Review*, November 21. Available at https://www.bostonreview. net/articles/making-communities-safe-without-the-police.

Allen, Stephen. 2008. "Mental Health Treatment and the Criminal Justice System." *Journal of Health and Biomedical Law* 4:153-91.

Alliance for Safety and Justice. 2020. *Toward Shared Safety: The First-Ever National Survey of America's Safety Gaps.* Oakland, CA: Alliance for Safety and Justice.

Alonso, José M., Rhys Andrews, and Vanesa Jorda. 2019. "Do Neighbourhood Renewal Programs Reduce Crime Rates? Evidence from England." *Journal of Urban Economics* 110:51-69.

American Civil Liberties Union (ACLU). 2014. *War Comes Home: The Excessive Militarization of American Policing.* New York: American Civil Liberties Union.

American Civil Liberties Union (ACLU). 2015. *Stop and Frisk in Chicago.* New York: American Civil Liberties Union. Accessed December 14, 2022. Available at https://www.aclu-il.org/sites/default/files/wp-content/uploads/2015/03/ACLU_Stopand-Frisk_6.pdf.

American Civil Liberties Union (ACLU). 2017. "91 Percent of Americans Support Criminal Justice Reform ACLU Polling Finds." November 16. New York: American Civil Liberties Union. Available at https://www.aclu.org/press-releases/91-percent-americans-support-criminal-justice-reform-aclu-polling-finds.

American Civil Liberties Union (ACLU). 2020. "Stop-and-Frisk Data Reveals Ineffective Policing, Troubling Racial Disparities." June 16. New York: American Civil Liberties Union. Available at https://www.aclu.org/press-releases/aclu-analysis-dc-stop-and-frisk-data-reveals-ineffective-policing-troubling-racial.

American Civil Liberties Union (ACLU). 2022. "Stop-and-Frisk Data: New York." New York: American Civil Liberties Union. Accessed December 14, 2022. Available at https://www.nyclu.org/en/stop-and-frisk-data.

An Garda Síochána. 2017. *Garda Crime Prevention and Reduction Strategy—Putting Prevention First.* Dublin: An Garda Síochána.

Andrews, Edmund. 2016. "Stanford Researchers Develop New Statistical Test That Shows Racial Profiling in Police Traffic Stops." *Stanford News*, June 28. Available at https://news.stanford.edu/2016/06/28/stanford-researchers-develop-new-statistical-test-shows-racial-profiling-police-traffic-stops.

Antenangeli, Leonardi, and Matthew R. Durose. 2021. *Recidivism of Prisoners Released in 24 States in 2008: A 10-Year Follow-Up Period (2008–2018).* Washington, DC: Bureau of Justice Statistics.

Aristotle. 2012 [350 BCE]. *Aristotle's "Nicomachean Ethics."* Translated by Robert C. Bartlett and Susan D. Collins. Chicago: Chicago University Press.

Armenta, Amada, and Isabela Alvarez. 2017. "Policing Immigrants or Policing Immigration? Understanding Local Law Enforcement Participation in Immigration Control." *Sociology Compass* 11:312453 (https://doi.org/10.1111/soc4.12453).

Armstrong, Jason. 2020. "A Letter to the American Public: We Need to Increase the Quantity and Quality of Police Training." *Police 1*, July 9. Available at https://www.police1.com/police-training/articles/a-letter-to-the-american-public-we-need-to-increase-the-quantity-and-quality-of-police-training-PEIoRJqWTIG55dqy.

Asher, Jeff, and Ben Horwitz. 2021. "How Do the Police Actually Spend Their Time?" *New York Times*, November 8. Available at https://www.nytimes.com/2020/06/19/upshot/unrest-police-time-violent-crime.html.

Ashworth, Andrew, Andrew von Hirsch, and Julian Roberts, eds. 2009. *Principled Sentencing: Readings on Theory and Policy.* Portland, OR: Hart Publishing.

Associated Press. 2020. *Widespread Desire for Policing and Criminal Justice Reform.* Chicago: NORC at the University of Chicago.

Avery, Joseph, and Joel Cooper, eds. 2020. *Bias in the Law: A Definitive Look at Racial Prejudice in the U.S. Criminal Justice System.* Lanham, MD: Rowman & Littlefield.

Bacon, John. 2021. "Philadelphia to Become First Major U.S. City to Ban Minor Traffic Stops to Promote Equity, Curb 'Negative Interactions' with Police." *USA Today*, October 31. Available at https://www.usatoday.com/story/news/nation/2021/10/31/philadelphia-ban-minor-police-traffic-stops/6224286001.

Balfour, Margaret E., Arlene Hahn Stephenson, Ayesha Delany-Brumsey, Jason Winsky, and Matthew L. Goldman. 2022. "Cops, Clinicians, or Both? Collaborative Approaches to Responding to Behavioral Health Emergencies." *Psychiatric Services* 73:658-69.

Balko, Radley. 2014. *Rise of the Warrior Cop: The Militarization of America's Police Forces.* New York: Public Affairs.

Balko, Radley. 2021. "The Bogus Backlash against Progressive Prosecutors." *Washington Post*, June 14. Available at https://www.washingtonpost.com/opinions/2021/06/14/bogus-backlash-against-progressive-prosecutors.

Ballard, Jamie. 2020. "Most Americans Feel Safe in Their Own Community, Big Cities Still Scare Many." September 8. London: YouGovAmerica. Available at https://today.yougov.com/topics/politics/articles-reports/2020/09/08/economist-cities-safety-poll-data.

Bandes, Susan, Marie Pryor, Erin M. Kerrison, and Phillip A. Goff. 2019. "The Mismeasure of *Terry* Stops: Assessing the Psychological and Emotional Harms of Stop and Frisk to Individuals and Communities." *Behavioral Sciences and the Law* 37:176-94.

Banks, Duren, Joshua Hendrix, Matthew Hickman, and Tracey Kyckelhahn. 2016. *National Sources of Law Enforcement Employment Data.* Washington, DC: Bureau of Justice Statistics.

Bardach, Eugene, and Eric M. Ptashnik. 2020. *A Practical Guide for Policy Analysis: The Eightfold Path to More Effective Problem Solving.* 6th ed. New York: Sage.

Barned-Smith, St. John, and Eric Dexheimer. 2020. *Blistering Government Report Blasts Poor Training, Oversight of Texas Law Enforcement.* Austin, TX: Texas Sunset Advisory Commission.

Barrett, Brian. 2020. "The Pentagon's Hand-Me-Downs Helped Militarize Police. Here's How." *Wired*, July 2. Available at https://www.wired.com/story/pentagon-hand-me-downs-militarize-police-1033-program.

Baumer, Eric P. 2013. "Reassessing and Redirecting Research on Race and Sentencing." *Justice Quarterly* 30:231-61.

Baumgartner, Frank, Derek Epp, and Kelsey Shoub. 2018. *What 20 Million Traffic Stops Tells Us about Policing and Race.* New York: Cambridge University Press.

Bayley, David. 1996. *Police for the Future.* New York: Oxford University Press.

Beauchamp, Zack. 2020. "What the Police Really Believe." *Vox*, July 7. Available at https://www.vox.com/policy-and-politics/2020/7/7/21293259/police-racism-violence-ideology-george-floyd.

Beckett, Katherine, Monica Bell, and Forrest Stuart. 2021. "From Crisis to Care." *Inquest*, September 2. Available at https://inquest.org/from-crisis-to-care.

Bell, Monica C. 2017. "Police Reform and the Dismantling of Legal Estrangement." *The Yale Law Journal* 126:2054-150.

Bender, Doris, and Friedrich Lösel. 2012. "Child Social Skills Training in the Prevention of Antisocial Development and Crime." Pp. 102-29 in *The Oxford Handbook of Crime Prevention*, edited by Brandon C. Welsh and David P. Farrington. Oxford: Oxford University Press.

Bennett, John. 2020. "Research Shows Black Drivers More Likely to Be Stopped by Police." NYU, May 5. Available at https://www.nyu.edu/about/news-publications/news/2020/may/black-drivers-more-likely-to-be-stopped-by-police.html.

Bhuiyan, Johana. 2021. "Major Camera Company Can Sort People by Race, Alert Police When It Spots Uighurs." *Los Angeles Times*, February 9. Available at https://www.latimes.com/business/technology/story/2021-02-09/dahua-facial-recognition-china-surveillance-uighur.

Blair, Clancy, and C. Cybele Raver. 2016. "Poverty, Stress, and Brain Development: New Directions for Prevention and Intervention." *Academic Pediatrics* 16:S30-36.

Bland, Nick, Amy Calder, Nicholas R. Fyfe, Simon Anderson, James Mitchell, and Susan Reid. 2021. "Public Policy Reform and Police Prevention Practice: A Journey Upstream?" *Policing* 15:1882-93.

Blumberg, Daniel, Michael Schlosser, Konstantinos Papazoglou, Sarah Creighton, and Chuck Kaye. 2019. "New Direction in Police Academy Training: A Call to Action." *International Journal of Environmental Research and Public Health* 16(24):4941.

Bolger, P. Colin, and Glenn D. Walters. 2019. "The Relationship between Police Procedural Justice, Police Legitimacy and People's Willingness to Co-operate with Law Enforcement: A Meta-Analysis." *Journal of Criminal Justice* 60:93-99.

Boston Globe Editorial Board. 2020. "City Must Confront Racial Bias of Stop-and-Frisk." *Boston Globe*, June 17. Available at https://www.bostonglobe.com/2020/06/17/opinion/city-must-confront-racial-bias-stop-and-frisk.

Bottoms, Anthony E., and Justice Tankebe. 2012. "Beyond Procedural Justice: A Dialogic Approach to Legitimacy in Criminal Justice." *Journal of Criminal Law and Criminology* 102:119-70.

Braga, Anthony A., and Brenda J. Bond. 2008. "Policing Crime and Disorder Hot Spots: A Randomized Controlled Trial." *Criminology* 46:577-608.

Braga, Anthony A., Rod K. Brunson, and Kevin M. Drakulich. 2019. "Race, Place, and Effective Policing." *Annual Review of Sociology* 45:535-55.

Braga, Anthony A., Brandon S. Turchan, Andrew V. Papachristos, and David M. Hureau. 2019. "Hot Spots Policing and Crime Reduction: An Update of an Ongoing Systematic Review and Meta-Analysis." *Journal of Experimental Criminology* 15:289-311.

Braga, Anthony A., and David L. Weisburd. 2019. "Problem-Oriented Policing: The Disconnect Between Principles and Practice." Pp. 182-204 in *Police Innovation: Contrasting Perspectives*, 2nd ed., edited by David L. Weisburd and Anthony A. Braga. New York: Cambridge University Press.

Braga, Anthony A., Brandon C. Welsh, and Cory Schnell. 2015. "Can Policing Disorder Reduce Crime? A Systematic Review and Meta-Analysis." *Journal of Research in Crime and Delinquency* 52:567-88.

Braithwaite, John. 2002. *Restorative Justice and Responsive Regulation.* New York: Oxford University Press.

Branas, Charles, Shani Buggs, Jeffrey A. Butts, Anna Harvey, Erin M. Kerrison, Tracy Meares, Andrew V. Papachristos, John Pfaff, Alex R. Piquero, Joseph Richardson Jr., Caterina G. Roman, and Daniel Webster. 2020. *Reducing Violence without Police: A Review of Research Evidence.* New York: John Jay Research and Evaluation Center.

Branas, Charles C., Michelle C. Kondo, Sean M. Murphy, Eugenia C. South, Daniel Polsky, and John M. MacDonald. 2016. "Urban Blight Remediation as a Cost-Beneficial Solution to Firearm Violence." *American Journal of Public Health* 106:2158-64.

Branas, Charles C., Eugenia South, Michelle C. Kondo, Bernadette C. Hohl, Philippe Bourgois, Douglas J. Wiebe, and John M. MacDonald. 2018. "Citywide Cluster Randomized Trial to Restore Blighted Vacant Land and Its Effects on Violence, Crime, and Fear." *PNAS* 115:2946-51.

Brenan, Megan. 2020. "Amid Pandemic, Confidence in Key U.S. Institutions Surges." Gallup, August 12. Available at https://news.gallup.com/poll/317135/amid-pandemic-confidence-key-institutions-surges.aspx.

Brown, Samantha J., Daniel P. Mears, Nicole L. Collier, Andrea N. Montes, George B. Pesta, and Sonja E. Siennick. 2020. "Education vs. Punishment? Silo Effects and the School-to-Prison Pipeline." *Journal of Research in Crime and Delinquency* 57:403-43.

Browning, Matthew, and Bruce Arrigo. 2020. "Stop and Risk: Policing, Data, and the Digital Age of Discrimination." *American Journal of Criminal Justice* 46:298-316.

Brunson, Rod K., and Brian A. Wade. 2019. "'Oh, Hell, No, We Don't Talk to Police': Insights on the Lack of Cooperation in Police Investigations of Urban Gun Violence." *Criminology and Public Policy* 18:623-48.

Brunson, Rod K., and Jody Miller. 2006. "Gender, Race, and Urban Policing: The Experience of African American Youths." *Gender and Society* 20:531-52.

Bucerius, Sandra M., Temitope B. Oriola, and Daniel J. Jones. 2021. "Policing with a Public Health Lens—Moving Towards an Understanding of Crime as a Public Health Issue." *The Police Journal* 95:421-35.

Buckwalter-Poza, Rebecca, and Sean McElwee. 2021. "Oregon Poll: Replace Police with Trained First Responders." *The Appeal,* March 17. Available at https://the-appeal.org/the-lab/polling-memos/oregon-poll-replace-police-with-trained-first-responders.

Buehler, Emily D. 2021. *State and Local Law Enforcement Training Academies, 2018—Statistical Tables.* Washington, DC: Bureau of Justice Statistics. Available at https://www.ojp.gov/library/publications/state-and-local-law-enforcement-training-academies-2018-statistical-tables.

Bump, Philip. 2020. "Over the Past 60 Years, More Spending on Police Hasn't Necessarily Meant Less Crime." *Washington Post,* June 7. Available at https://www.washingtonpost.com/politics/2020/06/07/over-past-60-years-more-spending-police-hasnt-necessarily-meant-less-crime.

Burke, Ronald J., ed. 2017. *Stress in Policing: Sources, Consequences, and Interventions.* New York: Routledge.

Caplan, Joel, Leslie Kennedy, Jeremy Barnum, and Eric Piza. 2015. "Risk Terrain Modeling for Spatial Risk Assessment." *Cityscape* 17:7-16.

Center for Evidence-Based Crime Policy (CEBCP). 2010. *What Works in Policing.* Fairfax, VA: George Mason University, Center for Evidence-Based Crime Policy. Available at https://cebcp.org/evidence-based-policing/what-works-in-policing.

Centers for Disease Control (CDC). 2018. *CDC-Kaiser ACE Study.* Atlanta, GA: Centers for Disease Control and Prevention. Available at https://www.cdc.gov/violenceprevention/aces/about.html.

Chalfin, Aaron. 2015. *Economic Costs of Crime.* New York: Wiley.

Chalfin, Aaron, Benjamin Hensen, Jason Lerner, and Lucie Parker. 2019. *Can Street Lighting Reduce Crime?* Chicago: Urban Labs.

Cheatham, Amelia, and Lindsay Maizland. 2020. "How Police Compare in Different Democracies." *Council on Foreign Relations*, November 12. Available at https://www.cfr.org/backgrounder/how-police-compare-different-democracies.

Chiu, Allyson, Alex Horton, and Jennifer Jenkins. 2018. "Scarred by School Shootings." *Washington Post*, March 21. Available at https://www.washingtonpost.com/graphics/2018/local/us-school-shootings-history.

Choudhury, Nusrat. 2018. "Stop-and-Frisk Settlement in Milwaukee Lawsuit Is a Wakeup Call for Police Nationwide." July 13. New York: American Civil Liberties Union. Available at https://www.aclu.org/news/criminal-law-reform/stop-and-frisk-settlement-milwaukee-lawsuit.

Chroust, Anton-Hermann, and David L. Osborn. 1942. "Aristotle's Conception of Justice." *Notre Dame Law Review* 17:129-43.

Cipriano, Andrea. 2020. "Public Confidence in Police 'Lowest in 20 Years.'" *The Crime Report*, October 9. Available at https://thecrimereport.org/2020/10/09/public-confidence-in-police-lowest-in-20-years.

Cipriano, Andrea. 2021a. "From Student to Criminal: Are School Resource Officers Doing More Harm Than Good?" *The Crime Report*, April 9. Available at https://thecrimereport.org/2021/04/09/from-student-to-criminal-are-school-resource-officers-doing-more-harm-than-good.

Cipriano, Andrea. 2021b. "Policing Task Force Calls for Chokehold Ban, Curbs on No-Knock Warrants." *The Crime Report*, January 27. Available at https://thecrimereport.org/2021/01/27/policing-task-force-calls-for-chokehold-ban-curbs-on-no-knock-warrants.

Clinton, William J. 1996. "The President's Radio Address." October 26. Washington, DC: The White House. Available at https://www.presidency.ucsb.edu/documents/the-presidents-radio-address-285.

Cobbina-Dungy, Jennifer E., and Delores Jones-Brown. 2023. "Too Much Policing: Why Calls Are Made to Defund the Police." *Punishment and Society* 25:3-20.

Cohen, Elior. 2020. *The Effect of Housing Assistance on Recidivism to Homelessness, Economic, and Social Outcomes.* Los Angeles: University of California.

Collins, Charles R., Jennifer Watling Neal, and Zachary P. Neal. 2014. "Transforming Individual Civic Engagement into Community Collective Efficacy: The Role of Bonding Social Capital." *American Journal of Community Psychology* 54:328-34.

Colover, Sarah, and Paul Quinton. 2018. *Neighbourhood Policing: Impact and Implementation*. Ryton-on-Dunsmore, UK: College of Policing.

Connery, Chelsea. 2020. *The Prevalence and the Price of Police in Schools*. Storrs, CT: University of Connecticut, Center for Education Policy Analysis.

Cordner, Gary. 2014. "Community Policing." Pp. 148-71 in *The Oxford Handbook of Police and Policing*, edited by Michael D. Reisig and Robert J. Kane. New York: Oxford University Press.

Council of State Governments Justice Center. 2019. *Police-Mental Health Collaborations: A Framework for Implementing Effective Law Enforcement Responses for People Who Have Mental Health Needs*. New York: Council of State Governments Justice Center.

Coviello, Decio, and Nicola Persico. 2015. "An Economic Analysis of Black-White Disparities in the New York Police Department's Stop-and-Frisk Program." *Journal of Legal Studies* 44:315-60.

Crabtree, Steve. 2020. "Most Americans Say Policing Needs 'Major Changes.'" *Gallup News*, July 22. Available at https://news.gallup.com/poll/315962/americans-say-policing-needs-major-changes.aspx.

Crowl, Justin. 2017. "The Effect of Community Policing on Fear and Crime Reduction, Police Legitimacy and Job Satisfaction: An Empirical Review of the Evidence." *Police Practice and Research*, 18:449-62.

Cullen, Francis T., Bonnie S. Fisher, and Brandon K. Applegate. 2000. "Public Opinion about Punishment and Corrections." *Crime and Justice* 27:1-79.

Cullen, Francis T., Cheryl L. Jonson, and Daniel P. Mears. 2017. "Reinventing Community Corrections." *Crime and Justice* 46:27-93.

Data for Progress. 2020. *Voters Support Federal Grants for Community Based Emergency and Non-Emergency Crisis Response*. San Francisco: Data for Progress.

Davis, Elizabeth, Anthony Whyde, and Lynn Langton. 2018. *Contacts between Police and the Public, 2015*. Washington, DC: Bureau of Justice Statistics.

Davis, Robert. 2020. "What It's Going to Take to Fix Policing." New York: Brennan Center for Justice. Available at https://www.brennancenter.org/our-work/research-reports/what-its-going-take-fix-policing.

Dempsey, Charles, Cameron Quanbeck, Clarissa Bush, and Kelly Kruger. 2020. "Decriminalizing Mental Illness: Specialized Policing Responses." *CNS Spectrums* 25:181-95.

Den Heyer, Garth. 2021. "Police Strategy Development: The New Zealand Police Prevention Strategy." *Police Practice and Research* 22:127-40.

Dewan, Shalia, and Richard Oppel Jr. 2015. "In Tamir Rice Case, Many Errors by Cleveland Police, Then a Fatal One." *New York Times*, January 22. Available at https://www.nytimes.com/2015/01/23/us/in-tamir-rice-shooting-in-cleveland-many-errors-by-police-then-a-fatal-one.html.

Dexheimer, Eric, and St. John Barned-Smith. 2021. "Vehicle Searches Are Often Fruitless Police Traffic Stops." *Houston Chronicle*, November 4. Available at https://www.houstonchronicle.com/politics/texas/article/Texas-police-search-thousands-of-drivers-and-find-16589982.php.

DiSalvo, Daniel. 2020. "The Trouble with Police Unions." *National Affairs* 53 (Fall). Available at https://www.nationalaffairs.com/publications/detail/the-trouble-with-police-unions.

Doleac, Jennifer L. 2018. "New Evidence that Access to Health Care Reduces Crime." *Brookings*, January 3. Available at https://www.brookings.edu/blog/up-front/2018/01/03/new-evidence-that-access-to-health-care-reduces-crime.

Drake, Elizabeth K., Steve Aos, and Marna G. Miller. 2009. "Evidence-Based Public Policy Options to Reduce Crime and Criminal Justice Costs: Implications in Washington State." *Victims and Offenders* 4:170-96.

Drug Policy Facts. 2020. "Total Annual Arrests in the U.S. by Type of Offense." Accessed December 13, 2022. Available at https://www.drugpolicyfacts.org/node/235.

Durkan, Jenny. 2021. *Executive Summary: Executive Order to Reimagine Policing and Community Safety in Seattle.* Seattle, WA: City of Seattle. Available at https://publicola.com/wp-content/uploads/2021/07/IDT-Report-on-Reimagining-Policing-and-Community-Safety-in-Seattle3361.pdf.

Eder, Steve, Michael Keller, and Blacki Migliozzi. 2021. "As New Police Reform Laws Sweep Across the U.S., Some Ask: Are They Enough?" *New York Times*, April 18. Available at https://www.nytimes.com/2021/04/18/us/police-reform-bills.html.

Edwards, Frank, Hedwig Lee, and Michael Esposito. 2018. "Risk of Being Killed by Police Use of Force in the United States by Age, Race-Ethnicity, and Sex." *PNAS* 116(34):16793-98. Available at https://www.pnas.org/doi/10.1073/pnas.1821204116.

Eisen, Lauren-Brooke, and Inimai M. Chettiar. 2016. *The Complex History of the Controversial 1994 Crime Bill.* New York: Brennan Center for Justice.

Ekins, Emily. 2016. *Policing in America: Understanding Public Attitudes toward the Police.* Washington DC: Cato Institute.

Ekins, Emily. 2020. "Poll: 63% of Americans Favor Eliminating Qualified Immunity for Police." Washington DC: Cato Institute. Available at https://www.cato.org/survey-reports/poll-63-americans-favor-eliminating-qualified-immunity-police#.

Engel, Robin S. 2003. *How Police Supervisory Styles Influence Patrol Officer Behavior.* Washington, DC: National Institute of Justice.

Engel, Robin S. 2005. "Citizens' Perceptions of Procedural and Distributive Injustice During Traffic Stops with Police." *Journal of Research in Crime and Delinquency* 42:445-81.

Eugene Police Crime Analysis Unit. 2020. *CAHOOTS Program Analysis.* Eugene, OR: Eugene Police Crime Analysis Unit.

Farrington, David P., Hannah Gaffney, Friedrich Lösel, and Maria M. Ttofi. 2017. "Systematic Reviews of the Effectiveness of Developmental Prevention Programs in Reducing Delinquency, Aggression, and Bullying." *Aggression and Violent Behavior* 33:91-106.

Farrington, David P., Rolf Loeber, and Maria M. Ttofi. 2012. "Risk and Protective Factors for Offending." Pp. 46-69 in *The Oxford Handbook of Crime Prevention*, edited by Brandon C. Welsh and David P. Farrington. Oxford: Oxford University Press.

Fellner, Jamie. 2009. *Decades of Disparity Drug Arrests and Race in the United States.* New York: Human Rights Watch.

Ferner, Matt. 2021. "Voters Want to See a Significant Shift of Internal Police Resources, Expect City Leaders to Prioritize Solving Murders." Safer Cities. Accessed

September 30, 2021. Available at https://safercitiesresearch.com/the-latest/voters-want-resource-shift-policing-more-murders-solved.

Fialk, Amanda. 2020. "Cops Shouldn't Be First at Scene in Mental Health Crisis. NYC Pilot Program Needed Nationwide." *USA Today*, December 2. Available at https://www.usatoday.com/story/opinion/policing/2020/12/02/cops-shouldnt-first-mental-health-call-ny-program-needed-nationwide-column/6422931002.

Finlaw, Sarah. 2020. "Governor Baker Signs Police Reform Legislation." Boston: Massachusetts Government. Available at https://www.mass.gov/news/governor-baker-signs-police-reform-legislation.

Firman, Sam. 2019. "Scottish Violence Reduction Unit (SVRU): A Public Health Approach to Ending Violence." London: Shift Relationships Project. Available at https://shiftdesign.org/case-study-svru.

Flack, Eric, and Jordan Fisher. 2020. "DMV Police Are Called on Tens of Thousand of Mental Health Runs a Year. Most Don't Get Any Training on How to Handle." *WUSA9*, November 12. Available at https://www.wusa9.com/article/news/911-mentally-ill-crisis-intervention-training-police-mental-health-dc-police-secret-service-metro-transit-police-fairfax-montgomery/65-3270ab6a-e15c-4ecb-9605-de5490668ca2.

Flamm, Michael. 2019. "From Harlem to Ferguson: LBJ's War on Crime and America's Prison Crisis." *Origins*. Columbus: Ohio State University. Accessed December 13, 2022. Available at https://origins.osu.edu/article/harlem-ferguson-lbjs-war-crime-and-americas-prison-crisis?language_content_entity=en.

Forer, Lois G. 1994. *A Rage to Punish: The Unintended Consequences of Mandatory Sentencing.* New York: Norton.

Friedman, Barry. 2020. *Disaggregating the Police Function.* New York: New York University.

Fryer, Roland. 2017. "An Empirical Analysis of Racial Differences in Police Use of Force." Cambridge, MA: Harvard University. Available at https://scholar.harvard.edu/files/fryer/files/empirical_analysis_tables_figures.pdf.

Fuller, Doris, Richard Lamb, Michael Biasotti, and John Snook. 2015. *Overlooked in the Undercounted: The Role of Mental Illness in Fatal Law Enforcement Encounters.* Arlington, VA: Treatment Advocacy Center.

Ganz, Jason, Charlotte Swasey, and Ethan Winter. 2020. "Voters Support Protests, Have Lost Trust in Police." San Francisco: Data for Progress. Available at https://www.dataforprogress.org/blog/2020/6/6/voters-support-reforms-have-lost-trust-in-police.

Gelb, Michael. 2020. "Public Confidence in Police at Record Low." *The Crime Report*, August 12. Available at https://thecrimereport.org/2020/08/12/public-confidence-in-police-at-record-low-gallup.

Gest, Ted. 2020. "Policing Experts Say Reform Possible without 'Defunding.'" *The Crime Report*, November 16. Available at https://thecrimereport.org/2020/11/16/policing-experts-say-reform-possible-without-defunding.

Gibbs, Jack P. 1975. *Crime, Punishment, and Deterrence.* New York: Elsevier.

Gill, Charlotte, David L. Weisburd, Cody W. Telep, Zoe Vitter, and Trevor Bennett. 2014. "Community-Oriented Policing to Reduce Crime, Disorder and Fear and Increase Satisfaction and Legitimacy among Citizens: A Systematic Review." *Journal of Experimental Criminology* 10:399-428.

Gillooly, Jessica. 2020. "How 911 Callers and Call-Takers Impact Police Encounters within the Public: The Case of the Henry Louis Gates, Jr. Arrest." *Criminology and Public Policy* 19:787-803.

Glock, Judge, and Devon Kurtz. 2020. *Reforming America's Police Unions to Ensure Justice.* Austin, TX: Cicero Institute.

Goh, Li S. 2022. "Did De-Escalation Successfully Reduce Serious Use of Force in Camden County, New Jersey? A Synthetic Control Analysis of Force Outcomes." *Criminology and Public Policy* 20:207-41.

Goldstein, Herman. 2018. "On Problem-Oriented Policing: the Stockholm Lecture." *Crime Science* 7(13) (https://doi.org/10.1186/s40163-018-0087-3).

Gomes, Hugo S., Ângela Maia, and David P. Farrington. 2018. "Measuring Offending: Self-Reports, Official Records, Systematic Observation and Experimentation." *Crime Psychology Review* 4:26-44.

Gomes, Hugo S., David P. Farrington, Ângela Maia, and Marvin D. Krohn. 2019. "Measurement Bias in Self-Reports of Offending: A Systematic Review of Experiments." *Journal of Experimental Criminology* 15:313-39.

Gottfredson, Denise C., Scott Crosse, Zhiqun Tang, Erin L. Bauer, Michele A. Harmon, Carol A. Hagen, and Angela D. Greene. 2020. "Effects of School Resource Officers on School Crime and Responses to School Crime." *Criminology and Public Policy* 19:905-40.

Gould, Mark. 1993. "Legitimation and Justification: The Logic of Moral and Contractual Solidarity in Weber and Durkheim." *Current Perspectives in Social Theory* 13:205-25.

Graham, David A. 2021. "Why Do Police Keep Shooting Into Moving Cars?" *The Atlantic*, May 21. Available at https://www.theatlantic.com/ideas/archive/2021/05/andrew-brown-police-shootings-moving-vehicles/618938.

Graham, David A. 2022. "The Stumbling Block to One of the Most Promising Police Reforms." *The Atlantic*, February 22. Available at https://www.theatlantic.com/ideas/archive/2022/02/mental-health-crisis-police-intervention/622842.

Gramlich, John. 2020a. *Four-in-Ten U.S. Drug Arrests in 2018 Were for Marijuana Offenses—Mostly Possession.* Washington, DC: Pew Research Center.

Gramlich, John. 2020b. *What the Data Says (and Doesn't Say) about Crime in the United States.* Washington, DC: Pew Research Center.

Gramlich, John. 2021. *What We Know about the Increase in U.S. Murders in 2020.* Washington, DC: Pew Research Center.

Gray, Sharon. 2007. *Community Safety Workers: An Exploratory Study of Some Emerging Crime Prevention Occupations.* Montreal: International Centre for the Prevention of Crime.

Griffin, Patricia A., Kirk Heilburn, Edward Mulvey, David DeMatteo, and Carol Schubert. 2015. *Promoting Community Alternatives for Individuals with Serious Mental Illness.* New York: Oxford University Press.

Gutierrez, David. 2021. *Why Police Training Must be Reformed.* Cambridge, MA: Harvard Kennedy School Institute of Politics.

Harcourt, Bernard E. 2001. *Illusion of Order: The False Promise of Broken Windows Policing.* Cambridge, MA: Harvard University Press.

Harcourt, Bernard E., and Jens Ludwig. 2006. "Broken Windows: New Evidence from New York City and a Five-City Social Experiment." *University of Chicago Law Review* 73:271-320.

Harrell, Erika, and Elizabeth Davis. 2020. *Contacts Between Police and the Public, 2018—Statistical Tables.* Washington, DC: Bureau of Justice Statistics. Available at https://bjs.ojp.gov/library/publications/contacts-between-police-and-public-2018-statistical-tables.

Harris, David. 2020. *Racial Profiling: Past, Present, and Future?* Washington, DC: American Bar Association.

Harrison, Robert. 2021. *Stop, Start, or Continue? A National Survey of the Police About Traffic Stops.* Santa Monica, CA: RAND.

Hatten, David, and Eric Piza. 2022. "When Crime Moves, Where Does It Go? Analyzing the Spatial Correlates of Robbery Incidents Displaced by a Place-based Policing Intervention." *Journal of Research in Crime and Delinquency* 59:128-62.

Hayes, Tara O'Neill. 2020. *The Economic Costs of the U.S. Criminal Justice System.* Washington, DC: American Action Forum.

Hayes, Tara O'Neill, and Margaret Barnhorst. 2020. *Incarceration and Poverty in the United States.* Washington, DC: American Action Forum.

Heaton, Paul, Sandra Mayson, and Megan Stevenson. 2017. "The Downstream Consequences of Misdemeanor Pretrial Detention." *Stanford Law Review* 69:711-94.

Heilbroner, David. 1990. *Rough Justice: Days and Nights of a Young D.A.* New York: Pantheon.

Heinze, Justin E., Allison Krusky-Morey, Kevin J. Vagi, Thomas M. Reischl, Susan Franzen, Natalie K. Pruett, Rebecca M. Cunningham, and Marc A. Zimmerman. 2018. "Busy Streets Theory: The Effects of Community-Engaged Greening on Violence." *American Journal of Community Psychology* 62:101-9.

Herscowitz, Eva. 2021. "The Rocky Road to a More Robust 911 System." *The Crime Report,* September 20. Available at https://thecrimereport.org/2021/09/20/the-rocky-road-to-a-more-robust-911-system.

Hinkle, Joshua, David Weisburd, Cody Telep, and Kevin Peterson. 2020. "Problem Oriented Policing for Reducing Crime and Disorder: An Updated Systematic Review and Meta-Analysis." *Campbell Systematic Reviews* 16:1-86.

Hinton Elizabeth. 2015. "'A War within Our Own Boundaries': Lyndon Johnson's Great Society and the Rise of the Carceral State." *The Journal of American History* 102:100-112.

Hinton, Elizabeth. 2021. *America on Fire: The Untold History of Police Violence and Black Rebellion Since the 1960s.* London: Liveright.

Home Office. 2011. *A New Approach to Fighting Crime.* London: Home Office.

Horton, Jake. 2021. "How U.S. Police Training Compares with the Rest of the World." *BBC,* May 18. Available at https://www.bbc.com/news/world-us-canada-56834733.

Howard, Philip K. 1994. *The Death of Common Sense: How Law Is Suffocating America.* New York: Random House.

Hughes, Michelle, and Whitney Tucker. 2018. "Poverty as an Adverse Childhood Experience." *NCMJ* 79:124-26.

Human Rights Watch. 2020. "A Roadmap for Re-imagining Public Safety in the United States." New York: Human Rights Watch. Available at https://www.hrw.org/news/2020/08/12/roadmap-re-imagining-public-safety-united-states.

Hvistendahl, Mara. 2016. "Can 'Predictive Policing' Prevent Crime before It Happens?" *Science*, September 26. Available at https://www.science.org/content/article/can-predictive-policing-prevent-crime-it-happens.

Irwin, Amos. 2020. *The Community Responder Model.* Washington, DC: Center for American Progress.

Ivković, Sanja K., Maki Haberfeld, and Robert Peacock. 2018. "Decoding the Code of Silence." *Criminal Justice Policy Review* 29:172-89.

Jackman, Tom. 2021. "For a Second Year, Most U.S. Police Departments Decline to Share Information on Their Use of Force." *Washington Post*, June 9. Available at https://www.washingtonpost.com/nation/2021/06/09/police-use-of-force-data.

Jenkins, Austin. 2021. "With 12 New Laws, Washington State Joins Movement to Overhaul Policing." *National Public Radio*, May 18. Available at https://www.npr.org/2021/05/18/997974519/a-dozen-police-reform-bills-signed-into-law-in-washington-state.

Jennings, Wesley G., and Alex R. Piquero. 2012. "Parent Training and the Prevention of Crime." Pp. 89-101 in *The Oxford Handbook of Crime Prevention*, edited by Brandon C. Welsh and David P. Farrington. Oxford: Oxford University Press.

Jones, J. Daniel. 2020. "The Potential Impacts of Pandemic Policing on Police Legitimacy: Planning Past the COVID-19 Crisis." *Policing* 14:579-86.

Joseph, Janice. 2022. "Invisible Police Lethal Violence against Black Women in the United States: An Intersectional Approach." *Peace Review* 34:177-86.

Junger-Tas, Josine, and Ineke H. Marshall. 199. "The Self-Report Methodology in Crime Research." *Crime and Justice* 25:291-367.

Karma, Roge. 2020a. "4 Ideas to Replace Traditional Police Officers." *Vox*, June 24. Available at https://www.vox.com/2020/6/24/21296881/unbundle-defund-the-police-george-floyd-rayshard-brooks-violence-european-policing.

Karma, Roge. 2020b. "Want to Fix Policing? Start with a Better 911 System." *Vox*, August 10. Available at https://www.vox.com/2020/8/10/21340912/police-violence-911-emergency-call-tamir-rice-cahoots.

Karma, Roge. 2020c. "We Train Police to Be Warriors—and Then Send Them Out to Be Social Workers: The Fatal Mismatch at the Heart of American Policing." *Vox*, July 31. Available at https://www.vox.com/2020/7/31/21334190/what-police-do-defund-abolish-police-reform-training.

Keizer, Kees, Siegwart Lindenberg, and Linda Steg. 2008. *The Spreading of Disorder.* Washington, DC: Science Magazine.

Kelly, William R. 2015. *Criminal Justice at the Crossroads: Transforming Crime and Punishment.* New York: Columbia University Press.

Kelly, William R. 2016. *The Future of Crime and Punishment: Smart Policies for Reducing Crime and Saving Money.* Lanham, MD: Rowman & Littlefield.

Kelly, William R. 2021. *The Crisis in the American Criminal Courts*. Lanham, MD: Rowman & Littlefield.

Kelly, William R., and Robert Pitman. 2018. *Confronting Underground Justice: Reinventing Plea Bargaining for Effective Criminal Justice Reform*. Lanham, MD: Rowman & Littlefield.

Kelly, William R, Robert Pitman, and William Streusand. 2017. *From Retribution to Public Safety: Disruptive Innovation of American Criminal Justice*. Lanham, MD: Rowman & Littlefield.

Kessler, Judd, Sarah Tahamont, Alexander Gelber, and Adam Isen. 2021. *The Effects of Youth Employment on Crime: Evidence from New York City Lotteries*. Cambridge, MA: National Bureau of Economic Research.

Khazan, Olga. 2021. "American Police Are Inadequately Trained." *The Atlantic*, April 22. Available at https://www.theatlantic.com/politics/archive/2021/04/daunte-wright-and-crisis-american-police-training/618649.

Kindy, Kimberly. 2021. "Dozens of States Have Tried to End Qualified Immunity. Police Officers and Unions Helped Beat Nearly Every Bill." *Washington Post*, October 7. Available at https://www.washingtonpost.com/politics/qualified-immunity-police-lobbying-state-legislatures/2021/10/06/60e546bc-0cdf-11ec-aea1-42a8138f132a_story.html.

Kindy, Kimberly, Julie Tate, Jennifer Jenkins, and Ted Mellnik. 2021. "Police Shootings of Children Spark New Outcry, Calls for Training to Deal with Adolescents in Crisis." *Washington Post*, May 12. Available at https://www.washingtonpost.com/nation/2021/05/12/children-police-shootings.

Kochel, Tammy Rinehart, and Jacinta M. Gau. 2021. "Examining Police Presence, Tactics, and Engagement as Facilitators of Informal Social Control in High-Crime Areas." *Justice Quarterly* 38:301-21.

Kochel, Tammy Rinehart, and David Weisburd. 2019. "The Impact of Hot Spots Policing on Collective Efficacy: Findings from a Randomized Field Trial." *Justice Quarterly* 36:900-928.

Koper, Christopher, Cynthia Lum, Xiaoyun Wu, and Noah Fritz. 2020. "Proactive Policing in the United States: A National Survey." *Policing* 43:861-76.

Kramer, Rory, and Brianna Remster. 2018. "Stop, Frisk, and Assault? Racial Disparities in Police Use of Force During Investigatory Stops." *Law and Society Review* 52:960-93.

Kraska, Peter B. 2007. "Militarization and Policing—Its Relevance to 21st Century Police." *Policing* 1:501-13.

Kroman, David. 2021. "King County Crisis Services Ask for Clarity on Police Intervention." *Crosscut*, September 30. Available at https://crosscut.com/news/2021/09/king-county-crisis-services-ask-clarity-police-intervention.

Krug, Etienne G., Linda L. Dahlberg, James A. Mercy, Anthony B. Zwi, and Rafael Lozano. 2002. *World Report on Violence and Health*. Geneva: World Health Organization.

Kupchik, Aaron. 2010. *Homeroom Security: School Discipline in an Age of Fear*. New York: New York University Press.

Lake Research Partners. 2017. *Community Reinvestment Study for Urban Institute and Public Welfare Foundation*. Washington, DC: Lake Research Partners.

Langer, Gary. 2021. "Six in 10 Favor Doing More to Hold Police Accountable." *ABC News*, April 23. Available at https://abcnews.go.com/Politics/10-favor-hold-police-accountable-poll/story?id=77218405.

Lantigua-Williams, Juleyka. 2016. "How Much Can Better Training Do to Improve Policing?" *The Atlantic*, July 13. Available at https://www.theatlantic.com/politics/archive/2016/07/police-training/490556.

Latessa, Edward J., Shelley J. Listwan, and Deborah Koetzle. 2014. *What Works (and Doesn't) in Reducing Recidivism*. Waltham, MA: Anderson Publishing.

Lattimore, Pamela. 2022. "Reflections on Criminal Justice Reform: Challenges and Opportunities." *American Journal of Criminal Justice* 47:1071-98.

Lau, Tim. 2020. *Predictive Policing Explained*. New York: Brennan Center for Justice.

Law Enforcement Assisted Diversion (LEAD). 2022a. "Core Principles." Seattle, WA: Law Enforcement Assisted Diversion. Available at https://www.leadbureau.org/resources.

Law Enforcement Assisted Diversion (LEAD). 2022b. "The LEAD National Support Bureau." Seattle, WA: Law Enforcement Assisted Diversion. Available at https://www.leadbureau.org/home.

Law Enforcement Assisted Diversion (LEAD). 2022c. "What Is LEAD?" Seattle, WA: Law Enforcement Assisted Diversion. Available at https://www.leadbureau.org/about-lead.

Lee, Nathaniel. 2021. "America Has Spent Over a Trillion Dollars Fighting the War on Drugs. 50 Years Later, Drug Use in the U.S. Is Climbing Again." *CNBC*, June 17. Available at https://www.cnbc.com/2021/06/17/the-us-has-spent-over-a-trillion-dollars-fighting-war-on-drugs.html.

Lee, Stephanie, Steve Aos, Elizabeth Drake, Annie Pennucci, Marna Miller, and Laurie Anderson. 2012. *Return on Investment: Evidence-Based Options to Improve State-wide Outcomes*. Olympia: Washington State Institute for Public Policy.

Lenehan, Rose. 2017. *What "Stop-and-Frisk" Really Means: Discrimination and Use of Force*. Northampton, MA: Prison Policy Initiative.

Lentz, Susan A., and Robert H. Chaires. 2007. "The Invention of Peel's Principles: A Study of Policing 'Textbook' History." *Journal of Criminal Justice* 35:69-79.

Lepore, Jill. 2020. "The Invention of the Police: Why Did American Policing Get So Big, So Fast? The Answer, Mainly, Is Slavery." *The New Yorker*, July 13. Available at https://www.newyorker.com/magazine/2020/07/20/the-invention-of-the-police.

Levchak, Philip J. 2017. "Do Precinct Characteristics Influence Stop-and-Frisk in New York City? A Multi-Level Analysis of Post-Stop Outcomes." *Justice Quarterly* 34:377-406.

Levchak, Philip J. 2021. "Stop-and-Frisk in New York City: Estimating Racial Disparities in Post-Stop Outcomes." *Journal of Criminal Justice* 73:101784.

Levine, Harry, Loren Siegal, and Gabriel Sayegh. 2013. *One Million Police Hours*. New York: Drug Policy Alliance. Available at https://drugpolicy.org/sites/default/files/One_Million_Police_Hours.pdf.

Li, Weihua and Illica Mahajan. 2021. "Police Say Demoralized Officers Are Quitting in Droves, Labor Data Says No." New York: The Marshall Project. Available at https://www.themarshallproject.org/2021/09/01/police-say-demoralized-officers-are-quitting-in-droves-labor-data-says-no.

Linder, Courtney. 2020. "Why Hundreds of Mathematicians Are Boycotting Predictive Policing." *Popular Mechanics*, July 20. Available at https://www.popularmechanics.com/science/math/a32957375/mathematicians-boycott-predictive-policing.

Lipsey, Mark W., and Francis T. Cullen. 2007. "The Effectiveness of Correctional Rehabilitation: A Review of Systematic Reviews." *Annual Review of Law and Social Science* 3:297-320.

Loeffler, Charles E., and Daniel S. Nagin. 2022. "The Impact of Incarceration on Recidivism." *Annual Review of Criminology* 5:15.1-.20.

Lopez, German. 2020. "Police Officers Are Prosecuted for Murder in Less than 2 Percent of Fatal Shootings." *Vox*, December 14. Available at https://www.vox.com/21497089/derek-chauvin-george-floyd-trial-police-prosecutions-black-lives-matter.

Lösel, Friedrich, and Doris Bender. 2012. "Child Social Skills Training in the Prevention of Antisocial Development and Crime." Pp. 102-29 in *The Oxford Handbook of Crime Prevention*, edited by Brandon C. Welsh and David P. Farrington. New York: Oxford University Press.

Lum, Cynthia, and Christopher S. Koper. 2017. *Evidence-Based Policing: Translating Research into Practice*. New York: Oxford University Press.

Lum, Cynthia, Christopher S. Koper, Charlotte Gill, Julie Hibdon, Cody Telep, and Laurie Robinson. 2016. *An Evidence-Assessment of the Recommendations of the President's Task Force on 21st Century Policing—Implementation and Research Priorities*. Fairfax, VA: George Mason University.

Lum, Cynthia, Christopher S. Koper, and Xiaoyun Wu. 2022. "Can We Really Defund the Police? A Nine-Agency Study of Police Response to Calls for Service." *Police Quarterly* 25:255-80.

Lum, Cynthia, Christopher S. Koper, Xiaoyun Wu, William Johnson, and Megan Stoltz. 2020. "Examining the Empirical Realities of Proactive Policing through Systematic Observations and Computer-Aided Dispatch Data." *Police Quarterly* 23:283-310.

Lum, Cynthia, and Daniel S. Nagin. 2017. "Reinventing American Policing." *Crime and Justice* 46:339-93.

Lyon, Ed. 2019. "Illinois Calculates the High Costs of Recidivism." *Prison Legal News*, February 5. Available at https://www.prisonlegalnews.org/news/2019/feb/5/illinois-calculates-high-costs-recidivism.

Mack, Marvin. 2021. "How America's State Police Got Military Weapons." *Insider*, April 28. Available at https://www.businessinsider.com/how-did-local-police-acquire-surplus-military-weapons-2020-8.

MacKenzie, Doris L. 2006. *What Works in Corrections? Reducing the Criminal Activities of Offenders and Delinquents*. Cambridge: Cambridge Press.

Madeo, M. 2018. *Half of Americans Have Family Members Who Have Been Incarcerated*. Montgomery, AL: Equal Justice Initiative. Available at https://eji.org/news/half-of-americans-have-family-members-who-have-been-incarcerated.

Manning, Peter K. 2005. "The Study of Policing." *Police Quarterly* 8:23-43.

Marchment, Zoe, and Paul Gill. 2021. "Systematic Review and Meta-Analysis of Risk Terrain Modeling (RTM) as a Spatial Forecasting Method." *Crime Science* 10(12) (https://doi.org/10.1186/s40163-021-00149-6).

Martin, Greg. 2019. "Researchers Find Little Evidence for 'Broken Windows Theory,' Say Neighborhood Disorder Doesn't Cause Crime." *PHYS*, May 16. Available at https://phys.org/news/2019-05-evidence-broken-windows-theory-neighborhood.html.

Masterson, Matt. 2017. "Chicago School-Based Officers Need More Training, Oversight." *WTTW News*, February 8. Available at https://news.wttw.com/2017/02/08/report-chicago-school-based-officers-need-more-training-oversight.

Mastrofski, Stephen D. 2019. "Community Policing: A Skeptical View." Pp. 45-70 in *Police Innovation: Contrasting Perspectives*, 2nd ed., edited by David L. Weisburd and Anthony A. Braga. New York: Cambridge University Press.

Mazumder, Shom. 2020. "What Black People Really Think about the Police." *The New Republic*, December 15. Available at https://newrepublic.com/article/160532/what-black-people-think-police.

Mbekeani-Wiley, Michelle. 2017. *Handcuffs in Hallways: The State of Policing in Chicago Public Schools*. Chicago: Sargent Shriver National Center on Poverty Law.

McCollister, Kathryn E., Michael T. French, and Hai Fang. 2010. "The Cost of Crime to Society: New Crime-Specific Estimates for Policy and Program Evaluation." *Drug Alcohol Dependence* 108-98-109.

McCorkel, Jill. 2020. "Police Unions Are One of the Biggest Obstacles to Transforming Policing." *The Conversation*, June 12. Available at https://theconversation.com/police-unions-are-one-of-the-biggest-obstacles-to-transforming-policing-140227.

McLaughlin, Michael, Carrie Pettus-Davis, Derek Brown, Chris Veeh, and Tanya Renn. 2016. *The Economic Burden of Incarceration in the U.S.* St. Louis, MO: Washington University.

McNamara, Joseph. 2006. "Fifty Shots." *Wall Street Journal*, November 29. Available at https://www.wsj.com/articles/SB116476867027935258.

Meares, Tracey L. 2021. "Clashing Narratives of Policing? The Quest for Lawful versus Effective Policing and the Possibility of Abolition as a Solution." Pp. 25-38 in *The Ethics of Policing: New Perspectives on Law Enforcement*, edited by Ben Jones and Eduardo Mendieta. New York: New York University Press.

Mears, Daniel P. 2001. "The Immigration-Crime Nexus: Toward an Analytic Framework for Assessing and Guiding Theory, Research, and Policy." *Sociological Perspectives* 44:1-19.

Mears, Daniel P. 2004. "Mental Health Needs and Services in the Criminal Justice System." *Houston Journal of Health Law and Policy* 4:255-84.

Mears, Daniel P. 2010. *American Criminal Justice Policy: An Evaluation Approach to Increasing Accountability and Effectiveness*. New York: Cambridge University Press.

Mears, Daniel P. 2012. "The Front End of the Juvenile Court: Intake and Informal vs. Formal Processing." Pp. 573-605 in *The Oxford Handbook of Juvenile Crime and Juvenile Justice*, edited by Barry C. Feld and Donna M. Bishop. New York: Oxford University Press.

Mears, Daniel P. 2017. *Out-of-Control Criminal Justice: The Systems Improvement Solution for More Safety, Justice, Accountability, and Efficiency.* New York: Cambridge University Press.

Mears, Daniel P. 2019. "Creating Systems That Can Improve Safety and Justice (and Why Piecemeal Change Won't Work)." *Justice Evaluation Journal* 2:1-17.

Mears, Daniel P. 2022. "Bridging the Research-Policy Divide to Advance Science and Policy: The 2022 Bruce Smith, Sr. Award Address to the Academy of Criminal Justice Sciences." *Justice Evaluation Journal* (https://doi.org/10.1080/24751979.2022.2062255).

Mears, Daniel P., and Sarah Bacon. 2009. "Improving Criminal Justice through Better Decisionmaking: Lessons from the Medical System." *Journal of Criminal Justice* 37:142-54.

Mears, Daniel P., and Joshua C. Cochran. 2015. *Prisoner Reentry in the Era of Mass Incarceration.* Thousand Oaks, CA: Sage.

Mears, Daniel P., Joshua C. Cochran, William D. Bales, and Avinash S. Bhati. 2016. "Recidivism and Time Served in Prison." *Journal of Criminal Law and Criminology* 106:83-124.

Mears, Daniel P., Joshua C. Cochran, and Francis T. Cullen. 2015. "Incarceration Heterogeneity and Its Implications for Assessing the Effectiveness of Imprisonment on Recidivism." *Criminal Justice Policy Review* 26:691-712.

Mears, Daniel P., Joshua C. Cochran, and Andrea M. Lindsey. 2016. "Offending and Racial and Ethnic Disparities in Criminal Justice: A Conceptual Framework for Guiding Theory and Research and Informing Policy." *Journal of Contemporary Criminal Justice* 32:78-103.

Mears, Daniel P., Miltonette O. Craig, Eric A. Stewart, and Patricia Y. Warren. 2017. "Thinking Fast, Not Slow: How Cognitive Biases May Contribute to Racial Disparities in the Use of Force in Police-Citizen Encounters." *Journal of Criminal Justice* 53:12-24.

Mears, Daniel P., Joshua J. Kuch, Andrea M. Lindsey, Sonja E. Siennick, George B. Pesta, Mark A. Greenwald, and Thomas G. Blomberg. 2016. "Juvenile Court and Contemporary Diversion: Helpful, Harmful, or Both?" *Criminology and Public Policy* 15:953-81.

Mears, Daniel P., and Andrea M. Lindsey. 2016. "Speeding in America: A Critique of, and Alternatives to, Officer-Initiated Enforcement." *Criminal Justice Review* 41:55-74.

Mears, Daniel P., Andrea N. Montes, Nicole L. Collier, Sonja E. Siennick, George B. Pesta, Samantha J. Ladwig, and Thomas G. Blomberg. 2019. "The Benefits, Risks, and Challenges of Get-Tough and Support-Oriented Approaches to Improving School Safety." *Criminal Justice Policy Review* 30:1342-67.

Mears, Daniel P., Melissa Moon, and Angela J. Thielo. 2017. "Columbine Revisited: Myths and Realities about the Bullying-School Shootings Connection." *Victims and Offenders* 12:939-55.

Meijer, Albert, and Martijn Wessels. 2019. "Predictive Policing: Review of Benefits and Drawbacks." *International Journal of Public Administration* 42:1031-39.

Merrick, Melissa, Derek Ford, Katie Ports, and Angie Guinn. 2018. "Prevalence of Adverse Childhood Experiences from the 2011–2015 Behavioral Risk Factor Surveillance System in 23 States." *JAMA Pediatrics* 172:1038-44.

Merton, Robert. 1957. *Social Theory and Social Structure*. Glencoe, IL: The Free Press.

Messner, Steven F., and Richard Rosenfeld. 2009. "Institutional Anomie Theory: A Macro-Sociological Explanation of Crime." Pp. 209-24 in *Handbook on Crime and Deviance*, edited by Marvin D. Krohn, Alan J. Lizotte, and Gina P. Hall. New York: Springer.

Miller, Ted R., Mark A. Cohen, David I. Swedler, Bina Ali, and Delia V. Hendrie. 2021. "Incidence and Costs of Personal and Property Crimes in the USA, 2017." *Journal of Benefit-Cost Analysis* 12:24-54.

Montes, Andrea N., Daniel P. Mears, Nicole L. Collier, George B. Pesta, Sonja E. Siennick, and Samantha J. Brown. 2021. "Blurred and Confused: The Paradox of Police in Schools." *Policing: A Journal of Policy and Practice* 15:1546-64.

Morgan, Rachel, and Jennifer Truman. 2020. *Criminal Victimization, 2019*. Washington, DC: Bureau of Justice Statistics.

Morin, Rich, Kim Parker, Renee Stepler, and Andrew Mercer. 2017. *Behind the Badge: Amid Protests and Calls for Reform, How Police View Their Jobs, Key Issues and Recent Fatal Encounters between Blacks and Police*. Washington, DC: Pew Research Center.

Moskos, Peter. 2008. *Cop in the Hood: My Year Policing Baltimore's Eastern District*. Princeton, NJ: Princeton University Press.

Moyer, Ruth, John M. Macdonald, Greg Ridgeway, and Charles C. Branas. 2019. "Effect of Remediating Blighted Vacant Land on Shootings: A Citywide Cluster Randomized Trial." *American Journal of Public Health* 109:140-44.

Mrazek, Patricia J., and Robert J. Haggerty, eds. 1994. *Reducing Risks for Mental Disorders: Frontiers for Preventive Intervention Research*. Washington, DC: National Academy Press.

Muhammad, Khalil G. 2019. *The Condemnation of Blackness: Race, Crime, and the Making of Modern Urban America*. Boston: Harvard University Press.

Nagin, Daniel S., Alex R. Piquero, Elizabeth S. Scott, and Laurence Steinberg. 2006. "Public Preferences for Rehabilitation versus Incarceration of Juvenile Offenders: Evidence from a Contingent Valuation Survey." *Criminology and Public Policy* 5:627-51.

Nation's Health, The. 2010. "Report Finds Most U.S. Inmates Suffer from Substance Abuse or Addiction." *The Nation's Health* 40(3):E11.

National Emergency Number Association. 2021. "9-1-1 Statistics." Alexandria, VA: NENA 9-1-1 Association. Available at https://www.nena.org/page/911Statistics.

National Registry of Exonerations. 2022. *The National Registry of Exonerations.* East Lansing: Michigan State University. Accessed December 14, 2022. Available at https://www.law.umich.edu/special/exoneration/Pages/about.aspx.

National Research Council. 2004. *Fairness and Effectiveness in Policing: The Evidence.* Washington, DC: National Academies Press.

Neusteter, Rebecca. 2021. "Leading the Field: Rebecca Neusteter." August 30. San Francisco: Code for America. Available at https://codeforamerica.org/news/leading-the-field-rebecca-neusteter.

Neusteter, Rebecca, Maris Mapolski, Mawia Khogali, and Megan O'Toole. 2019. *The 911 Call Processing System: A Review of the Literature as it Relates to Policing.* New York: Vera Institute.

Neusteter, Rebecca, Megan O'Toole, Mawia Khogali, Abdul Rad, Frankie Wunschel, Sarah Schaffidi, Marilyn Sinkewicz, Maris Mapolski, Paul DeGrandis, Daniel Bodah, and Henessy Pineda. 2020. *Understanding Police Enforcement: A Multicity 911 Analysis.* New York: Vera Institute.

Neusteter, Rebecca, Ram Subramanian, Jennifer Trone, Mawia Khogali, and Cindy Reed. 2019. *Gatekeepers: The Role of Police in Ending Mass Incarceration.* New York: Vera Institute.

New Zealand Police. 2017. *Prevention First National Operating Manual.* Wellington: New Zealand Police. Available at https://www.police.govt.nz/sites/default/files/publications/prevention-first-2017.pdf.

Nix, Justin, Bradley A. Campbell, Edward H. Byers, and Geoffrey P. Alpert. 2017. "A Bird's Eye View of Civilians Killed by Police in 2015." *Criminology and Public Policy* 16:309-40.

Noppe, Jannie, Antoinette Verhage, and Anjuloi Van Damme. 2017. "Police Legitimacy: An Introduction." *Policing* 40:474-79.

NORC. 2020. *Widespread Desire for Policing and Criminal Justice Reform.* Chicago: University of Chicago, NORC.

O'Brien, Daniel T., Chelsea Farrell, and Brandon C. Welsh. 2019. "Looking through Broken Windows: The Impact of Neighborhood Disorder on Aggression and Fear of Crime Is an Artifact of Research Design." *Annual Review of Criminology* 2:53-71.

Ofer, Udi. 2016. "Getting It Right: Building Effective Civilian Review Boards to Oversee Police." *Seton Hall Law Review* 46:1033-62.

Office of Civil Rights Evaluation. 2018. *Police Use of Force: An Examination of Modern Policing Practices.* Washington, DC: The United States Commission on Civil Rights.

Office of Community Oriented Policing Services. 2015. *The President's Task Force on 21st Century Policing Implementation Guide: Moving from Recommendations to Action.* Washington, DC: Office of Community Oriented Policing Services.

Office of the Inspector General for the NYPD (OIG-NYPD). 2016. *An Analysis of Quality-of-Life Summonses, Quality-of-Life Misdemeanor Arrests, and Felony Crime in New York City, 2010–2015.* New York: Office of the Inspector General for the NYPD.

Office of Juvenile Justice and Delinquency Prevention. 2015. *Protective Factors Against Delinquency*. Washington, DC: Office of Juvenile Justice and Delinquency Prevention.

Office of Juvenile Justice and Delinquency Prevention. 2020. *Arrests by Offense, Age, and Gender*. Washington, DC: Office of Juvenile Justice and Delinquency Prevention.

Ohmer, Mary L. 2010. "How Theory and Research Inform Citizen Participation in Poor Communities: The Ecological Perspective and Theories on Self- and Collective Efficacy and Sense of Community." *Journal of Human Behavior in the Social Environment* 20:1-19.

Ohmer, Mary L. 2016. "Strategies for Preventing Youth Violence: Facilitating Collective Efficacy Among Youth and Adults." *Journal for the Society for Social Work and Research* 7:681-705.

Open Society Foundations. 2002. "Majority of Americans Think U.S. Criminal Justice System Is Broken, Ineffective; See Need for Change." February 12. New York: Open Society Foundations. Available at https://www.opensocietyfoundations.org/newsroom/majority-americans-think-us-criminal-justice-system-broken-ineffective-see-need.

Oudekerk, Barbara, and Danielle Kaeble. 2021. *Probation and Parole in the United States, 2019*. Washington, DC: Bureau of Justice Statistics.

Page, Susan, and Ella Lee. 2021. "Exclusive: In Poll, Only 1 in 5 Say Police Treat People Equally Even as Worries about Crime Surge." *USA Today*, July 8. Available at https://www.usatoday.com/story/news/politics/2021/07/08/poll-worries-crime-most-say-police-dont-treat-all-equally/7880911002.

Parker, Kim, and Kiley Hurst. 2021. *Growing Share of Americans Say They Want More Spending on Police in their Area*. Washington, DC: Pew Research Center.

Parsons, Jim, and Frankie Wunschel. 2020. "Changing Police Practices Means Changing 911." September 29. New York: Vera Institute. Available at https://www.vera.org/news/changing-police-practices-means-changing-911.

Pearl, Betsy. 2018. *Ending the War on Drugs: By the Numbers*. Washington, DC: Center for American Progress.

Pearl, Betsy. 2020. *Beyond Policing: Investing in Offices of Neighborhood Safety*. Washington, DC: Center for American Progress.

Perry, Walter L., Brian McInnis, Carter C. Price, Susan Smith, and John S. Hollywood. 2013. *Predictive Policing*. Santa Monica, CA: RAND.

Peters, Mark, and Philip Eure. 2016. *An Analysis of Quality-of-Life-Summonses, Quality-of-Life Misdemeanor Arrests, and Felony Crime in New York City, 2010–2015*. New York: New York City Department of Investigation.

Peterson, Randy. 2018. *The Conservative Case for Policing Reforms*. Austin, TX: Texas Public Policy Foundation.

Pew Charitable Trusts. 2021. "New Research Suggests 911 Call Centers Lack Resources to Handle Behavioral Health Crises." October 26. Philadelphia, PA: Pew Charitable Trusts. Available at https://www.pewtrusts.org/en/research-and-analysis/issue-briefs/2021/10/new-research-suggests-911-call-centers-lack-resources-to-handle-behavioral-health-crises.

Pew Research Center. 2020. *Majority of Public Favors Giving Civilians the Power to Sue Police Officers for Misconduct.* Washington, DC: Pew Research Center.

Peyton, Kyle, Michael Sierra-Arévalo, and David G. Rand. 2019. "A Field Experiment on Community Policing and Police Legitimacy." *PNAS*, 116:19894-98.

Piaget, Jean. 1932. *The Moral Judgment of the Child.* Glencoe, IL: The Free Press.

Pierson, Emma, Camelia Simoiu, Jan Overgoor, Sam Corbett-Davies, Daniel Jenson, Amy Shoemaker, Vignesh Ramachandran, Phoebe Barghouty, Cheryl Philips, Ravi Shroff, and Sharad Goel. 2020. "A Large-Scale Analysis of Racial Disparities in Police Stops across the United States." *Nature Human Behaviour* 4:736-45.

Piquero, Alex R., and Wesley G. Jennings. 2012. "Parent Training and the Prevention of Crime." Pp. 89-101 in *The Oxford Handbook of Crime Prevention*, edited by Brandon C. Welsh and David P. Farrington. New York: Oxford University Press.

Piven, Frances F., and Richard A. Cloward. 1993. *Regulating the Poor: The Functions of Public Welfare.* New York: Vintage.

Piza, Eric L., and Brandon C. Welsh, eds. 2022. *The Globalization of Evidence-Based Policing: Innovations in Bridging the Research-Practice Divide.* New York: Routledge.

Police Executive Research Forum. 2019. *The Workforce Crisis, and What Police Agencies Are Doing about It.* Washington, DC: Police Executive Research Forum.

Police Executive Research Forum. 2020. "PERF Daily Covid-19 Report." Washington, DC: Police Executive Research Forum. Available at https://www.policeforum.org/covidaugust3.

Police Executive Research Forum. 2021. "What Police Reform in America Really Needs to Look Like." Washington, DC: Police Executive Research Forum. Available at https://www.policeforum.org/trending22may21.

Police Foundation, The. 2022. *A New Mode of Protection: Redesigning Policing and Public Safety for the 21st Century.* London: The Police Foundation.

Policy Development and Research (PD&R) Edge. 2014. "Collaborative Community Efforts Help Create Safer, Stronger Neighborhoods." *PD&R Edge*, March 10. Available at https://www.huduser.gov/portal/pdredge/pdr_edge_featd_article_031014.html.

Pratt, Travis C., and Francis T. Cullen. 2005. "Assessing Macro-Level Predictors and Theories of Crime: A Meta-Analysis." *Crime and Justice* 32:373-450.

President's Task Force on 21st Century Policing. 2015. *Final Report of the President's Task Force on 21st Century Policing.* Washington, DC: Office of Community Oriented Policing Services.

Purnell, Spence. 2020. "Ending the War on Drugs Is Key to Long-Term Police Reform." *Reason*, June 17. Available at https://reason.org/commentary/ending-the-war-on-drugs-is-key-to-long-term-police-reform.

Rahr, Sue, and Stephen Rice. 2015. *From Warriors to Guardians: Recommitting American Police Culture to Democratic Ideals.* Washington, DC: National Institute of Justice.

Raine, Adrian. 2018. "The Biological Crime: Implications for Society and the Criminal Justice System." *Revista de Psiquatria do Rio Grande do Sul* 30:5-8.

Raine, Adrian, and Yaling Yang. 2006. "Neural Foundations to Moral Reasoning and Antisocial Behavior." *Social Cognitive and Affective Neuroscience* 1:203-13.

RAND. 2022. "Zero Tolerance and Aggressive Policing (And Why to Avoid It) in Depth." Santa Monica, CA: RAND. Available at https://www.rand.org/pubs/tools/TL261/better-policing-toolkit/all-strategies/zero-tolerance/in-depth.html.

Rawlings, Philip. 1994. "The Idea of Policing: A History." *Policing and Society* 5:129-49.

Rawls, John. 1999. *A Theory of Justice*. Rev. ed. Cambridge, MA: Harvard University Press.

Ray, Rashawn, and Clark Neily. 2021. *A Better Path Forward for Criminal Justice: Police Reform*. Washington, DC: The Brookings Institution.

Reisig, Michael D. 2010. "Community and Problem-Oriented Policing." *Crime and Justice* 39:1-53.

Richardson, Rashida, Jason Schultz, and Kate Crawford. 2019. "Dirty Data, Bad Predictions: How Civil Rights Violations Impact Police Data, Predictive Policing Systems, and Justice." *New York University Law Review* 94:192-228.

Riley, Emily. 2020. "What 'Defunding Police' Really Means to Americans." *The Crime Report*, October 2. Available at https://thecrimereport.org/2020/10/02/what-defunding-police-really-means.

Rodriguez, Isidoro. 2021. "Can We Lower Urban Violence without Police?" *The Crime Report*, February 26. Available at https://thecrimereport.org/2021/02/26/can-we-lower-urban-violence-without-police.

Roeder, Oliver, Lauren-Brooke Eisen, and Julia Bowling. 2015. *What Caused the Crime Decline?* New York: Brennan Center for Justice.

Romero, Anthony. 2020. "Reimagining the Role of Police." June 5. New York: American Civil Liberties Union. Available at https://www.aclu.org/news/criminal-law-reform/reimagining-the-role-of-police.

Rosenbaum, Dennis P. 2019. "The Limits of Hot Spots Policing." Pp. 314-46 in *Police Innovation: Contrasting Perspectives*, 2nd ed., edited by David L. Weisburd and Anthony A. Braga. New York: Cambridge University Press.

Rosenfeld, Richard. 2006. "Connecting the Dots: Crime Rates and Criminal Justice Evaluation Research." *Journal of Experimental Criminology* 2:309-19.

Rossi, Peter H., Mark W. Lipsey, and Howard E. Freeman. 2004. *Evaluation: A Systematic Approach*. 7th ed. Thousand Oaks, CA: Sage.

Rubin, Edward L., and Malcolm M. Feeley. 2022. "Criminal Justice through Management: From Police, Prosecutors, Courts, and Prisons to a Modern Administrative Agency." *Oregon Law Review* 100:261-355.

Rubin, Joel, and Ben Poston. 2020. "LAPD Responds to a Million 911 Calls a Year, but Relatively Few for Violent Crimes." *Washington Post*, July 5. Available at https://www.latimes.com/california/story/2020-07-05/lapd-911-calls-reimagining-police.

Russell-Brown, Katheryn. 2021. *The Color of Crime: Racial Hoaxes, White Crime, Media Messages, Police Violence, and Other Race-Based Harms*. 3rd ed. New York: New York University Press.

Ryan, Julia. 2011. *A Natural Connection: The Role of Public Safety in Community Development*. New York: Local Initiatives Support Coalition (LISC).

Saletan, William. 2021. "Americans Don't Want to Defund the Police. Here's What They Do Want." *Slate*, October 17. Available at https://slate.com/news-and-politics/2021/10/police-reform-polls-white-black-crime.html.

Sampson, Robert J. 2012. *Great American City: Chicago and the Enduring Neighborhood Effect*. Chicago: University of Chicago Press.

Sampson, Robert J., and Stephen W. Raudenbush. 2001. *Disorder in Urban Neighborhoods—Does It Lead to Crime?* Washington, DC: National Institute of Justice.

Sampson, Robert J., Stephen W. Raudenbush, and Felton Earls. 1997. "Neighborhoods and Violent Crime: A Multilevel Study of Collective Efficacy." *Science* 277:918-24.

Sampson, Robert J., and Patrick S. Sharkey. 2015. "Violence, Cognition, and Neighborhood Inequality in America." Pp. 320-39 in *Social Neuroscience: Brain, Mind, and Society*, edited by Russell K. Schutt, Larry J. Seidman, and Matcheri S. Keshavan. Cambridge, MA: Harvard University Press.

Samuels, Paul N. 2016. "Public Opinion Favors Criminal Justice and Drug Policy Reform, Making Now the Time to Act." Washington, DC: Legal Action Center. Available at https://www.lac.org/news/public-opinion-favors-criminal-justice-and-drug-policy-reform-making-now-the-time-to-act.

Sanchez, Ray, and Holly Yan. 2018. "Florida Gov. Rick Scott Signs Gun Bill." *CNN*, March 9. Available at https://www.cnn.com/2018/03/09/us/florida-gov-scott-gun-bill/index.html.

Santos, Rachel B. 2013. *Crime Analysis with Crime Mapping*. Thousand Oaks, CA: Sage.

Santos, Rachel B. 2014. "The Effectiveness of Crime Analysis for Crime Reduction: Cure or Diagnosis?" *Journal of Contemporary Criminal Justice* 30:147-68.

Santos, Rachel B. 2019. "Predictive Policing: Where's the Evidence?" Pp. 366-96 in *Police Innovation*, 2nd ed., edited by David Weisburd and Anthony A. Braga. New York: Cambridge University Press.

Santos, Rachel B. 2022. *Crime Analysis with Crime Mapping*. New York: Sage.

Scheiber, Noam, Farah Stockman, and David J. Goodman. 2020. "How Police Unions Became Such Powerful Opponents to Reform Efforts." *New York Times*, June 6. Available at https://www.nytimes.com/2020/06/06/us/police-unions-minneapolis-kroll.html.

Schuck, Amie M., and Cara E. Rabe-Hemp. 2022. "Breaking the Code of Silence: The Importance of Control Systems and Empathy toward Outgroups." *Criminal Justice and Behavior* (https://doi.org/10.1177/00938548221105219).

Schulte, Gabriela. 2021. "Plurality Says Relations Between Police, People of Color Have Gotten Worse in Last Year." *The Hill*, May 25. Available at https://thehill.com/hilltv/what-americas-thinking/555381-poll-plurality-of-voters-say-relations-between-police-and.

Schweig, Sarah. 2014. "Healthy Communities May Make Safe Communities: Public Health Approaches to Violence Prevention." *NIJ Journal* 273:52-59.

Seattle Police Monitor. 2016. *The Seattle Police Monitor's Sixth Systemic Assessment Regarding Supervision*. Seattle, WA: Seattle Police Monitor. Available at https://www.seattle.gov/documents/Departments/Police/Compliance/Sixth_Systemic_Assessment_Supervision_Assessment.pdf.

Sentencing Project, The. 2013. *The Facts about Dangers of Added Police in Schools.* Washington, DC: The Sentencing Project.

Sharkey, Patrick. 2018. *Uneasy Peace: The Great Crime Decline, the Renewal of City Life, and the Next War on Violence.* New York: Norton.

Sharkey, Patrick, Gerard Torrats-Espinosa, and Delaram Takyar. 2017. "Community and the Crime Decline: The Causal Effect of Local Nonprofits on Violent Crime." *American Sociological Review* 82:1214-40.

Sherman, Lawrence W. 1983. "Patrol Strategies for Police." Pp. 145-63 in *Crime and Public Policy,* edited by James Q. Wilson. San Francisco: Institute for Contemporary Studies.

Sherman, Lawrence W., Patrick R. Gartin, and Michael E. Buerger. 1989. "Hot Spots of Predatory Crime: Routine Activities and the Criminology of Place." *Criminology* 27:27-56.

Sierra-Arévalo, Michael. 2020. "American Policing and the Danger Imperative." *Law and Society Review* 55:70-103.

Simpson, Brett. 2021. "Why Cars Don't Deserve the Right of Way." *The Atlantic,* October 15. Available at https://www.theatlantic.com/ideas/archive/2021/10/end-police-violence-get-rid-traffic-cop/620378.

Sinyangwe, Samuel. 2021. "Mapping Police Violence Database." Mapping Police Violence. Available at https://mappingpoliceviolence.us.

Skogan, Wesley G. 1995. "Crime and the Racial Fears of White Americans." *Annals of the American Academy of Political and Social Science* 539:59-71.

Skogan, Wesley G. 2012. "Disorder and Crime." Pp. 173-88 in *The Oxford Handbook of Crime Prevention,* edited by Brandon C. Welsh and David P. Farrington. Oxford: Oxford University Press.

Skogan, Wesley G. 2019. "Community Policing." Pp. 27-44 in *Police Innovation: Contrasting Perspectives,* 2nd ed., edited by David L. Weisburd and Anthony A. Braga. New York: Cambridge University Press.

Skolnick, Jerome. 1966. *Justice without Trial: Law Enforcement in Democratic Society.* New York: Wiley.

Skolnick, Jerome. 2002. "Corruption and the Blue Code of Silence." *Police Practice and Research* 3:7-19.

Smith, Robert, Liz Frondigoun, Denise Martin, Ross Campbell, and Linda Thomas. 2018. *An Independent Assessment of the "Prevention First" Crime Prevention Strategy in Ayrshire.* Glasgow: University of the West of Scotland.

Snider, Jill, and Maya Szilak. 2021. "Is It Time to Rethink 'Broken Windows' Policing?" *The Crime Report,* September 3. Available at https://thecrimereport.org/2021/09/03/is-it-time-to-rethink-broken-windows-policing.

Snow, Mark D., Lindsay C. Malloy, and Naomi E. S. Goldstein. 2021. "Information Gathering in School Contexts: A National Survey of School Resource Officers." *Law and Human Behavior* 45:356-69.

Snyder, David, and William R. Kelly. 1977. "Conflict Intensity, Media Sensitivity and the Validity of Newspaper Data." *American Sociological Review* 42:105-23.

South, Eugenia. 2021. "To Combat Gun Violence, Clean Up the Neighborhood." *New York Times*, October 8. Available at https://www.nytimes.com/2021/10/08/opinion/gun-violence-biden-philadelphia.html.

Speri, Alice. 2019. "Police Make More than 10 Million Arrests a Year, but That Doesn't Mean They're Solving Crimes." *The Intercept*, January 31. Available at https://theintercept.com/2019/01/31/arrests-policing-vera-institute-of-justice.

St. Martin, Greg. 2019. "Do More Broken Windows Mean More Crime?" May 15. Boston, MA: Northeastern University. Available at https://news.northeastern.edu/2019/05/15/northeastern-university-researchers-find-little-evidence-for-broken-windows-theory-say-neighborhood-disorder-doesnt-cause-crime.

Stanford Open Policing Project. 2022. "The Stanford Open Policing Project." Palo Alto, CA: Stanford University. Available at https://openpolicing.stanford.edu.

Statista Research Department. 2011. "Rate of Law Enforcement Officers in the United States from 1981–2001." Hamburg, DE: Statista Research Department. Available at https://www.statista.com/statistics/191706/rate-of-law-enforcement-officers-in-the-us-since-1981.

Stellin, Susan. 2019. "Is the 'War on Drugs' Over? Arrest Statistics Say No." *New York Times*, November 5. Available at https://www.nytimes.com/2019/11/05/upshot/is-the-war-on-drugs-over-arrest-statistics-say-no.html.

Stolper, Harold, and Jeff Jones. 2018. *Criminalizing Poverty: The Enduring Discriminatory Practice of Stop and Frisk: An Analysis of Stop-and-Frisk Policing in NYC.* New York: Community Service Society.

Stoughton, Seth, Jeffery J. Nobel, and Geoffrey P. Albert. 2020. "How to Actually Fix America's Police." *The Atlantic*, June 3. Available at https://www.theatlantic.com/ideas/archive/2020/06/how-actually-fix-americas-police/612520.

Sullivan, Becky. 2021. "With Slow Progress on Federal Level, Police Reform Remains Patchwork Across U.S." *National Public Radio*, April 27. Available at https://www.npr.org/2021/04/27/990580272/with-slow-progress-on-federal-level-police-reform-remains-patchwork-across-u-s.

Tabachnik, Sam. 2020. "How Do Cops Spend Their Time? As Denver Debates Police Funding, These Numbers Offer an Inside Look." *Denver Post*, September 6. Available at https://www.denverpost.com/2020/09/06/denver-police-officer-time-job-funding-data.

Tallon, Jennifer A., Melissa Labriola, and Joseph Spadafore. 2018. *Creating Off-Ramps: A National Review of Police-Led Diversion Programs.* New York: Center for Court Innovation.

Task Force on Policing. 2022. *Policing By the Numbers.* Washington, DC: Council on Criminal Justice. Accessed December 14, 2022. Available at https://counciloncj.foleon.com/policing/assessing-the-evidence/policing-by-the-numbers.

Taylor, Ralph B. 2000. *Breaking Away from Broken Windows.* New York: Routledge.

Tchekmedyian, Alene. 2022. "Majority of L.A. County Sheriff's Deputies Did Not Complete Training Requirements, Audit Says." *Los Angeles Times*, March 11. Available at https://www.latimes.com/california/story/2022-03-11/los-angeles-county-sheriffs-deputies-training-deficiencies-audit.

Telep, Cody W., and Julie Hibdon. 2018. "Community Crime Prevention in High-Crime Areas: The Seattle Neighborhood Group Hot Spots Project." *City and Community* 17:1143-67.

Telep, Cody W., David Weisburd, Sean Wire, and David Farrington. 2016. "Protocol: Increased Police Patrol Presence Effects on Crime and Disorder." *Campbell Systematic Reviews* 12:1-35.

Texas Department of Public Safety. 2020. *2020 Motor Vehicle Stop Data Report.* Austin, TX: Texas Department of Public Safety.

Thompson, Ben. 2022. *Thousands of 911 Calls Diverted to Mental Health Specialists.* Austin, TX: City of Austin.

Thompson, Cheryl. 2021. "Fatal Police Shootings of Unarmed Black People Reveal Troubling Patterns." *National Public Radio*, January 25. Available at https://www.npr.org/2021/01/25/956177021/fatal-police-shootings-of-unarmed-black-people-reveal-troubling-patterns.

Thusi, India, and Robert L. Carter. 2016. *Transforming the System.* New York: The Opportunity Agenda.

Tonry, Michael H. 2011. *Punishing Race: A Continuing American Dilemma.* New York: Oxford University Press.

Tonry, Michael H. 2012. "Race, Ethnicity, and Punishment." Pp. 53-82 in *The Oxford Handbook of Sentencing and Corrections*, edited by Joan Petersilia and Kevin R. Reitz. New York: Oxford University Press.

Tonry, Michael H. 2014. "Why Crime Rates Are Falling throughout the Western World." *Crime and Justice* 43:1-63.

Treatment Advocacy Center. 2016. *Serious Mental Illness (SMI) Prevalence in Jails and Prisons.* Arlington, VA: Treatment Advocacy Center, Office of Research and Public Affairs.

Trotta, Daniel. 2020. "U.S. Mayors Identify Police Unions as an Obstacle to Reform." *Reuters*, August 13. Available at https://www.reuters.com/article/us-global-race-usa-police/u-s-mayors-identify-police-unions-as-an-obstacle-to-reform-idUSKCN2592N1.

Tyler, Tom R. 2006. *Why People Obey the Law.* Princeton, NJ: Princeton University Press.

Tyler, Tom R., and Tracey Meares. 2020. "Revisiting Broken Windows: The Role of the Community and the Police in Promoting Community Engagement." *New York University Annual Survey of American Law* 76:637-56.

Uchida, Craig D. 1989. "Development of the American Police: An Historical Overview." Pp. 14-30 in *Critical Issues in Policing: Contemporary Readings*, edited by Roger G. Dunham and Geoffrey P. Alpert. Long Grove IL: Waveland Press.

United Nations. 2002. *ECOSOC Resolution 2002/13.* New York: United Nations.

University of Cincinnati Center for Police Research and Policy. 2021a. *Assessing the Impact of Law Enforcement Assisted Diversion (LEAD): A Review of Research.* Cincinnati, OH: University of Cincinnati.

University of Cincinnati Center for Police Research and Policy. 2021b. *Assessing the Impact of Mobile Crisis Teams: A Review of Research.* Cincinnati, OH: University of Cincinnati.

U.S. Census Bureau. 2020. "American Community Survey 5-Year Data (2009–2019)." Washington, DC: U.S. Census Bureau. Available at https://www.census.gov/data/developers/data-sets/acs-5year.html.

U.S. Department of Housing and Urban Development. 2016. "Neighborhoods and Violent Crime." *Evidence Matters* Summer:16-24.

U.S. Department of Justice. 2011. *Investigation of the New Orleans Police Department*. Washington, DC: U.S. Department of Justice. Available at https://www.justice.gov/sites/default/files/crt/legacy/2011/03/17/nopd_report.pdf.

U.S. Department of Justice. 2017. *An Interactive Guide to the Civil Rights Division's Police Reforms*. Washington, DC: U.S. Department of Justice. Available at https://www.justice.gov/crt/page/file/922456/download.

USAFacts. 2020. "Police Departments in the U.S.: Explained." Available at https://usafacts.org/articles/police-departments-explained.

Van Dijk, Auke J., Victoria Herrington, Nick Crofts, Robert Breunig, Scott Burris, Helen Sullivan, John Middleton, Susan Sherman, and Nicholas Thomson. 2019. "Law Enforcement and Public Health: Recognition and Enhancement of Joined-Up Solutions." *The Lancet* 393:287-94.

Vannette, David L., and Jon A. Krosnick, eds. 2018. *The Palgrave Handbook of Survey Research*. Cham, Switzerland: Palgrave Macmillan.

Vera Institute. 2018. *Emerging Issues in Policing*. New York: Vera Institute. Available at https://www.vera.org/publications/emerging-issues-in-american-policing-digest/volume-1/digest.

Vera Institute. 2021a. *Investing in Evidence-Based Alternatives to Policing: Community Violence Intervention*. New York: Vera Institute.

Vera Institute. 2021b. *Investing in Evidence-Based Alternatives to Policing: Non-Police Responses to Traffic Safety*. New York: Vera Institute.

Vera Institute. 2022. "What Policing Costs: A Look at Policing in America's Biggest Cities." New York: Vera Institute. Accessed December 13, 2022. Available at https://www.vera.org/publications/what-policing-costs-in-americas-biggest-cities.

Vitale, Alex S. 2020. "Five Myths About Policing." *Washington Post*, June 26. Available at https://www.washingtonpost.com/outlook/five-myths/five-myths-about-policing/2020/06/25/65a92bde-b004-11ea-8758-bfd1d045525a_story.html.

Vito, Anthony, George Higgins, and Gennaro Vito. 2021. "Police Stop and Frisk and the Impact of Race: A Focal Concerns Theory Approach." *Social Sciences* 10:1-13.

von Hirsch, Andrew. 1976. *Doing Justice: The Choice of Punishments*. New York: Hill and Wang.

Walker, Samuel. 1977. *A Critical History of Police Reform: The Emergence of Professionalism*. Lexington, MA: Lexington Books.

Wang, Ke, Yongqiu Chen, and Jizhi Zhang. 2020. *Indicators of School Crime and Safety: 2019*. Washington, DC: U.S. Department of Education.

Warren, Jenifer. 2022. "Homicides Continued to Increase in Major U.S. Cities in 2021, but at Slower Pace." January 26. Washington, DC: Council on Criminal Justice. Available at https://counciloncj.org/2021-year-end-crime-report.

Washington Post Editorial Board. 2020. "Sending Armed Police Officers Isn't the Right Answer for Every Emergency." *Washington Post*, October 16. Available at https://www.washingtonpost.com/opinions/sending-armed-police-officers-isnt-the-right-answer-for-every-emergency/2020/10/16/606b0cd0-0cae-11eb-b1e8-16b59b92b36d_story.html?outputType=amp.

Washington Post Editorial Board. 2021. "Reimagine Safety." *Washington Post*, March 16. Available at https://www.washingtonpost.com/opinions/interactive/2021/reimagine-safety.

Washington Post. 2022. "Fatal Force." Accessed December 14, 2022. Available at https://www.washingtonpost.com/graphics/investigations/police-shootings-database/?itid=sf_Investigations_unaccountable_p001_f001.

Washington State Institute for Public Policy. 2020. *Updated Inventory of Evidence-Based, Research-Based, and Promising Practices: For Prevention and Intervention Services for Children and Juveniles in the Child Welfare, Juvenile Justice, and Mental Health Systems.* Olympia: Washington State Institute for Public Policy.

Waxman, Olivia B. 2017. "How the U.S. Got Its Police Force." *Time*, May 18. Available at https://time.com/4779112/police-history-origins.

Weber, Max. 1978 [1922]. *Economy and Society.* Translated and edited by Guenther Roth and Claus Wittich. Berkeley: University of California Press.

Weichselbaum, Simone. 2020. "One Roadblock to Police Reform: Veteran Officers Who Train Recruits." New York: The Marshall Project. Available at https://www.themarshallproject.org/2020/07/22/one-roadblock-to-police-reform-veteran-officers-who-train-recruits.

Weichselbaum, Simone, Emily R. Siegel, and Andrew Blankstein. 2021. "Police Face a 'Crisis of Trust' with Black Motorists. One State's Surprising Policy May Help." *NBC News*, October 7. Available at https://www.nbcnews.com/news/us-news/traffic-stops-are-flashpoint-policing-america-reformers-are-winning-big-n1280594.

Weill-Greenberg, Elizabeth. 2021. "Brooklyn Center Mayor Unveils Plan to Decrease Police Traffic Enforcement Powers." *The Appeal*, May 8. Available at https://theappeal.org/brooklyn-center-police-traffic-enforcement-plan.

Weisburd, David L., and Anthony A. Braga, eds. 2019. *Police Innovation: Contrasting Perspectives.* 2nd ed. New York: Cambridge University Press.

Weisburd, David L., Anthony A. Braga, Elizabeth R. Groff, and Alese Wooditch. 2017. "Can Hot Spots Policing Reduce Crime in Urban Areas? An Agent-Based Simulation." *Criminology* 55:137-73.

Weisburd, David L., Shawn Bushway, Cynthia Lum, and Sue Ming-Yang. 2004. "Trajectories of Crime at Places: A Longitudinal Study of Street Segments in the City of Seattle." *Criminology* 42:283-321.

Weisburd, David L., Michael Davis, and Charlotte Gill. 2015. "Increasing Collective Efficacy and Social Capital at Crime Hot Spots: New Crime Control Tools for Police." *Policing* 9:265-74.

Weisburd, David L., Charlotte Gill, Alese Wooditch, William Barritt, and Jody Murphy. 2021. "Building Collective Action at Crime Hot Spots: Findings from a Randomized Field Experiment." *Journal of Experimental Criminology* 17:161-91.

Weisburd, David L., and Malay Majmundar, eds. 2018. *Proactive Policing: Effects on Crime and Communities.* Washington DC: National Academies Press.

Weisburd, David L., Cody W. Telep, Heather Vovak, Taryn Zastrow, Anthony A. Braga, and Brandon Turchan. 2022. "Incorporating Procedural Justice into Hot Spots Policing: Lessons from a Multicity Randomized Trial." *Translational Criminology* Fall:6-8.

Weisburd, David L., Clair White, and Alese Wooditch. 2020. "Does Collective Efficacy Matter at the Micro Geographic Level? Findings from a Study of Street Segments." *The British Journal of Criminology* 60:873-91.

Weitzer, Ronald. 2015. "American Policing Under Fire: Misconduct and Reform." *Society* 52:475-80.

Welsh, Brandon C., and David P. Farrington. 2012. "Science, Politics, and Crime Prevention: Towards a New Crime Policy." *Journal of Criminal Justice* 40:128-33.

Westervelt, Eric. 2020. "Mental Health and Police Violence: How Crisis Intervention Teams Are Failing." *National Public Radio*, September 18. Available at https://www.npr.org/2020/09/18/913229469/mental-health-and-police-violence-how-crisis-intervention-teams-are-failing.

Wexler, Chuck. 2021. *Looking Back and Looking Ahead on Police Reform*. Washington, DC: Police Executive Research Forum.

Whitaker, Amir, Sylvia Torres-Guillén, Michelle Morton, Harold Jordan, Stefanie Coyle, Angela Mann, and Wei-Ling Sun. 2019. *Cops and No Counselors: How the Lack of School Mental Health Counselors Is Harming Students*. New York: American Civil Liberties Union.

Willison, Janeen B., Evelyn F. McCoy, Carla Vasquez-Noriega, and Travis Reginal. 2018. *Using the Sequential Intercept Model to Guide Local Reform: An Innovation Fund Case Study*. Washington, DC: Justice Policy Center.

Witkin, Gordon. 2021. "The Vexing Obstacle to Police Reform: A Cop's Miserable Life." *Washington Monthly*, July 14. Available at https://washingtonmonthly.com/2021/07/14/the-vexing-obstacle-to-police-reform-a-cops-miserable-life.

Woods, Jordan B. 2021. "Traffic Without the Police." *Stanford Law Review* 73:1471-549.

Worden, Robert E., and Sarah McLean. 2017. *Mirage of Police Reform*. Oakland: University of California Press.

Worden, Robert E., and Sarah McLean. 2018. "Discretion and Diversion in Albany's LEAD Program." *Criminal Justice Policy Review* 29:584-610.

Wunschel, Frankie, and Daniel Bodah. 2020. *A New Way of 911 Call Taking: Criteria Based Dispatching*. New York: Vera Institute.

Yesberg, Julia Anne, and Ben Bradford. 2021. "Policing and Collective Efficacy: A Rapid Evidence Assessment." *International Journal of Police Science and Management* 23:417-30.

Index

About the Authors

William R. Kelly, PhD, is professor in the Department of Sociology and director of the Center for Criminology and Criminal Justice Research at the University of Texas at Austin. He is the author of and contributor to several books and articles on criminal justice, law, and policy, including *Criminal Justice at the Crossroads* (2015), *Confronting Underground Justice* (2018), and *The Crisis in the American Courts* (2021).

Daniel P. Mears, PhD, is distinguished research professor in the College of Criminology and Criminal Justice at Florida State University. A fellow of the American Society of Criminology and recipient of the Bruce Smith Sr. award from the Academy of Criminal Justice Sciences, Mears conducts research on crime and policy. His work appears in journal articles and books, including the award-winning *American Criminal Justice Policy* (2010) and *Out-of-Control Criminal Justice* (2017).

www.ingramcontent.com/pod-product-compliance
Lightning Source LLC
Chambersburg PA
CBHW031411270326
41929CB00010BA/1415

9 781538 179208